# Historical Documents in American Education

*Edited with Introductions by*

**Tony W. Johnson**
*West Chester University*

**Ronald F. Reed**
*formerly of Texas Wesleyan University*

**Allyn and Bacon**

Boston ■ London ■ Toronto ■ Sydney ■ Tokyo ■ Singapore

*For Clora Love Johnson*

**Vice-President:** *Paul A. Smith*
**Executive Editor & Publisher:** *Stephen D. Dragin*
**Editorial Assistant:** *Barbara Strickland*
**Marketing Manager:** *Kathleen Morgan*
**Editorial Production Service:** *Grace Sheldrick, Wordsworth Associates Editorial Services*
**Manufacturing Buyer:** *Chris Marson*
**Cover Administrator:** *Kristina Mose-Libon*
**Electronic Composition:** *Omegatype Typography, Inc.*

Internet: www.ablongman.com

Between the time Website information is gathered and published, some sites may have closed. Also, the transcription of URLs can result in typographical errors. The publisher would appreciate notification where these occur so that they may be corrected in subsequent editions.

**Library of Congress Cataloging-in-Publication Data**

Historical documents in American education / edited and with introductions by Tony W. Johnson, Ronald F. Reed.
    p.  cm.
    Includes bibliographical references.
    ISBN 0-8013-3314-8
      1. Education—United States—History—Sources.  I. Johnson, Tony W.  II. Reed, Ronald F.

    LA205 .H52 2002
    370'.973—dc21

                                                    2001022716

Printed in the United States of America
10  9  8  7  6  5  4  3  2  1      06  05  04  03  02  01

# CONTENTS

# PREFACE

Historical Documents in American Education, much like its companion volume, *Philosophical Documents in Education,* assumes that potential and practicing educators can become better professionals by reading, thinking about, and discussing the historical roots of the educational enterprise to which they aspire or belong. This anthology of documents and other historical material brings these historically significant events to you so that you can understand and use them to inform your own teaching.

*Historical Documents in American Education* is designed for use in a social foundations of education classroom as the point of departure for engaging prospective and practicing educators in a serious conversation about the role of education, past and present, in American society. This text, too, like *Philosophical Documents in Education,* is meant to serve as an invitation to further examine the issues and events that continue to define education in the United States. The hope is that readers and instructors will recognize the limits of this or any anthology and go beyond the documents and selections to further investigate and understand the historical roots of contemporary U.S. education.

The anthology is not intended to be comprehensive. In seeking to connect contemporary issues to their historical antecedents, *Historical Documents in American Education* has a particular focus or perspective that, admittedly, reflects the perspective and/or biases of the person compiling it.

Like *Philosophical Documents in Education, Historical Documents in American Education* is deliberately lean in hopes of making the historical legacies of present-day education accessible to a wider audience. The text is organized into four thematic units and includes nineteen chapters. Each chapter begins with a brief introductory essay that helps make the court cases and/or other documents relevant to the reader. Each chapter concludes with a series of questions designed to focus the reader on the key issues discussed in the text and documents.

The text is organized more or less chronologically, beginning with the Puritans, and continuing up to the present time. The concluding chapters of the first two parts discuss contemporary manifestations of the dominant historical themes in American education. Part III discusses various retreats from our nation's commitment to common schooling for all children and traces the education of African Americans and other so-called child races from the late nineteenth century to the present day. Parts I and III are similar in that most of the documents included are relevant court cases. Admittedly, court cases do not tell the whole story; but an understanding of our society's educational controversies is not possible without an appreciation for the role our courts play in addressing conflicts over race and religion. Finally, Part IV introduces the reader to key contemporary educational issues and provides the historical context for these ongoing conflicts.

Throughout the text, there is a conscious attempt to connect the historical antecedents with more contemporary issues. The focus in Part I, "Religion and Education: Its Roots and Continuing Legacy," is on the purpose of education for both the Biblical commonwealth of the Massachusetts Bay Colony and Thomas Jefferson's more secular democratic republic.

Even though their visions of society are significantly different, education is so crucial for both the Puritans and Jefferson that it had to be more than just a familial responsibility. Herein lie the roots of the idea that education is a societal or state responsibility and, based on their varying visions of the ideal society, for the conflict over the role religion should play in our schools. As discussed in Chapters 3, 4, and 5, this conflict emerged as a twentieth-century phenomenon once the First Amendment prescription that "congress shall make no law respecting the establishment of religion or prohibiting the free exercise thereof" began to be applied to actions of state governments in the closing decades of the nineteenth century.

Part II, "Localized versus Centralized Control of Schooling: Past and Present," emphasizes the importance of the local or district school during the early national period of the United States. Chapter 6 focuses on these district schools as "pure little democracies" and on the importance of Noah Webster's use of spelling and language to forge a sense of nationalism. Chapter 7 focuses on the crusade by Horace Mann and other reformers for a revival of the common school as the panacea for the triple threat of immigration, industrialization, and urbanization. Chapters 8 and 9 discuss the new structure of schooling known as the "one best system," the "feminization of the teaching profession," and the nature of textbooks written and used in the nineteenth century. Part II concludes with a discussion of educational vouchers as a modern version of the debate over who controls or should control the schools.

Part III, "Retreat from Commonality: Education of "Child Races," begins with a discussion of industrial training as the appropriate education for Negroes and other so-called child races. The ideas of both Booker T. Washington and W. E. B. Du Bois are included. Issues revolving around the segregated facilities for colored and Whites are discussed, as is the courts' implementation of the "separate but equal" doctrine of the *Plessy* decision. In this context, the educational experiences of Mexican Americans are compared to those of earlier immigrants and African Americans. Progressing chronologically, chapters in Part III discuss the landmark *Brown* decisions and justifications for moving toward affirmative action. In addition to chronicling our nation's retreat from the goal of a common education for all students, related educational issues that continue to influence our educational policy and practice are discussed.

Part IV, "Contemporary Issues: Equity, Inclusion, and Abuse," examines three current issues with long historical roots. In Chapter 17, San Antonio, Texas, is offered as a case study to illustrate how our traditional way of funding schools often produces great inequities among neighboring school districts. Here again, the question of control resurfaces since the source of funding often determines who controls the schools. Chapter 18 chronicles the recent treatment of children with special needs in our schools. Drawing parallels to others outside the U.S. mainstream, our history of ignoring children with special needs by isolating them into segregated facilities is discussed. Recent court cases and legislation are cited as we struggle to embrace and implement inclusive practices as the educational ideal for all students. Finally, by focusing on the historical abuses of high-stakes testing, specifically the uses of Binet's IQ test and the overreliance on the Scholastic Aptitude Test (SAT), Chapter 19 cautions readers not to jump too quickly on the current testing bandwagon.

This introduction to *Historical Documents in American Education,* along with the brief essay that begins each chapter, provides the readers with advanced organizers to help them understand the historical documents and their connections to contemporary educational issues. The goal is to unlock the door to a greater appreciation and understanding of education's importance in a democratic society. Once that door is opened, you, the reader, are encouraged to go beyond the selections that comprise this text; genuine understanding requires, as Jerome Bruner suggests, that you to "go beyond the information given." Suggestions for further reading are included at the end of part section to facilitate this first step.

The authors express their gratitude for the helpful remarks and suggestions of the reviewers: James A. Johnson, Northern Illinois University; and Linda Eisenmann, University of Massachusetts—Boston.

---

# In Memoriam

Ronald F. Reed died suddenly and unexpectedly of a heart attack on August 23, 1998. We had discussed the development of *Historical Documents in American Education* earlier that summer and envisioned it as a complement to our *Philosophical Documents in Education* text. Although he did not live to see the completed work, by inviting and enabling potential and practicing educators to better understand the historical antecedents to contemporary educational issues, *Historical Documents in American Education* contributes to and continues Ron's educational legacy.

*Tony W. Johnson*

# PART ONE

# Religion and Education
## Its Roots and Continuing Legacy

# CHAPTER

# 1 The Biblical Commonwealth

Most of us are familiar with *Mayflower*'s journey to Plymouth and the establishment of a colony there by the Pilgrims in 1621. The Pilgrims are perhaps best known for beginning that uniquely American celebration known as Thanksgiving. Aside from this, the Pilgrims had little impact on the development of what is now known as the United States of America or on its educational system. Of much greater significance are the Puritans, who settled nearby a few years later (1629) in the Massachusetts Bay area.

Both the Puritans and the Pilgrims came to the New World to practice their own religious beliefs, but the Pilgrims tolerated people with perspectives different from their own. The Puritans refused to accept and even persecuted people who refused to believe as they did. Alarmed by the religious turmoil engulfing Europe at this time and especially opposed to the Anglican Church in their home country, the Puritans migrated to the New World to establish a true Biblical commonwealth. Often referring to the settlement established on the Massachusetts Bay as the City or Beacon on the Hill, this new, pure Biblical commonwealth was intended to serve as a beacon lighting the path toward ultimate salvation.

In establishing the Massachusetts Bay Colony as a Biblical commonwealth, the Puritans knowingly created a "theocracy," or rule by religious men. The notion of separation of church and state was alien to the Puritans because they believed that both the norms of society and the norms of the church were grounded in Biblical law. Their Biblical commonwealth was antithetical to democracy in that the religious leaders were supposedly blessed with a special understanding of God's word and were authorized, indeed compelled, to ensure that all inhabitants of the colony lived in accordance with God's law. Embracing the teachings of John Calvin, Puritans believed that humankind was innately depraved and could be saved only through the grace of God. The Puritans established in the wilderness an entire society based on this premise, and their leaders were not above using force to literally "beat the devil" out of those people unwilling or unable to comply with the Biblical laws of the society. This belief that we are born with the devil within us has been used—indeed continues to be used—to explain and justify the use of corporal punishment in our schools.

The Puritan theology was undeniably harsh and forbidding in its outlook, but Puritans were not ignorant or anti-intellectual. Of the initial settlers migrating to the New World, a high percentage of them were university educated. Despite its harshness, Puritanism was a rational religion. As heirs to both the Renaissance and the Reformation, Puritans were convinced that reading the Bible was the Christian's sacred duty. Although they understood that knowing God's Word was not sufficient for ensuring grace, the Puritans also understood that knowing how to read, understand, and comply with God's law was an absolute necessity if their new commonwealth was to fulfill its destiny of lighting the path to salvation. In short, literacy—for the Puritans—was both a religious and civic necessity.

On the frontier of the New World, where the daily struggle to survive often superseded the crucial goal of transmitting God's transcendent truths to each new generation, ensuring a literate population was especially difficult. To combat this problem, the leaders of the Massachusetts Bay Colony recognized the importance of education for their vision of creating a "city on a hill." Education was an absolute necessity for the Puritans, resulting—some have suggested—in the establishments of schools before "privies" or outhouses were built. At first, these schools were individual efforts not sanctioned by the commonwealth, but as the settlement expanded, community leaders became increasingly concerned that children on the fringes of the community were not being taught to read and understand the Puritan tenets and the societal laws derived from these principles.

In 1635—six years after the first settlers landed—the first Latin Grammar school was established in Boston. This secondary school—destined to become famous for the favorite sons it produced—prepared young men for college and the university. A year later the Puritans established Harvard College. Although it may seem strange to us that within seven years after establishing the Massachusetts Bay Colony the Puritans found it necessary to create a college, it was absolutely essential for their vision of a Biblical commonwealth destined to guide the rest of the world to salvation. A college was required to prepare the next generation of educated community leaders and clergymen to replace those migrating from England. The gnawing fear that some day their store of trained and learned leaders—both cleric and civilian—might run out led the Puritan fathers to stress secondary and higher education.

Fearing that settlers along the frontier might neglect their parental and societal duty, the General Court of the Massachusetts Bay Colony in 1642 enacted a law requiring all parents to provide for their offspring or for apprentices under their charge instruction in the reading of Puritan tenets and in the principle laws of the Colony. The selectmen, the rulers of the community, were charged with inspecting homes and workshops to verify that this responsibility was being met. Although not always enforced, this law planted a seed that bore fruit more than two centuries later with passage of the first compulsory school law in the United States. With this action in 1642, the Massachusetts General Court established the precedent that education is more than a familial responsibility. Education—the teaching of Puritan tenets and the societal laws derived from them—was so crucial for their vision of a Biblical commonwealth that it must be a societal as well as a familial responsibility.

In 1647, the General Court of the Massachusetts Bay Colony took a more forceful step by enacting a law ordering every town of 50 or more households to offer instruction in reading and writing. Towns or villages of this size were required to establish a school and hire a teacher. Furthermore, for towns of 100 or more households, the law required that instruction in Latin grammar be provided so that students might be "fitted for the university." In effect, this 1647 law mandated that towns of a specified size establish elementary and secondary schools. Known as the "ould deluder Satan act," this legislation sought to ensure that the Word of God and the laws based on it would remain the birthright of every inhabitant of this Biblical commonwealth. Such a law was essential in order to prevent Satan from sabotaging this grand and glorious scheme of preparing the world for ultimate salvation.

In these schools—first in the Massachusetts Bay Colony and eventually throughout New England and beyond—the Bible was the primary text. Over time other writers and their writings rose up to buttress the inspired Word. As their titles suggest, these texts were unabashedly religious. John Cotton's *Spiritual Milk for Babes Drawn from the Breasts of Testaments* is an early illustrative example. The most famous and most widely used of such texts was *The New England Primer.* Much more dour and second in popularity to the *Primer* was Michael Wigglesworth's *The Day of Doom or a Poetical Description of the Great and Last Judgment. With a Short Discourse About Eternity.*

This Puritan view that education was so important that it must be both a societal as well as a familial responsibility has had a major impact on the nature of education in this country. Herein lies the origin of the belief that education is, first and foremost, a societal responsibility. Although its harshness mellowed over time, Puritanism and a secularized version of its ethic continue to influence our society's commitment to education as a public good.

## Massachusetts School Law of 1642*

This court, taking into consideration the great neglect of many parents and masters in training up their children in learning, and labor, and other implyments which may be proffitable to the common wealth, do hereupon order and decree, that in euery towne the chosen men appointed for managing the prudentiall affajres of the same shall henceforth stand charged with the care of the redresse of this evil, so as they shalbee sufficiently punished by fines for the neglect thereof, upon presentment of the grand jury, or other information or complaint in any Court within this jurisdiction; and for this end they, or the greater number of them, shall have power to take account from time to time of all parents and masters, and of their children, concerning their calling and implyment of their children, especially of their ability to read and understand the principles of religion and the capitall lawes of this country, and to impose fines upon such as shall refuse to render such accounts to them when they shall be required; and they shall have power, with consent of any Court or the magistrate, to put forth apprentices the children of such as they shall [find] not to be able and fitt to imploy and bring up...and they are to take care of such as are sett to keep cattle be set to some other imployment withall; as spinning upon the rock, knitting, weaving tape, etc. and that boyes and girles be not sufferd to converse together, so as may occasion any wanton, dishonest, or immodest behavior; and for their better performance of this trust committed to them, they may divide the towne amongst them, appointing to every of the said townesmen a certaine number of families to have special oversight of. They are also to provide that a sufficient quantity of materialls, as hemp, flaxe, etc., may be raised in their severall

---

*From Nathaniel B. Shurtleff, ed., *Records of the Governor and Company of Massachusetts Bay in New England* (Boston, 1853–1854), vol. II. pp. 6–7.

townes, and tooles and implements provided for working out the same; and for their assistance in this so needful and beneficiall imployment, if they meete with any difficulty or opposition which they cannot well master by their own power, they may have recourse to some of the magistrates, who shall take such course for their help and incuragment as the occasion shall require according to justice, and the said townsmen, at the next Court in those limits, after the end of their year, shall give a breife account in writing of their proceedings herein, provided that they have bene so required by some Court or magistrate a month at least before; and this order to continew for two yeares, and till the Court shall take further order.

# Violation by the Town of Topsfield of the
# Massachusetts School Law of 1642 (1668)*

Warrant to the constable of Topsfield, dated Mar. 2, 1668: "Whereas the law published by the Honered Generall Court lib. I, pag 76, doe require all Townes from time to time to dispose of all single persons and inmates within their Towns to service or otherwise and in pag. 16, tit. children & youth, It is required of the selectmen that they see that all youth under family Government be taught to read perfectly the english tongue, have knowledge in the capital laws, and be taught some orthodox catechism, and that they be brought up to some honest employment, profitable to themselves and to the commonwealth, and in case of neglect, on the part of famaly Governours, after admonition given them, the sayd selectmen are required, with the helpe of two magistrates, or next court of that shire, to take such children or apprentices from them, and place them forth with such as will looke more straitly to them. The neglect wherof, as by sad experience from court to court abundantly appears, doth occasion much sin and prophanes to increase among us, to the dishonor of God, and the ensueing of many children and servants, by the dissolute lives and practices of such as doe live from under family Government and is a great discouragement to most family governours, who consciently indeavour to bring up their youth in all christian nurture, as the laws of God and this commonwealth doth require;" said constable was ordered to acquaint the selectmen of the town that "the court doth expect and will require that the sayd laws be accordingly attended, the prevalency of the former neglect notwithstanding, and you are also required to take a list of the names of those young persons within the bounds of your Town, and all adjacent farmes, though out of all Towne bounds, who do live from under family government viz. doe not serve their parents or masters, as children apprentices, hired servants, or journeymen ought to do, and usually did in our native country, being subject to there commands & discipline and the same you are to returne to the next court to be held at Ipswich the 30 day of this month, etc.; signed by Robert Lord, cleric; and served by Thomas Dorman, constable of Topsfield, who returned that he had made the selectmen acquainted with Mathew Hooker, who was all that he found in the town."

*From *Records and Files of the Quarterly Courts of Essex County, Massachusetts, 1636–1671* (Salem, Mass., 1911–1914); vol. IV. p. 212.

## Massachusetts School Law of 1647*

It being one chiefe project of that ould deluder, Satan, to keepe men from the knowledge of the Scriptures, as in former times by keeping them in an unknowne tongue, so in these latter times by perswading from the used of tongues, that so at least the true sence and meaning of the originall might be clouded by false glosses of saint seeming deceivers, that learning may not be buried in the grave of our fathers in the church and commonwealth, the Lord assisting our endeavors,—

It is therefore ordered, that every towneship in this jurisdiction after the Lord hath increased them to the number of 50 housholders, shall then forthwith appoint one within their towne to teach all such children as shall resort to him to write and reade, whose wages shall be paid either by the parents or masters of such children, or by the inhabitants in generall, by way of supply, as the maior part of those that order the prudentials of the towne shall appoint; provided, those that send their children be not oppressed by paying much more than they can have them taught for in other townes; and it is further ordered, that where any towne shall increase to the number of 100 families or houshoulders, they shall set up a grammer schoole, the master thereof being able to instruct youth so farr as they may be fited for the university, provided, that if any towne neglect the performance hereof above one yeare, that every such towne shall pay £5 to the next schoole till they shall performe this order.

*From Nathaniel B. Shurtleff, ed., *Records of the Governor and Company of Massachusetts Bay in New England* (Boston, 1853–1854), vol. II, p. 203.

## Connecticut School Law of 1650*

Forasmuch as the good Education of Children is of singular behoofe and benefitt to any Commonwealth; and whereas many parents and masters are too indulgent and negligent of theire duty in that kind;

It is therefore ordered by this Courte and Authority thereof, that the Select men of euery Towne in the several precincts and quarters where they dwell, shall have a vigilant eye over their brethern and neighbors, to see, first, that none of them shall suffer so much barbarism in any of their families, as not to endeavor to teach by themselves or others, their children and apprentices so much learning as may enable them perfectly to read the English tongue, and knowledge of the capital laws, upon penalty of twenty shillings for each neglect therein; also, that all masters of families, do, once a week, at least catechise their children and servants, in the grounds and principles of religion; and if any be unable to do so much, that then, at the least, they procure such children or apprentices to learn some short orthodox catechism, without book, that they may be able to answer to the questions that shall be propounded to them out of such catechisms by their parents or masters, or any

*As quoted in *American Journal of Education,* vol. IV, p. 660.

selectmen, when they shall call them to a trial of what they have learned in this kind; and further, that all parents and masters do breed and bring up their children and apprentices in some honest lawful [calling,] labor, or employment, either in husbandry or some other trade profitable for themselves and the commonwealth, if they will not nor can not train them up in learning, to fit them for higher employments, and if any of the selectmen, after admonition by them given to such masters of families, shall find them still negligent of their duty, in the particulars aforementioned, whereby children and servants become rude, stubborn and unruly, the said selectmen, with the help of two magistrates, shall take such children or apprentices from them, and place them with some masters for years, boys until they come to twenty-one, and girls to eighteen years of age complete, which will more strictly look unto and force them to submit unto government, according to the rules of this order, if by fair means and former instructions they will not be drawn unto it.

# John Eliot Request's a College for Massachusetts Bay (1636)*

Now for your selfe to come, I doe earnestly desire it, If God so move your heart, & not only for the common wealth sake; but also for Larnings sake, which I know you love, & will be ready to furder, & indeede we want store of such men, as will furder that, for if we norish not Larning both church & common wealth will sinke: & because I am upon this poynt I beseech you let me be bould to make one motion, for the furtheranc of Larning among us: God hath bestowed upon you a bounty full blessing; now if you should please, to imploy but one mite, of that greate welth which God hath given, to erect a schoole of larning, a colledg among us; you should doe a most glorious work, acceptable to God & man; & the commemoration of the first founder of the means of Larning, would be a perpetuating of your name & honour among us.

\* \* \*

I humbly thank you for your tender care of vs, &, for your great respect to our name, in the defenc of it, against the gainsayers, I humbly thank you for putting vs in mind, of such waighty & necessary matters: for my owne part I have often spake of the wrighting a history, & some doe record the most memorable passages: but none yet have sett themselves apart for it: & for a library, & a place for the exercize of Larning, its my earnest desire & prayre, that God would stir vp the heart of some well wishers to Larning, to make an onsett in that kind, & indeed Sir I know none, every way more fitt then your selfe: I beseech you therfore consider of it, & doe that which may comfort vs: & where as a library is your first project, & then a college; I conceive vpon our experiens, that we shall most neede convenient chambers, to entertaine students at first, & a little room I feare, will hould all our first stock of bookes, & as they increase we may inlarge the roome: but with vs in our young beginings, men want purses to make such buildings: & therfore publik exercizes

*From Franklin M. Wright, "A College First Proposed, 1633: Unpublished Letters of Apostle Eliot and William Hammond to Sir Simonds D'Ewes," in *Harvard Library Bulletin,* vol. VIII, pp. 273–74, 276.

of larning be not yet sett on foote, though we have many larned men, both gentlemen & ministers: but had we a place fitted, we should have our tearmes & seasons for disputations, & lectures, not only in divinity: but in other arts & sciences, & in law also: for that would be very material for the wellfaire of our common wealth: & now I will say no more, but pray that the Lord would move your heart (which yet I hope is allready moved) to be the first founder of so gloryous a worke, as this is.

# Description of the Founding of Harvard College (1636)*

### In Respect of the Colledge, and the Proceedings of Learning Therein

**1.** After God had carried us safe to *New-England,* and wee had builded our houses, provided necessaries for our liveli-hood, rear'd convenient places for Gods worship, and setled the Civill Government: One of the next things we longed for, and looked after was to advance Learning and perpetuate it to Posterity, dreading to leave an illiterate Ministery to the Churches, when our present Ministers shall lie in the Dust. And as wee were thinking and consulting how to effect this great Work; it pleased God to stir up the heart of one Mr. *Harvard* (a godly Gentleman, and a lover of Learning, there living amongst us) to give the one halfe of his Estate (it being in all about 1700.1.) towards the erecting of a Colledge, and all his Library: after him another gave 300.1. others after them cast in more, and the publique hand of the State added the rest: the Colledge was, by common consent, appointed to be at *Cambridge,* (a place very pleasant and accommodate) and is called (according to the name of the first founder) *Harvard Colledge.*

The Edifice is very faire and comely within and without, having in it a spacious Hall; (where they daily meet at Common Lectures) Exercises, and a large Library with some Bookes to it, the gifts of diverse of our friends their Chambers and studies also fitted for, and possessed by the Students, and all other roomes of Office necessary and convenient, with all needfull Offices thereto belonging: And by the side of the Colledge a faire *Grammar* Schoole, for the training up of young Schollars, and fitting of them for *Academicall Learning,* that still as they are judged ripe, they may be received into the Colledge of this Schoole: Master *Corlet* is the Mr., who hath very well approved himselfe for his abilities, dexterity and painfulnesse, in teaching and education of the youth under him.

Over the Colledge is master *Dunster* placed, as President, a learned conscionable and industrious man, who hath so trained up, his Pupills in the tongues and Arts, and so seasoned them with the principles of Divinity and Christianity, that we have to our great comfort, (and in truth) beyond our hopes, beheld their progresse in Learning and godlinesse also; the former of these hath appeared in their publique declamations in *Latine* and *Greeke,* and Disputations Logicall and Philosophicall, which they have beene wonted (besides their ordinary Exercises in the Colledge-Hall) in the audience of the Magistrates,

---

*From "New England's First Fruits," as quoted in Perry Miller and Thomas H. Johnson, eds., *The Puritans* (New York, 1938), pp. 701–2.

Ministers, and other Schollars, for the probation of their growth in Learning upon set dayes, constantly once every moneth to make and uphold: The latter hath been manifested in sundry of them by the savoury breathings of their Spirits in their godly conversation. Insomuch that we are confident, if these early blossomes may be cherished and warmed with the influence of the friends of Learning and lovers of this pious worke, they will by the help of God, come to happy maturity in a short time.

Over the Colledge are twelve Overseers chosen by the generall Court, six of them are of the Magistrates, the other six of the Ministers, who are to promote the best good of it, and (having a power of influence into all persons in it) are to see that every one be diligent and proficient in his proper place.

## Selections from the Earliest Extant Copy of the New England Primer (1727)*

A — In *Adam's* Fall
We Sinned all.

B — Thy Life to Mend
This *Book* Attend.

C — The *Cat* doth play
And after flay.

D — A *Dog* will bite
A Thief at night.

E — An *Eagles* flight
Is out of fight.

F — The Idle *Fool*
Is whipt at School.

*From Paul Leicester Ford, ed., *The New England Primer* (New York, 1897), no pagination.

G — As runs the *Glass*,
Mans life doth pass.

H — My *Book* and *Heart*
Shall never part.

J — *Job* feels the *Rod*
Yet blesses GOD.

K — Our *KING* the
good
No man of blood.

L — The *Lion* bold
The *Lamb* doth hold.

M — The *Moon* gives light
In time of night.

N — *Nightingales* sing
In Time of Spring.

O — The *Royal Oak*
it was the Tree
That sav'd His
Royal Majestie.

P — *Peter* denies
His Lord and cries.

Q — Queen *Esther* comes
in Royal State
To Save the JEWS
from dismal Fate.

R — *Rachel* doth mourn
For her first born.

S — *Samuel* anoints
Whom God appoints.

T — *Time* cuts down all
Both great and small.

U — *Uriah's* beauteous Wife
Made *David* seek his
Life.

W — *Whales* in the Sea
God's Voice obey.

X — *Xerxes* the great did
die,
And so must you & I.

Y — *Youth* forward slips
Death soonest nips.

Z — *Zacheus* he
Did climb the Tree
His Lord to see.

*Now the Child being entred in his
Letters and Spelling, let him
learn these and such like Sentences by Heart, whereby he will
be both instructed in his Duty,
and encouraged in his Learning.*

### The Dutiful Child's Promises,

I Will fear GOD, and honour the KING.
  I will honour my Father & Mother.
I will Obey my Superiours.
I will Submit to my Elders.
I will Love my Friends.
I will hate no Man.
I will forgive my Enemies, and pray to
    God for them.
I will as much as in me lies keep all God's
    Holy Commandments.

I will learn my Catechism.
I will keep the Lord's Day Holy,
I will Reverence God's Sanctuary,
*For our GOD is a consuming Fire,*

*An Alphabet of Lessons for Youth.*

**A** Wise Son makes a glad Father, but a foolish Son is the heaviness of his Mother.

**B** Etter is a little with the fear of the Lord, than great treasure and trouble therewith.

**C** Ome unto CHRIST all ye that labour and are heavy laden, and He will give you rest.

**D** O not the abominable thing which I hate, saith the Lord.

**E** Xcept a Man be born again, he cannot see the Kingdom of God.

**F** Oolishness is bound up in the heart of a Child, but the rod of Correction shall drive it far from him.

**G** Rieve not the Holy Spirit.

**H** Oliness becomes God's House for ever.

**I** T is good for me to draw near unto God.

**K** Eep thy Heart with all Diligence, for out of it are the issues of Life.

**L** Iars shall have their part in the lake which burns with fire and brimstone.

**M** Any are the Afflictions of the Righteous, but the Lord delivers them out of them all.

**N** OW is the accepted time, now is the day of Salvation.

**O** Ut of the abundance of the heart the mouth speaketh.

**P** Ray to thy Father which is in secret, and thy Father which sees in secret, shall reward thee openly.

**Q** Uit you like Men, be strong, stand fast in the Faith.

**R** Emember thy Creator in the days of thy Youth.

**S** Alvation belongeth to the Lord.

B                    Trust

**T** Rust in God at all times ye peopl. pour out your hearts before him.

**U** Pon the wicked God shall rain an horrible Tempest.

**W** O to the wicked, it shall be ill with him, for the reward of his hands shall be given him.

**E** **X** Hort one another daily while is is called to day, lest any of you be hardened through the deceitfulness of Sin.

**Y** Oung Men ye have overcome the wicked one.

**Z** Eal hath consumed me, because thy enemies have forgotten the words of God.    *Choice Sentences.*

1. Praying will make thee leave sinning, or sinning will make thee leave praying.

2. Our Weakness and Inabilities break not the bond of our Duties.

3. What we are afraid to speak before Men, we should be afraid to think before God.

The

*Good Children must,*
*Fear God all Day,     Love Christ alway,*
*Parents obey,          In Secret Pray,*
*No false thing say,    Mind little Play,*
*By no Sin stray,       Make no delay,*
           *In doing Good.*

*Awake, arise, behold thou hast*
*Thy Life a Leaf, thy Breath a Blast;*
*As Night lye down prepar'd to have*
*Thy sleep, thy death, thy bed, thy grave.*

**Learn these four Lines by Heart.**

*Have Communion with few.*
*Be Intimate with ONE.*
*Deal justly with all.*
*Speak Evil of none.*

**The Names and Order of the Books**
**of the Old and New-Testament.**

**G** Enesis          Leviticus
    Exodus           Numbers

# Michael Wigglesworth, "The Day of Doom" (1662)*

* * *

*Then were brought near with trembling fear,*
*a number numberless,*
*Of Blind Heathen, and brutish men*
*that did God's Law transgress;*

CLVII

*Whose wicked ways Christ open lays,*
*and makes their sins appear,*
*They making pleas their case to ease,*
*if not themselves to clear.*
*"Thy Written Word," say they, "good Lord,*
*we never did enjoy;*
*We ne'er refus'd, nor it abus'd;*
*Oh, do not us destroy!"*

* * *

CLXVI

*Then to the Bar all they drew near*
*Who died in infancy,*
*And never had or good or bad*
*effected pers'nally;*
*But from the womb unto the tomb*
*were straightway carried,*
*(Or at the least ere they transgress'd)*
*Who thus began to plead:*

CLXVII

*"If for our own transgressi-on,*
*or disobedience,*
*We here did stand at thy left hand,*
*just were the Recompense;*
*But Adam's guilt our souls hath spilt,*
*his fault is charg'd upon us;*
*And that alone hath overthrown*
*and utterly undone us.*

CLXVIII

*"Not we, but he ate of the Tree,*
*Whose fruit was interdicted;*

---

*From the *Proceedings of the Massachusetts Historical Society,* vol. XII, pp. 83–93.

*Yet on us all of his sad Fall*
*the punishment's inflicted.*
*How could we sin that had not been,*
*or how is his sin our,*
*Without consent, which to prevent*
*we never had the pow'r?*

CLXIX

*"O great Creator why was our Nature*
*depraved and forlorn?*
*Why so defil'd, and made so vil'd,*
*whilst we were yet unborn?*
*If it be just, and needs we must*
*transgressors reckon'd be,*
*Thy Mercy, Lord, to us afford,*
*which sinners hath set free.*

CLXX

*"Behold we see Adam set free,*
*and sav'd from his trespass,*
*Whose sinful Fall hath split us all,*
*and brought us to this pass.*
*Canst thou deny us once to try,*
*or Grace to us to tender,*
*When he finds grace before thy face,*
*who was the chief offender?"*

CLXXI

*Then answered the Judge most dread:*
*"God doth such doom forbid,*
*That men should die eternally*
*for what they never did.*
*But what you call old Adam's Fall,*
*and only his Trespass,*
*You call amiss to call it his,*
*both his and yours it was.*

CLXXII

*"He was design'd of all Mankind*
*to be a public Head;*
*A common Root, whence all should shoot,*
*and stood in all their stead.*
*He stood and fell, did ill or well,*
*not for himself alone,*
*But for you all, who now his Fall*
*and trespass would disown.*

CLXXIII

*"If he had stood, then all his brood*
*had been established*
*In God's true love never to move,*
*nor once awry to tread;*
*Then all his Race my Father's Grace*
*should have enjoy'd for ever,*
*And wicked Sprites by subtile sleights*
*could them have harmed never.*

CLXXIV

*"Would you have griev'd to have receiv'd*
*through Adam so much good,*
*As had been your for evermore,*
*if he at first had stood?*
*Would you have said, 'We ne'er obey'd*
*nor did thy laws regard;*
*It ill befits with benefits,*
*us, Lord, to so reward?'*

CLXXV

*"Since then to share in his welfare,*
*You could have been content,*
*You may with reason share in his treason,*
*and in the punishment.*
*Hence you were born in state forlorn,*
*with Natures so depraved;*
*Death was your due because that you*
*had thus yourselves behaved.*

CLXXVI

*"You think 'If we had been as he,*
*whom God did so betrust,*
*We to our cost would ne'er have lost*
*all for a paltry lust.'*
*Had you been made in Adam's stead,*
*you would like things have wrought,*
*And so into the self-same woe,*
*yourselves and yours have brought.*

CLXXVII

*"I may deny you once to try,*
*or Grace to you to tender,*
*Though he finds Grace before my face*
*who was the chief offender;*

*Else should my Grace cease to be Grace,*
*for it would not be free,*
*If to release whom I should please*
*I have no liberty.*

CLXXVIII

*"If upon one what's due to none*
*I frankly shall bestow,*
*And on the rest shall not think best*
*compassion's skirt to throw,*
*Whom injure I? will you envy*
*and grudge at others' weal?*
*Or me accuse, who do refuse*
*yourselves to help and heal?*

CLXXIX

*"Am I alone of what's my own,*
*no Master or no Lord?*
*And if I am, how can you claim*
*what I to some afford?*
*Will you demand Grace at my hand,*
*and challenge what is mine?*
*Will you teach me whom to set free,*
*and thus my Grace confine?*

CLXXX

*"You sinners are, and such a share*
*as sinners, may expect;*
*Such you shall have, for I do save*
*none but mine own Elect.*
*Yet to compare your sin with their*
*who liv'd a longer time,*
*I do confess yours is much less,*
*though every sin's a crime.*

CLXXXI

*"A crime it is, therefore in bliss*
*you may not hope to dwell;*
*But unto you I shall allow*
*the easiest room in Hell."*
*The glorious King thus answering,*
*they cease, and plead no longer;*
*Their Consciences must needs confess*
*his Reasons are the stronger.*

\* \* \*

CCII

*Oh piercing words, more sharp than swords!*
*What! to depart from Thee,*
*Whose face before for evermore*
*the best of Pleasures be!*
*What! to depart (unto our smart),*
*from thee* Eternally!
*To be for aye banish'd away*
*with Devil's company!*

CCIII

*What! to be sent to Punishment,*
*and flames of burning Fire!*
*To be surrounded, and eke confounded*
*with God's revengeful Ire!*
*What! to abide, not for a tide,*
*these Torments, but for Ever!*
*To be releas'd, or to be eas'd,*
*not after years, but Never!*

CCIV

*Oh fearful Doom! now there's no room*
*for hope or help at all;*
*Sentence is past which aye shall last;*
*Christ will not it recall.*
*Then might you hear them rend and tear*
*the Air with their out-cries;*
*The hideous noise of their sad voice*
*ascendeth to the Skies.*

CCV

*They wring their hands, their caitiff-hands,*
*and gnash their teeth for terror;*
*They cry, they roar for anguish sore,*
*and gnaw their tongues for horror.*
*But get away without delay,*
*Christ pities not your cry;*
*Depart to Hell, there may you yell,*
*and roar Eternally.*

# Q U E S T I O N S

**1.** How were the Pilgrims and the Puritans alike? How were they different?

**2.** What is a theocracy?

**3.** What impact has the Puritan belief in the innate depravity of humankind had on the educational beliefs in the United States?

**4.** Why was education so important for the Puritans?

**5.** Why was it necessary to establish Harvard College seven years after Puritans settled in the Massachusetts Bay area?

**6.** What were the long-range consequences of the school laws passed by the Massachusetts General Court in 1642 and 1647?

**7.** Describe the founding of Harvard College, including the characteristics of the twelve overseers.

**8.** Do you agree that the use of religious or moral vignettes to illustrate and emphasize each letter of the alphabet is an appropriate pedagogical strategy? Why or why not?

**9.** Would you use Michael Wigglesworth's work *The Day of Doom* in a class of fifth graders? Why or why not?

# CHAPTER

# 2 Education as the Safeguard of Liberty

In continuing our investigation of the origins of American educational ideas, we must not forget Thomas Jefferson, our third president and the author of the Declaration of Independence, who was both a scientist and a philosopher. The essence of Jefferson's educational legacy may be best captured in his own statement characterizing his life as a continuous struggle against "every form of tyranny against the mind of man."

In combating this tyranny, Jefferson is perhaps best known as the primary author of the Declaration of Independence. Of this achievement he was deservedly proud, for in it he exposed the tyranny of the British monarchies over the colonies. He is also well known for his authorship of the statutes for religious freedom in Virginia, freeing the state from the tyranny of organized religion. The Virginia House of Burgesses enacted his "Bill for Establishing Religious Freedom" in 1786, prohibiting the commonwealth from establishing any religion as the official one. Unlike the Puritans, Jefferson believed—in matters of religion—that the state should neither promote nor impede the free exercise of religious beliefs. Although this statue applied only to the Colony of Virginia, it established the principle of separation of church and state that is the essence of the First Amendment to the U.S. Constitution.

Jefferson's hatred of tyranny was real. Espousing a protectionist theory of government, Jefferson argued that "experience hath shown even under the best forms, those entrusted with power, have in time and by slow operation perverted it into tyranny." According to Jefferson, a government's only purpose is to protect the inalienable rights of life, liberty, and the pursuit of happiness. But governments are no better than the individuals who comprise them. If they are to protect the citizenry's inalienable rights, then governmental officials must be properly educated and must remain accountable to the people they serve. In short, the liberties Americans fought for in the Revolutionary War are never safe but in the hand of the people themselves.

From this perspective, education becomes the ultimate safeguard of liberty. Only an educated people can create and maintain a government as a fortress against tyranny. Herein lies a paradox. From this perspective, education is so basic to the preservation of freedom that the government itself must take the responsibility for educating its children. Even though their visions of the ideal society are dramatically different, the Puritans and Jefferson share the belief that education is so important to the commonwealth that it is more than just a familial responsibility.

For Americans to protect their new-found liberties, Jefferson believed that citizens had to be literate and be able to appreciate the lessons of history. By emphasizing history,

Jefferson hoped the citizens of this new nation could recognize tyranny in all its forms and confront it when it raised its ugly head. Literacy, a free press, and some knowledge of history were sufficient, Jefferson believed, for the people to protect themselves. "When the press is free, and every man able to read, all is safe." A democratic republic presupposes an educated citizenry, but it also requires, according to Jefferson, that the people assuming leadership roles receive an appropriate kind of education. Leaders should be men of character with both virtuous and intellectual talents. In Jefferson's words, the leaders in a democracy must be drawn from the "natural aristocracy."

The idea of a natural aristocracy is central to Jefferson's educational ideas. We must, he argues, encourage intellectual and virtuous talent wherever we find it. Through education, society (the state) must "rake the gems for the rubbish." His "Bill for the More General Diffusion of Knowledge" called for the establishment of a state- or colonywide system of elementary schools offering three years of schooling free to every child in the commonwealth. In addition, Jefferson proposed that the state create 20 grammar or secondary schools across the state and offer scholarships to those promising young geniuses from poor families (one scholarship from each of the 100 elementary schools) to continue their study at the grammar school. These 100 public foundationers were to receive two more years of education. At this point, 20 of these most promising geniuses were selected to receive four more years of grammar school education at the public's expense.

Each year, the twenty grammar schools were to select and send ten of their most virtuous and intellectual students on to William and Mary College for three more years of study. By creating such a state-supported educational pyramid, Jefferson hoped to develop the educated citizenry that a democracy requires and to cultivate the real or natural aristocracy that such a government needs. Jefferson's legislative colleagues rejected this proposal as too costly, but in articulating the necessary relationship between democracy and education, Jefferson provided future generations with both a compelling rationale and a blueprint for a comprehensive state system of education.

Although Jefferson failed to become the father of universal education in the United States (Horace Mann would assume that mantle some fifty years later), he reinforced and Americanized the notion that education is so important for the commonwealth that it must be significantly a societal responsibility. When you combine this idea with his advocacy of the separation of church and state, the result is a very powerful educational legacy.

For more information about Jefferson's educational ideas, see Henry J. Perkinson, *Two Hundred Years of American Educational Thought* (New York: David Mckay, Inc., 1976), pp. 41–59.

# Thomas Jefferson on His Own Education (c. 1760)*

My father's education had been quite neglected; but being of a strong mind, sound judgment, and eager after information, he read much and improved himself, insomuch that he was chosen, with Joshua Fry, Professor of Mathematics in William and Mary College, to

*From Albert E. Bergh, ed., *The Writings of Thomas Jefferson* (Washington, 1905), vol. I, pp. 2–4.

continue the boundary line between Virginia and North Carolina, which had been begun by Colonel Byrd; and was afterwards employed with the same Mr. Fry, to make the first map of Virginia which had ever been made, that of Captain Smith being merely a conjectural sketch. They possessed excellent materials for so much of the country as is below the blue ridge; little being then known beyond that ridge. He was the third or fourth settler, about the year 1737, of the part of the country in which I live. He died, August 17th, 1757, leaving my mother a widow, who lived till 1776, with six daughters and two sons, myself the elder. To my younger brother he left his estate on James River, called Snowden, after the supposed birthplace of the family: to myself, the lands on which I was born and live.

He placed me at the English school at five years of age; and at the Latin at nine, where I continued until his death. My teacher, Mr. Douglas, a clergyman from Scotland, with the rudiments of the Latin and Greek languages, taught me the French; and on the death of my father, I went to the Reverend Mr. Maury, a correct classical scholar, with whom I continued two years; and then, to wit, in the spring of 1760, went to William and Mary college, where I continued two year. It was my great good fortune, and what probably fixed the destinies of my life, that Dr. William Small of Scotland, was then professor of Mathematics, a man profound in most of the useful branches of science, with a happy talent of communication, correct and gentlemanly manners, and an enlarged and liberal mind. He, most happily for me, became soon attached to me, and made me his daily companion when not engaged in the school; and from his conversation I got my first views of the expansion of science, and of the system of things in which we are placed. Fortunately, the philosophical chair became vacant soon after my arrival at college, he was appointed to fill it *per interim:* and he was the first who ever gave, in college, regular lectures in Ethics, Rhetoric and Belles Lettres. He returned to Europe in 1762, having previously filled up the measure of his goodness to me, by procuring for me, from his most intimate friend, George Wythe, a reception as a student of law, under his direction, and introduced me to the acquaintance and familiar table of Governor Fauquier, the ablest man who had ever filled that office. With him, and at his table, Dr. Small and Mr. Wythe, his *amici omnium horarum,* and myself, formed a *partie quarree,* and to the habitual conversations on these occasions I owed much instruction. Mr. Wythe continued to be my faithful and beloved mentor in youth, and my most affectionate friend through life. In 1767, he led me into the practice of the law at the bar of the General court, at which I continued until the Revolution shut up the courts of justice.

# Thomas Jefferson's "Bill for the More General Diffusion of Knowledge" (1779)*

### *Section I*

Whereas it appeareth that however certain forms of government are better calculated than others to protect individuals in the free exercise of their natural rights, and are at the same time themselves better guarded against degeneracy, yet experience hath shewn, that even under the best forms, those entrusted with power have, in time, and by slow operations,

*From Paul L. Ford, ed., *The Works of Thomas Jefferson* (New York, 1904), vol. II, pp. 414–26.

perverted it into tyranny; and it is believed that the most effectual means of preventing this would be, to illuminate, as far as practicable, the minds of the people at large, and more especially to give them knowledge of those facts, which history exhibiteth, that, possessed thereby of the experience of other ages and countries, they may be enabled to know ambition under all its shapes, and prompt to exert their natural powers to defeat its purposes; And whereas it is generally true that that people will he happiest whose laws are best, and are best administered, and that laws will be wisely formed, and honestly administered, in proportion as those who form and administer them are wise and honest; whence it becomes expedient for promoting the publick happiness that those persons, whom nature hath endowed with genius and virtue, should be rendered by liberal education worthy to receive, and able to guard the sacred deposit of the rights and liberties of their fellow citizens, and that they should be called to that charge without regard to wealth, birth or other accidental condition or circumstance; but the indigence of the greater number disabling them from so educating, at their own expence, those of their children whom nature hath fitly formed and disposed to become useful instruments for the public, it is better that such should be sought for and educated at the common expence of all, than that the happiness of all should be confined to the weak or wicked:

### Section II

Be it therefore enacted by the General Assembly, that in every county within this commonwealth, there shall be chosen annually, by the electors qualified to vote for Delegates, three of the most honest and able men of their county, to be called the Alderman of the county; and that the election of the said Aldermen shall be held at the same time and place, before the same persons, and notified and conducted in the same manner as by law is directed, for the annual election of Delegates for the county.

* * *

### Section IV

The said Aldermen on the first Monday in October, if it be fair, and if not, then on the next fair day, excluding Sunday, shall meet at the courthouse of their county, and proceed to divide their said county into hundreds, bounding the same by water courses, mountains, or limits, to be run and marked, if they think necessary, by the county surveyor, and at the county expence, regulating the size of the said hundreds, according to the best of their discretion, so as that they may contain a convenient number of children to make up a school, and be of such convenient size that all the children within each hundred may daily attend the school to be established therein, and distinguishing each hundred by a particular name; which division, with the names of the several hundreds, shall be returned to the court of the county and be entered of record, and shall remain unaltered until the increase or decrease of inhabitants shall render an alteration necessary, in the opinion of any succeeding Alderman, and also in the opinion of the court of the county.

### Section V

The electors aforesaid residing within every hundred shall meet on the third Monday in October after the first election of Aldermen, at such place, within their hundred, as the said Aldermen shall direct, notice thereof being previously given to them by such person residing within the hundred as the said Aldermen shall require who is hereby enjoined to obey such requisition, on pain of being punished by amercement and imprisonment. The electors being so assembled shall choose the most convenient place within their hundred for building a school-house. If two or more places, having a greater number of votes than any others, shall yet be equal between themselves, the Aldermen, or such of them as are not of the same hundred, on information thereof, shall decide between them. The said Aldermen shall forthwith proceed to have a school-house built at the said place, and shall see that the same shall be kept in repair, and, when necessary, that it be rebuilt; but whenever they shall think necessary that it be rebuilt, they shall give notice as before directed, to the electors of the hundred to meet at the said school-house on such a day as they shall appoint, to determine by vote, in the manner before directed, whether it shall be rebuilt at the same, or what other place in the hundred.

### Section VI

At every of those schools shall be taught reading, writing, and common arithmetick, and the books which shall be used therein for instructing the children to read shall be such as will at the same time make them acquainted with Graecian, Roman, English, and American history. At these schools all the free children, male and female, resident within the respective hundred, shall be intitled to receive tuition gratis, for the term of three years, and as much longer, at their private expence, as their parents, guardians, or friends shall think proper.

### Section VII

Over every ten of these schools (or such other number nearest thereto, as the number of hundreds of the county will admit, without fractional divisions) an overseer shall be appointed annually by the aldermen at their first meeting, eminent for his learning, integrity, and fidelity to the commonwealth, whose business and duty it shall be, from time to time, to appoint a teacher to each school, who shall give assurance of fidelity to the commonwealth, and to remove him as he shall see cause; to visit every school once in every half year at the least; to examine the scholars; see that any general plan of reading and instruction recommended by the visitors of William and Mary College shall be observed; and to superintend the conduct of the teacher in everything relative to his school.

### Section VIII

Every teacher shall receive a salary of ———— by the year, which, with the expences of building and repairing the school-houses, shall be provided in such manner as other county expences are by law directed to be provided and shall also have his diet, lodging, and washing found him, to be levied in like manner, save only that such levy shall be on the inhabitants of each hundred for the board of their own teacher only.

### Section IX

And in order that grammer schools may be rendered convenient to the youth in every part of the commonwealth, be it therefore enacted, that on the first Monday in November, after the first appointment of overseers for the hundred schools, if fair, and if not, then on the next fair day, excluding Sunday, after the hour of one in the afternoon, the said overseers appointed for the schools...shall fix on such place in some one of the counties in their district as shall be most proper for situating a grammer school-house, endeavoring that the situation be as central as may be to the inhabitants of the said counties, that it be furnished with good water, convenient to plentiful supplies of provision and fuel, and more than all things that it be healthy.

* * *

### Section X

The said overseers having determined the place at which the grammer school for their district shall be built, shall forthwith (unless they can otherwise agree with the proprietors of the circumjacent lands as to location and price) make application to the clerk of the county in which the said house is to be situated, who shall thereupon issue a writ, in the nature of a writ of ad quod damnum, directed to the sheriff of the said county commanding him to summon and impannel twelve fit persons to meet at the place so destined for the grammer school-house, on a certain day, to be named in the said writ, not less than five, nor more than ten, days from the date thereof; and also to give notice of the same to the proprietors and tenants of the lands to be viewed if they be found within the county, and if not, then to their agents therein if any they have. Which freeholders shall be charged by the said sheriff impartially, and to the best of their skill and judgment to view the lands round about the said place and to locate and circumscribe, by certain meets and bounds, one hundred acres thereof, having regard therein principally to the benefit and convenience of the said school, but respecting in some measure also the convenience of the said proprietors, and to value and appraise the same in so many several and distinct parcels as shall be owned or held by several and distinct owners or tenants, and according to their respective interests and estates therein. And after such location and appraisement so made, the said sheriff shall forthwith return the same under the hands and seats of the said jurors, together with the writ, to the clerk's office of the said county and the right and property of the said proprietors and tenants in the said lands so circumscribed shall be immediately devested and be transferred to the commonwealth for the use of the said grammer school, in full and absolute dominion, any want of consent or disability to consent in the said owners or tenants notwithstanding. But it shall not be lawful for the said overseers so to situate the grammer school-house, nor to the said jurors so to locate the said lands, as to include the mansion-house of the proprietor of the lands, nor the offices, curtilage, or garden, thereunto immediately belonging.

### Section XI

The said overseers shall forthwith proceed to have a house of brick or stone, for the said grammer school, with necessary offices, built on the said lands, which grammer school-house shall contain a room for the school, a hall to dine in, four rooms for a master and usher, and ten or twelve lodging rooms for the scholars.

### Section XII

To each of the said grammer schools shall be allowed out of the public treasury, the sum of ———— pounds, out of which shall be paid by the Treasurer, on warrant from the Auditors, to the proprietors or tenants of the lands located, the value of their several interests as fixed by the jury, and the balance thereof shall be delivered to the said overseers to defray the expense of the said buildings.

### Section XIII

In either of these grammer schools shall be taught the Latin and Greek languages, English Grammer, geography, and the higher part of numerical arithmetick, to wit, vulgar and decimal fractions, and the extrication of the square and cube roots.

### Section XIV

A visiter from each county constituting the district shall be appointed, by the overseers, for the county, in the month of October annually, either from their own body or from their county at large, which visiters, or the greater part of them, meeting together at the said grammer school on the first Monday in November, if fair, and if not, then on the next fair day, excluding Sunday, shall have power to choose their own Rector, who shall call and preside at future meetings, to employ from time to time a master, and if necessary, an usher, for the said school, to remove them at their will, and to settle the price of tuition to be paid by the scholars. They shall also visit the school twice in every year at the least, either together or separately at their discretion, examine the scholars, and see that any general plan of instruction recommended by the visiters, of William and Mary College shall be observed. The said masters and ushers, before they enter on the execution of their office, shall give assurance of fidelity to the commonwealth.

### Section XV

A steward shall be employed, and removed at will by the master, on such wages as the visiters shall direct; which steward shall see to the procuring provisions, fuel, servants for cooking, waiting, house cleaning, washing, mending, and gardening on the most reasonable terms; the expence of which, together with the steward's wages, shall be divided equally among all the scholars boarding either on the public or private expence. And the part of those who are on private expence, and also the price of their tuitions due to the master or usher, shall be paid quarterly by the respective scholars, their parents, or guardians, and shall be recoverable, if withheld, together with costs, on motion in any Court of Record, ten days notice thereof being previously given to the party, and a jury impannelled to try the issue joined, or enquire of the damages. The said steward shall also, under the direction of the visiters, see that the houses be kept in repair, and necessary enclosures be made and repaired, the accounts for which, shall, from time to time, be submitted to the Auditors, and on their warrant paid by the Treasurer.

### Section XVI

Every overseer of the hundred schools shall, in the month of September annually, after the most diligent and impartial examination and inquiry, appoint from among the boys who shall have been two years at the least at some one of the schools under his superintendance, and whose parents are too poor to give them farther education, some one of the best and most promising genius and disposition, to proceed to the grammer school of his district; which appointment shall be made in the court-house of the county and on the court day for that month if fair, and if not, then on the next fair day, excluding Sunday, in the presence of the Aldermen, or two of them at the least, assembled on the bench for that purpose, the said overseer being previously sworn by them to make such appointment, without favor or affection, according to the best of his skill and judgment, and being interrogated by the said Aldermen, either on their own motion, or on suggestions from their parents, guardians, friends, or teachers of the children, competitors for such appointment; which teachers the parents shall attend for the information of the Aldermen. On which interrogatories the said Aldermen, if they be not satisfied with the appointment proposed, shall have right to negative it; whereupon the said visiter may proceed to make a new appointment, and the said Aldermen again to interrogate and negative, and so toties quoties until an appointment be approved.

### Section XVII

Every boy so appointed shall be authorized to proceed to the grammer school of his district, there to be educated and boarded during such time as is hereafter limited; and his quota of the expences of the house together with a compensation to the master or usher for his tuition, at the rate of twenty dollars by the year, shall be paid by the Treasurer quarterly on warrant from the Auditors.

### Section XVIII

A visitation shall be held, for the purpose of probation, annually at the said grammer school on the last Monday in September, if fair, and if not, then on the next fair day, excluding Sunday, at which one third of the boys sent thither by appointment of the said overseers, and who shall have been there one year only, shall be discontinued as public foundationers, being those who, on the most diligent examination and enquiry, shall be thought to be the least promising genius and disposition; and of those who shall have been there two years, all shall be discontinued save one only the best in genius and disposition, who shall be at liberty to continue there four years longer on the public foundation, and shall thence forward be deemed a senior.

### Section XIX

The visiters for the districts which, or any part of which, be southward and westward of James river, as known by that name, or by the names of Fluvanna and Jackson's river, in every other year, to wit, at the probation meetings held in the years, distinguished in the Christian computation by odd numbers, and the visiters for all the other districts at their said meetings to be held in those years, distinguished by even numbers, after diligent examination and enquiry as before directed, shall chuse one among the said seniors, of the best learning and most hopeful genius and disposition, who shall be authorized by them to proceed to William and Mary College; there to be educated, boarded, and clothed, three years; the expence of which annually shall be paid by the Treasurer on warrant from the Auditors.

# Thomas Jefferson's "Bill for Establishing Religious Freedom" (1779)*

### *Section I*

Well aware that the opinions and belief of men depend not on their own will, but follow involuntarily the evidence proposed to their minds; that Almighty God hath created the mind free, and manifested his supreme will that free it shall remain by making it altogether insusceptible of restraint; that all attempts to influence it by temporal punishments, or burthens, or by civil incapacitations, tend only to beget habits of hypocrisy and meanness, and are a departure from the plan of the holy author of our religion, who being lord both of body and mind, yet choose not to propagate it by coercions on either, as was in his Almighty power to do, but to exalt it by its influence on reason alone; that the impious presumption of legislature and ruler, civil as well as ecclesiastical, who, being themselves but fallible and uninspired men, have assumed dominion over the faith of others, setting up their own opinions and modes of thinking as the only true and infallible, and as such endeavoring to impose them on others, hath established and maintained false religions over the greatest part of the world and through all time: That to compel a man to furnish contributions of money for the propagation of opinions which he disbelieves and abhors, is sinful and tyrannical; that even the forcing him to support this or that teacher of his own religious persuasion, is depriving him of the comfortable liberty of giving his contributions to the particular pastor whose morals he would make his pattern, and whose powers he feels most persuasive to righteousness; and is withdrawing from the ministry those temporary rewards, which proceeding from an approbation of their personal conduct, are an additional incitement to earnest and unremitting labours for the instruction of mankind; that our civil rights have no dependence on our religious opinions, any more than our opinions in physics or geometry; and therefore the proscribing any citizen as unworthy the public confidence by laying upon him an incapacity of being called to offices of trust or emolument, unless he profess or renounce this or that religious opinion, is depriving him injudiciously of those privileges and advantages to which, in common with his fellow-citizens, he has a natural right; that it tends also to corrupt the principles of that very religion it is meant to encourage, by bribing with a monopoly of worldly honours and emoluments, those who will externally profess and conform to it; that though indeed these are criminals who do not withstand such temptation, yet neither are those innocent who lay the bait in their way; that the opinions of men are not the object of civil government, nor under its jurisdiction; that to suffer the civil magistrate to intrude his powers into the field of opinion and to restrain the profession or propagation of principles on supposition of their ill tendency is a dangerous falacy, which at once destroys all religious liberty, because he being of course judge of that tendency will make his opinions the rule of judgment, and approve or condemn the sentiments of others only as they shall square with or differ from his own; that it is time enough for the rightful purposes of civil government for its officers to interfere when principles break out into overt acts against peace and good order; and finally, that truth is great

---

*From Paul L. Ford, ed., *The Works of Thomas Jefferson* (New York, 1904), vol II, pp. 438–441.

and will prevail if left to herself; that she is the proper and sufficient antagonist to error, and has nothing to fear from the conflict unless by human interposition disarmed of her natural weapons, free argument and debate; errors ceasing to be dangerous when it is permitted freely to contradict them.

### *Section II*

We the General Assembly of Virginia do enact that no man shall be compelled to frequent or support any religious worship, place, or ministry whatsoever, nor shall be enforced, restrained, molested, or burthened in his body or goods, or shall otherwise suffer, on account of his religious opinions or belief; but that all men shall be free to profess, and by argument to maintain, their opinions in matters of religion, and that the same shall in no wise diminish, enlarge, or affect their civil capacities.

## Q U E S T I O N S

1. Is Jefferson correct in suggesting that education is the safeguard of liberty?

2. In what way or ways did Jefferson's view of religion differ from that of the Puritans?

3. What is the relationship between tyranny and a protectionist theory of government?

4. Explain, in your own words, Jefferson's educational paradox.

5. What did Jefferson mean by a "Natural Aristocracy"?

6. What is education's role in fostering such an aristocracy?

7. Jefferson's colleagues rejected his proposal for a colonywide educational system as being too costly. Was this the real reason? Explain your answer.

8. How are Jefferson's and the Puritan visions of society alike? How are they different?

9. Describe the education of Thomas Jefferson.

10. Summarize Jefferson's arguments in support of religion and against a formal or established "state religion."

11. Compare your own education to that of Thomas Jefferson.

12. Describe in your words Jefferson's rationale for his "Bill for the More General Diffusion of Knowledge."

13. Are boys and girls considered equal in Jefferson's "Bill for the More General Diffusion of Knowledge"?

14. Does Jefferson's "Natural Aristocracy" include women? Explain your answer.

# CHAPTER

# 3

# Religion and the Schools

## Conflicting Values

As we discuss in the previous two chapters, the Puritans and Thomas Jefferson had similar yet conflicting visions of the role education should play in society. Although both considered education (specifically schooling) as a necessity for their respective visions of the ideal society, the theocracy (rule by religious men) of the Puritans is antithetical to the Jeffersonian ideal of a democratic republic. The religious perspective championed by the Puritans favored combining religious and secular authority into the hands of a select few. The selectmen of this Biblical commonwealth were to govern with absolute authority in accordance with the Puritans' understanding of the infallible word of God. From the Jeffersonian perspective, such a Puritan theocracy was tyranny of the highest order for it denied the basic human freedom of the free exercise of religion. If, as argued in the first two chapters, the U.S. educational system is grounded in these two conflicting visions of society, then conflicts over what role, if any, religion should play in our schools is inevitable.

As is illustrated in the Chapters 7, 8, 9, and 11, the influence of Protestantism—if not Puritanism—is pervasive in the development of our nation's education system. Although much less foreboding than the harsh doctrine of the early Puritans, religious tenets familiar to all Puritans dominated efforts to create a public system of schooling throughout much of the nineteenth century. Since the U.S. Constitution with its Jefferson-inspired Bill of Rights had been established before the nineteenth century, it seems odd that the first constitutional challenge regarding the relationship between religion and the schools did not occur until the first quarter of the twentieth century (1925).

To understand why the conflict between religion and the schools is largely a twentieth-century phenomenon, we must examine the Bill of Rights to the U.S. Constitution and its subsequent amendments. The Tenth Amendment to the U.S. Constitution states that rights and responsibilities not specifically identified as belonging to the federal government become the responsibility of the individual states. Because the U.S. Constitution is virtually silent regarding education, the responsibility for educating our citizenry has been assumed to be largely a local and state responsibility. Even though the free exercise and establishment clauses of the First Amendment support the Jeffersonian idea of the separation of church and state, this protection against the possible tyranny of religion applied only to legislation or policies established by the Congress (House and Senate) of the

United States of America. Not until the latter half of the nineteenth century—with the passage of the Fourteenth Amendment—were protections guaranteed by the Bill of Rights applied to legislative actions taken by state and local governments. For these reasons, the controversy between religion and the public school is a twentieth-century phenomenon.

## The Amendments to the United States Constitution

ARTICLES in addition to, and Amendment of the Constitution of the United States of America, proposed by Congress, and ratified by the Legislatures of the several States, pursuant to the fifth Article of the original Constitution.

### Article I

*[Articles I through X, now known as the Bill of Rights, were proposed on September 25, 1789, and declared in force on December 15, 1791.]*

Congress shall make no law respecting an establishment of religion, or prohibiting the free exercise thereof; or abridging the freedom of speech, or of the press; or the right of the people peaceably to assemble, and to petition the Government for a redress of grievances.

### Article II

A well regulated Militia, being necessary to the security of a free State, the right of the people to keep and bear Arms, shall not be infringed.

### Article III

No Soldier shall, in time of peace be quartered in any house, without the consent of the Owner, nor in time of war, but in a manner to be prescribed by law.

### Article IV

The right of the people to be secure in their persons, houses, papers, and effects, against unreasonable searches and seizures, shall not be violated, and no Warrants shall issue, but upon probable cause, supported by Oath or affirmation, and particularly describing the place to be searched, and the persons or things to be seized.

### Article V

No person shall be held to answer for a capital, or otherwise infamous crime, unless on a presentment or indictment of a Grand Jury, except in cases arising in the land or naval forces, or in the Militia, when in actual service in time of War or public danger; nor shall any person be subject for the same offence to be twice put in jeopardy of life or limb; nor shall be compelled in any criminal case to be a witness against himself, nor be deprived of life, liberty, or property, without due process of law; nor shall private property be taken for public use, without just compensation.

*Article VI*

In all criminal prosecutions, the accused shall enjoy the right to a speedy and public trial, by an impartial jury of the State and district wherein the crime shall have been committed, which district shall have been previously ascertained by law, and to be informed of the nature and cause of the accusation; to be confronted with the witnesses against him; to have compulsory process for obtaining witnesses in his favor, and to have the Assistance of Counsel for his defence.

*Article VII*

In Suits at common law, where the value in controversy shall exceed twenty dollars, the right of trial by jury shall be preserved, and no fact tried by a jury shall be otherwise re-examined in any Court of the United States, than according to the rules of the common law.

*Article VIII*

Excessive bail shall not be required, nor excessive fines imposed, nor cruel and unusual punishments inflicted.

*Article IX*

The enumeration in the Constitution, of certain rights, shall not be construed to deny or disparage others retained by the people.

*Article X*

The powers not delegated to the United States by the Constitution, nor prohibited by it to the States, are reserved to the States respectively, or to the people.

*Article XI*

[*Proposed March 4, 1794; declared ratified January 8, 1798*]

The Judicial power of the United States shall not be construed to extend to any suit in law or equity, commenced or prosecuted against one of the United States by Citizens of another State, or by Citizens or Subjects of any Foreign State.

*Article XII*

[*Proposed Decemer 9, 1803; declared ratified September 25, 1804*]

The Electors shall meet in their respective states and vote by ballot for President and Vice-President, one of whom, at least, shall not be an inhabitant of the same state with themselves; they shall name in their ballots the person voted for as President, and in distinct ballots the person voted for as Vice-President, and they shall make distinct lists of all persons voted for as President, and of all persons voted for as Vice-President, and of the number of votes for each, which lists they shall sign and certify, and transmit sealed to the seat of the government of the United States, directed to the President of the Senate;—The President of the Senate shall, in the presence of the Senate and House of Representatives, open all the certificates and the votes shall then be counted;—The person having the greatest number of votes for President, shall be the President, if such number be a majority of the whole number of Electors appointed; and if no person have such majority, then from the persons having the highest numbers not exceeding three on the list of those voted for as President, the House of Representatives shall choose immediately, by ballot, the President. But in choosing the President, the votes shall be taken by states, the representation from each state having one vote; a quorum for this purpose shall consist of a member or members from two-thirds of the states, and a majority of all the states shall be necessary to a choice. [And if the House of Representatives shall not choose a President whenever the right of choice shall devolve upon them, before the fourth day of March next following, then the Vice-President shall act as President, as in the case of the death or other constitutional disability of the President.][1]—The person having the greatest number of votes as Vice-President, shall be the Vice-President, if such number be a majority of the whole number of Electors appointed, and if no person have a majority, then from the two highest numbers on the list, the Senate shall choose the Vice-President; a quorum for the purpose shall consist of two-thirds of the whole number of Senators, and a majority of the whole number shall be necessary to a choice. But no person constitutionally ineligible to the office of President shall be eligible to that of Vice-President of the United States.

### Article XIII

[*Proposed January 31, 1865; declared ratified December 18, 1865*]

*Section 1.* Neither slavery nor involuntary servitude, except as a punishment for crime whereof the party shall have been duly convicted, shall exist within the United States, or any place subject to their jurisdiction.

*Section 2.* Congress shall have power to enforce this article by appropriate legislation.

### Article XIV

[*Proposed June 13, 1866; declared ratified July 28, 1868*]

*Section 1.* All persons born or naturalized in the United States, and subject to the jurisdiction thereof, are citizens of the United States and of the State wherein they reside. No State shall make or enforce any law which shall abridge the privileges or immunities of citizens of the United States; nor shall any State deprive any person of life, liberty, or property, without due process of law; nor deny to any person within its jurisdiction the equal protection of the laws.

*Section 2.* Representatives shall be apportioned among the several States according to their respective numbers, counting the whole number of persons in each State, excluding Indians not taxed. But when the right to vote at any election for the choice of electors for President and Vice President of the United States, Representatives in Congress, the Executive and Judicial officers of a State, or the members of the Legislature thereof, is denied to any of the male inhabitants of such State, being twenty-one years of age, and citizens of the United States, or in any way abridged, except for participation in rebellion, or other crime,

[1]Bracketed material superseded by Section 3 of the Twentieth Amendment.

the basis of representation therein shall be reduced in the proportion which the number of such male citizens shall bear to the whole number of male citizens twenty-one years of age in such State.

*Section 3.* No person shall be a Senator or Representative in Congress, or elector of President and Vice President, or hold any office, civil or military, under the United States, or under any State, who, having previously taken an oath, as a member of Congress, or as an officer of the United States, or as a member of any State legislature, or as an executive or judicial officer of any State, to support the Constitution of the United States, shall have engaged in insurrection or rebellion against the same, or given aid or comfort to the enemies thereof. But Congress may by a vote of two-thirds of each House, remove such disability.

*Section 4.* The validity of the public debt of the United States, authorized by law, including debts incurred for payment of pensions and bounties for services in suppressing insurrection or rebellion, shall not be questioned. But neither the United States nor any State shall assume or pay any debt or obligation incurred in aid of insurrection or rebellion against the United States, or any claim for the loss or emancipation of any slave; but all such debts, obligations and claims shall be held illegal and void.

*Section 5.* The Congress shall have power to enforce, by appropriate legislation, the provisions of this article.

## Article XV

[*Proposed February 26, 1869; declared ratified March 30, 1870*]

*Section 1.* The right of citizens of the United States to vote shall not be denied or abridged by the United States or by any State on account of race, color, or previous condition of servitude.

*Section 2.* The Congress shall have power to enforce this article by appropriate legislation.

## Article XVI

[*Proposed July 12, 1909; declared ratified February 25, 1913*]

The Congress shall have power to lay and collect taxes on incomes, from whatever source derived, without apportionment among the several States, and without regard to any census or enumeration.

## Article XVII

[*Proposed May 13, 1912; declared ratified May 31, 1913*]

The Senate of the United States shall be composed of two Senators from each State, elected by the people thereof, for six years; and each Senator shall have one vote. The electors in each State shall have the qualifications requisite for electors of the most numerous branch of the State legislatures.

When vacancies happen in the representation of any State in the Senate, the executive authority of such State shall issue writs of election to fill such vacancies: *Provided,* That the legislature of any State may empower the executive thereof to make temporary appointments until the people fill the vacancies by election as the legislature may direct.

This amendment shall not be so construed as to affect the election or term of any Senator chosen before it becomes valid as part of the Constitution.

## Article XVIII

*[Proposed December 18, 1917; declared ratified January 29, 1919; repealed by the Twenty-first Amendment December 5, 1933]*

*Section 1.* After one year from the ratification of this article the manufacture, sale, or transportation of intoxicating liquors within, the importation thereof into, or the exportation thereof from the United States and all territory subject to the jurisdiction thereof for beverage purposes is hereby prohibited.

*Section 2.* The Congress and the several States shall have concurrent power to enforce this article by appropriate legislation.

*Section 3.* This article shall be inoperative unless it shall have been ratified as an amendment to the Constitution by the legislatures of the several States, as provided in the Constitution, within seven years from the date of the submission hereof to the States by the Congress.

## Article XIX

*[Proposed June 4, 1919; declared ratified August 26, 1920]*

The right of citizens of the United States to vote shall not be denied or abridged by the United States or by any State on account of sex.

Congress shall have power to enforce this article by appropriate legislation.

## Article XX

*[Proposed March 2, 1932; declared ratified February 6, 1933]*

*Section 1.* The terms of the President and Vice President shall end at noon on the 20th day of January, and the terms of Senators and Representatives at noon on the 3d day of January, of the years in which such terms would have ended if this article had not been ratified; and the terms or their successors shall then begin.

*Section 2.* The Congress shall assemble at least once in every year, and such meeting shall begin at noon on the 3d day of January, unless they shall by law appoint a different day.

*Section 3.* If, at the time fixed for the beginning of the term of the President, the President elect shall have died, the Vice President elect shall become President. If a President shall not have been chosen before the time fixed for the beginning of his term, or if the President elect shall have failed to qualify, then the Vice President elect shall act as President until a President shall have qualified; and the Congress may by law provide for the case wherein neither a President elect nor a Vice President elect shall have qualified, declaring who shall then act as President, or the manner in which one who is to act shall be selected, and such person shall act accordingly until a President or Vice President shall have qualified.

*Section 4.* The Congress may by law provide for the case of the death of any of the persons from whom the House of Representatives may choose a President whenever the right of choice shall have devolved upon them, and for the case of the death of any of the persons from whom the Senate may choose a Vice President whenever the right of choice shall have devolved upon them.

*Section 5.* Sections 1 and 2 shall take effect on the 15th day of October following the ratification of this article.

*Section 6.* This article shall be inoperative unless it shall have been ratified as an ammendment to the Constitution by the legislatures of three-fourths of the several States within seven years from the date of its submission.

## Article XXI

[*Proposed February 20, 1933; declared ratified December 5, 1933*]

*Section 1.* The eighteenth article of amendment to the Constitution of the United States is hereby repealed.

*Section 2.* The transportation or importation into any State, Territory, or possession of the United States for delivery of use therein of intoxicating liquors, in violation of the laws thereof, is hereby prohibited.

*Section 3.* This article shall be inoperative unless it shall have been ratified as an amendment to the Constitution by conventions in the several States, as provided in the Constitution, within seven years from the date of the submission hereof to the States by the Congress.

## Article XXII

[*Proposed March 24, 1947; declared ratified March 1, 1951*]

*Section 1.* No person shall be elected to the office of the President more than twice, and no person who has held the office of President or acted as President, for more than two years of a term to which some other person was elected President shall be elected to the office of the President more than once. But this Article shall not apply to any person holding the office of President when this Article was proposed by the Congress, and shall not prevent any person who may be holding the office of President, or acting as President, during the term within which this Article becomes operative from holding the office of President or acting as President during the remainder of such term.

*Section 2.* This article shall be inoperative unless it shall have been ratified as an amendment to the Constitution by the legislatures of three-fourths of the several States within seven years from the date of its submission to the States by the Congress.

## Article XXIII

[*Proposed June 16, 1960; declared ratified April 3, 1961*]

*Section 1.* The District constituting the seat of Government of the United States shall appoint in such manner as the Congress may direct:

A number of electors of President and Vice President equal to the whole number of Senators and Representatives in Congress to which the District would be entitled if it were a State, but in no event more than the least populous state; they shall be in addition to those appointed by the States, but they shall be considered, for the purposes of the election of the

President and Vice President, to be electors appointed by a State; and they shall meet in the District and perform such duties as provided by the twelfth article of amendment.

*Section 2.* The Congress shall have power to enforce this article by appropriate legislation.

## Article XXIV

[*Proposed August 27, 1962; declared ratified February 4, 1964*]

*Section 1.* The right of citizens of the United States to vote in any primary or other election for President or Vice President, for electors for President or Vice President, or for Senator or Representative in Congress, shall not be denied or abridged by the United States or any State by reason of failure to pay any poll tax or other tax.

*Section 2.* The Congress shall have power to enforce this article by appropriate legislation.

## Article XXV

[*Proposed July 6, 1965; declared ratified February 23, 1967*]

*Section 1.* In case of removal of the President from office or of his death or resignation, the Vice President shall become President.

*Section 2.* Whenever there is a vacancy in the office of the Vice President, the President shall nominate a Vice President who shall take office upon confirmation by a majority vote of both Houses of Congress.

*Section 3.* Whenever the President transmits to the President pro tempore of the Senate and the Speaker of the House of Representatives his written declaration that he is unable to discharge the powers and duties of his office, and until he transmits to them a written declaration to the contrary, such powers and duties shall be discharged by the Vice President as Acting President.

*Section 4.* Whenever the Vice President and a majority of either the principal officers of the executive departments or of such other body as Congress may by law provide, transmit to the President pro tempore of the Senate and the Speaker of the House of Representatives their written declaration that the President is unable to discharge the powers and duties of his office, the Vice President shall immediately assume the powers and duties of the office as Acting President.

Thereafter, when the President transmits to the President pro tempore of the Senate and the Speaker of the House of Representatives his written declaration that no inability exists, he shall resume the powers and his duties of his office unless the Vice President and a majority of either the principal officers of the executive department or of such other body as Congress may by law provide, transmit within four days to the President pro tempore of the Senate and the Speaker of the House of Representatives their written declaration that the President is unable to discharge the powers and duties of his office. Thereupon Congress shall decide the issue, assembling within forty-eight hours for that purpose if not in session. If the Congress, within twenty-one days after receipt of the latter written declaration, or, if Congress is not in session, within twenty-one days after Congress is required to assemble, determines by two-thirds vote of both Houses that the President is unable to discharge the powers and duties of his office, the Vice President shall continue to discharge the same as Acting President; otherwise, the President shall resume the powers and duties of his office.

### Article XXVI

[*Proposed March 23, 1971; declared ratified July 5, 1971*]

*Section 1.* The right of citizens of the United States, who are eighteen years of age or older, to vote shall not be denied or abridged by the United States or by any State on account of age.

*Section 2.* The Congress shall have power to enforce this article by appropriate legislation.

### Proposed Equal Rights Amendment

[*Proposed March 22, 1972; declared ratified——*]

*Section 1.* Equality of rights under the law shall not be denied or abridged by the United States or by any State on account of sex.

*Section 2.* The Congress shall have the power to enforce, by appropriate legislation, the provisions of this article.

*Section 3.* This amendment shall take effect two years after the date of ratification.

### Amendment XXVII

[*Compensation of Members of Congress (1992)*]

No law, varying the compensation for the services of the Senators and Representatives, shall take effect, until an election of Representatives shall have intervened.


## QUESTIONS

1. Do you agree that conflict over the role religion should play in U.S. schools is inevitable?

2. How is a theocracy different from a democratic republic?

3. Why is the conflict between religion and the schools largely a twentieth-century phenomenon?

4. What, if anything, does this conflict have to do with the First Amendment? with the Tenth Amendment? with the Fourteenth Amendment?

# 4 Compulsion, Religion, and the Schools

## The Free Exercise Clause

During the latter half of the nineteenth century, most states passed compulsory school laws as a factorylike system of schooling began to emerge first in Massachusetts and New England in the 1840s and 1850s, then in the Midwest and middle-Atlantic states before the Civil War, and even in the southern and western states before the end of the nineteenth century. The development of this "one best system" of schooling is discussed more fully in Chapter 8, but it is important here to note that with the establishment of compulsory school laws and with the application of First Amendment protections to actions of state governments, legal conflicts over religion and the schools were inevitable.

These religious conflicts revolve around the "free exercise" and "establishment" clauses of the First Amendment. In short, the dictum "Congress shall make no law respecting an establishment of religion, or prohibiting the free exercise thereof" often conflicts with local and/or state norms and policies designed to foster a religious ethos in our schools.

The first major conflict over compulsory schooling and religious freedom ruled on by the United States Supreme Court was *Pierce v Society of Sisters* (1925). In 1922 the state of Oregon passed compulsory school law requiring every parent or guardian to send all children ages eight to sixteen to a public school. The law clearly intended to abolish parochial schools in Oregon because it compelled all children to attend public schools. Private schools objected, arguing that the law violated the First Amendment "free exercise" rights of people choosing to attend private or parochial schools. The Supreme Court agreed, stating that the "fundamental theory of liberty upon which all governments in this union repose excludes any general power or the State to standardize its children by forcing them to accept instruction from public teachers only." The U.S. Supreme Court declared the 1922 Oregon law unconstitutional.

In addition to declaring that children could not be forced to attend public schools, the Court recognized the power of the state to regulate education and to compel students to attend schools. The Court affirmed the right of the state to require that "teachers shall be of good moral character and patriotic disposition, that certain studies plainly essential to good citizenship must be taught, and that nothing be taught which is manifestly inimical to the public welfare." In short, while the Court ruled that a state may not compel children to attend public schools only, it confirmed that the state has the authority to make school attendance compulsory and to regulate both public and private schools. Based on the "free exercise" clause of the First Amendment, the Court declared the 1922 law unconstitutional. In affirming the principle that education is crucial for the common good, the Court officially recognized the state's responsibility for educating its citizenry.

These issues are complex. Here—as in most situations—a single decision did not clarify all issues related to the conflict between state and societal interests in promoting good citizenship and the child's right to the free exercise of religion. This question reappeared in the 1940s over the constitutionality of compulsory flag salute in U.S. public schools. In Minersville, Pennsylvania, teachers and students began the school day like their counterparts throughout country by saluting the U.S. flag and reciting the Pledge of Allegiance. Rather than participate in this mandatory activity, Lillian and William Gobitis were enrolled in a private school while their father went to court seeking an injunction to eliminate saluting the flag as a condition for his children's attendance at the Minersville public school. The Gobitis family claimed that compulsory flag salute violated their right to freely exercise their religion as guaranteed by the First Amendment. As Jehovah's Witnesses, the Gobitis family objected to compulsory flag salute, saying that it conflicted with their belief in the scripture, specifically the statement from Exodus declaring: "Thou shalt not make unto thee any graven image, or any likeness of anything that is in the heaven above, or that is in the earth beneath, or that is in the water under the earth. Thou shalt not bow down thyself to them, nor serve them." The state—through its agent, the Minersville Board of Education—responded that because saluting the flag is not a form of worship, mandatory flag salute does not deny students their free exercise rights.

In the decision handed down by the Supreme Court of the United States, the Court ruled that no right is absolute, even the right to practice religious beliefs. In an 8-to-1 ruling, the Court confirmed patriotism and loyalty as legitimate interests of the state and stated that it is proper for the public schools—as agents of the state—to foster "a common feeling for a common country."

Three years later (1943), in a similar case known as *West Virginia v Barnette,* the Supreme Court reversed itself. In this case, the high court sided with the children of Jehovah's Witnesses. While recognizing and respecting the state's desire to promote national unity (especially because the United States was a major combatant in World War II), the Court declared that compulsory flag salute was unconstitutional because it violated the free exercise clause of the First Amendment. Justice Robert Jackson made it clear that First Amendment freedoms are preferred freedoms. Some rights—driving a car, for example—can be restricted if the government has a legitimate reason and chooses reasonable means, but preferred rights require more protection. Freedom to exercise one's religious belief is such a preferred right and cannot be restricted unless the state can show compelling need for limiting it.

In short, public schools—as agents of the state—must be sensitive to the religious beliefs of their constituents. At the same time, public schools are prohibited from establishing or promoting one or any religious view over another. In short, thanks to our Puritan and Jeffersonian legacy, when it comes to religion, U.S. public schools are on a tightrope—protecting all, favoring none, and disparaging none.

# Decision on the Constitutional Right to Operate a Religious School (1925)*

*Appeals from the District Court of the U.S. for the District of Oregon*

*Mr. Justice McReynolds Delivered the Opinion of a Unanimous Court*

\* \* \*

The challenged Act, effective September 1, 1926, requires every parent, guardian or other person having control or charge or custody of a child between eight and sixteen years to send him to "a public school for the period of time a public school shall be held during the current year" in the district where the child resides; and failure so to do is declared a misdemeanor. There are exemptions—not specially important here—for children who are not normal, or who have completed the eighth grade, or who reside at considerable distances from any public school, or whose parents or guardians hold special permits from the County Superintendent. The manifest purpose is to compel general attendance at public schools by normal children, between eight and sixteen, who have not completed the eighth grade. And without doubt enforcement of the statute would seriously impair, perhaps destroy, the profitable features of appellees' business and greatly diminish the value of their property.

Appellee, the Society of Sisters, is an Oregon corporation, organized in 1880, with power to care for orphans, educate and instruct the youth, establish and maintain academies or schools, and acquire necessary real and personal property. It has long devoted its property and effort to the secular and religious education and care of children, and has acquired the valuable good will of many parents and guardians. It conducts interdependent primary and high schools and junior colleges, and maintains orphanages for the custody and control of children between eight and sixteen. In its primary schools many children between those ages are taught the subjects usually pursued in Oregon public schools during the first eight years. Systematic religious instruction and moral training according to the tenets of the Roman Catholic Church are also regularly provided.

\* \* \*

No question is raised concerning the power of the State reasonably to regulate all schools, to inspect, supervise and examine them, their teachers and pupils; to require that all children of proper age attend some school, that teachers shall be of good moral character and patriotic disposition, that certain studies plainly essential to good citizenship must be taught, and that nothing be taught which is manifestly inimical to the public welfare.

The inevitable practical result of enforcing the Act under consideration would be destruction of appellees' primary schools, and perhaps all other private primary schools for normal children within the State of Oregon. These parties are engaged in a kind of undertaking not inherently harmful, but long regarded as useful and meritorious. Certainly there is nothing in the present records to indicate that they have failed to discharge their obliga-

---

*From *Pierce et al. v. Society of Sisters,* 268 U.S. 510 (1925).

tions to patrons, students or the State. And there are no peculiar circumstances or present emergencies which demand extraordinary measures relative to primary education.

Under the doctrine of *Meyer* v. *Nebraska,* 262 U.S. 390, we think it entirely plain that the Act of 1922 unreasonably interferes with the liberty of parents and guardians to direct the upbringing and education of children under their control. As often heretofore pointed out, rights guaranteed by the Constitution may not be abridged by legislation which has no reasonable relation to some purpose within the competency of the State. The fundamental theory of liberty upon which all governments in this Union repose excludes any general power of the State to standardize its children by forcing them to accept instruction from public teachers only. The child is not the mere creature of the State; those who nurture him and direct his destiny have the right, coupled with the high duty, to recognize and prepare him for additional obligations.

\* \* \*

The decrees below are *affirmed.*

## Decision on Mandatory Saluting of the Flag (1940)*

### On Writ of Certiorari to the United States Circuit Court of Appeals for the Third Circuit

Frankfurter, J. A grave responsibility confronts this Court whenever in course of litigation it must reconcile the conflicting claims of liberty and authority. But when the liberty invoked is liberty of conscience, and the authority is authority to safeguard the nation's fellowship, judicial conscience is put to its severest test. Of such a nature is the present controversy.

Lillian Gobitis, aged twelve, and her brother William, aged ten, were expelled from the public schools of Minersville, Pennsylvania, for refusing to salute the national flag as part of a daily school exercise. The local Board of Education required both teachers and pupils to participate in this ceremony. The ceremony is a familiar one. The right hand is placed on the breast and the following pledge recited in unison: "I pledge allegiance to my flag, and to the Republic for which it stands; one nation indivisible, with liberty and justice for all." While the words are spoken, teachers and pupils extend their right hands in salute to the flag. The Gobitis family are affiliated with "Jehovah's Witnesses," for whom the Bible as the Word of God is the supreme authority. The children had been brought up conscientiously to believe that such a gesture of respect for the flag was forbidden by command of scripture.

The Gobitis children were of an age for which Pennsylvania makes school attendance compulsory. Thus they were denied a free education and their parents had to put them into private schools. To be relieved of the financial burden thereby entailed, their father, on behalf of the children and in his own behalf, brought this suit. He sought to enjoin the authorities from continuing to exact participation in the flag-salute ceremony as

*From *Minersville School District* v. *Gobitis,* 310 U.S. 586 (1940).

a condition of his children's attendance at the Minersville school. After trial of the issues, Judge Maris gave relief in the District Court on the basis of a thoughtful opinion; his decree was affirmed by the Circuit Court of Appeals. Since this decision ran counter to several per curiam dispositions of this Court, we granted certiorari to give the matter full reconsideration. By their able submissions, the Committee on the Bill of Rights of the American Bar Association and the American Civil Liberties Union, as friends of the Court, have helped us to our conclusion.

We must decide whether the requirement of participation in such a ceremony, exacted from a child who refuses upon sincere religious grounds, infringes without due process of law the liberty guaranteed by the Fourteenth Amendment.

Centuries of strife over the erection of particular dogmas as exclusive or all-comprehending faiths led to the inclusion of a guarantee for religious freedom in the Bill of Rights. The First Amendment, and the Fourteenth through its absorption of the First, sought to guard against repetition of those bitter religious struggles by prohibiting the establishment of a state religion and by securing to every sect the free exercise of its faith. So pervasive is the acceptance of this precious right that its scope is brought into question, as here, only when the conscience of individuals collides with the felt necessities of society.

Certainly the affirmative pursuit of one's convictions about the ultimate mystery of the universe and man's relation to it is placed beyond the reach of law. Government may not interfere with organized or individual expression of belief or disbelief. Propagation of belief—or even of disbelief in the supernatural—is protected, whether in church or chapel, mosque or synagogue, tabernacle or meetinghouse. Likewise the Constitution assures generous immunity to the individual from imposition of penalties for offending, in the course of his own religious activities, the religious views of others, be they a minority or those who are dominant in government.

But the manifold character of man's relations may bring his conception of religious duty into conflict with the secular interests of his fellow-men. When does the constitutional guarantee compel exemption from doing what society thinks necessary for the promotion of some great common end, or from a penalty for conduct which appears dangerous to the general good? To state the problem is to recall the truth that no single principle can answer all of life's complexities. The right to freedom of religious belief, however dissident and however obnoxious to the cherished beliefs of others—even of a majority—is itself the denial of an absolute. But to affirm that the freedom to follow conscience has itself no limits in the life of a society would deny that very plurality of principles which, as a matter of history, underlies protection of religious toleration. Compare Mr. Justice Holmes in Hudson County Water Co. v. McCarter, 209 U.S. 349, 355. Our present task then, as so often the case with courts, is to reconcile two rights in order to prevent either from destroying the other. But, because in safeguarding conscience we are dealing with interests so subtle and so dear, every possible leeway should be given to the claims of religious faith.

In the judicial enforcement of religious freedom we are concerned with a historic concept. See Mr. Justice Cardozo in Hamilton v. Regents, 293 U.S. 245, at page 265. The religious liberty which the Constitution protects has never excluded legislation of general scope not directed against doctrinal loyalties of particular sects. Judicial nullification of legislation cannot be justified by attributing to the framers of the Bill of Rights views for which there is no historic warrant. Conscientious scruples have not, in the course of the long struggle for religious toleration, relieved the individual from obedience to a general law not aimed at the promotion or restriction of religious beliefs. The mere possession of religious convictions which contradict the relevant concerns of a political society does not relieve the citizen from the discharge of political responsbilities. The necessity for this adjustment has again and again been recognized. In a number of situations the exertion of political authority has been sustained, while basic considerations of religious freedom have been left inviolate. Reynolds v. United States, 98 U.S. 145; Davis v. Beason, 133 U.S. 333; Selective Draft Law Cases, 245 U.S. 366; Hamilton v. Regents, 293 U.S. 245. In all these cases the general laws in question, upheld in their application to those who refused obedience from religious conviction, were manifestations of specific powers of government deemed by the legislature essential to secure and maintain that orderly, tranquil, and free society without which religious toleration itself is unattainable. Nor does the freedom of speech assured by Due Process move in a more absolute circle of immunity than that enjoyed by religious freedom. Even if it were assumed that freedom of speech goes beyond the historic concept of full opportunity to utter and to disseminate views, however heretical or offensive to dominant opinion, and includes freedom from conveying what may be deemed an implied but rejected affirmation, the question remains whether school children, like the Gobitis children, must be excused from conduct required of all the other children in the promotion of national cohesion. We are dealing with an interest inferior to none in the hierarchy of legal values. National unity is the basis of national security. To deny the legislature the right to select appropriate means for its attainment presents a totally different order of problem from that of the propriety of subordinating the possible ugliness of littered streets to the free expression of opinion through distribution of handbills. Compare Schneider v. State of New Jersey, 308 U.S. 147.

Situations like the present are phases of the profoundest problem confronting a democracy—the problem which Lincoln cast in memorable dilemma: "Must a government of necessity be too strong for the liberties of its people, or too weak to maintain its own existence?" No mere textual reading or logical talisman can solve the dilemma. And when the issue demands judicial determination, it is not the personal notion of judges of what wise adjustment requires which must prevail.

Unlike the instances we have cited, the case before us is not concerned with an exertion of legislative power for the promotion of some specific need or interest of secular society—the protection of the family, the promotion of the family, the promotion of health, the common defense, the raising of public revenues to defray the cost of government. But all these specific activities of government presuppose the existence of an organized political society. The ultimate foundation of a free society is the binding tie of cohesive sentiment. Such a sentiment is fostered by all those agencies of the mind and spirit which may serve to gather up the traditions of a people, transmit them from generation to generation, and thereby create that continuity of a treasured common life which constitutes a civilization. "We live by symbols." The flag is a symbol of our national unity, transcending all internal differences, however large, within the framework of the Constitution. This Court has had occasion to say that "…the flag is the symbol of the nation's power,—the emblem of freedom in its truest, best sense…. it signifies government resting on the consent of the governed; liberty regulated by law; the protection of the weak against the strong; security against the exercise of arbitrary power; and absolute safety for free institutions against foreign aggression." Halter v. Nebraska, 205 U.S. 34.

The case before us must be viewed as though the legislature of Pennsylvania had itself formally directed the flag-salute for the children of Minersville; had made no exemption for children whose parents were possessed of conscientious scruples like those of the Gobitis family; and had indicated its belief in the desirable ends to be secured by having its public school children share a common experience at those periods of development when their minds are supposedly receptive to its assimilation, by an exercise appropriate in time and place and setting, and one designed to evoke in them appreciation of the nation's hopes and dreams, its sufferings and sacrifices. The precise issue, then, for us to decide is whether the legislatures of the various states and the authorities in a thousand counties and school districts of this country are barred from determining the appropriateness of various means to evoke that unifying sentiment without which there can ultimately be no liberties, civil or religious. To stigmatize legislative judgment in providing for this universal gesture of respect for the symbol of our national life in the setting of the common school as a lawless inroad on that freedom of conscience which the Constitution protects, would amount to no less than the pronouncement of pedagogical and psychological dogma in a field where courts possess no marked and certainly no controlling competence. The influences which help toward a common feeling for the common country are manifold. Some may seem harsh and others no doubt are foolish. Surely, however, the end is legitimate. And the effective means for its attainment are still so certain and so unauthenticated by science as to preclude us from putting the widely prevalent belief in flag-saluting beyond the pale of legislative power. It mocks reason and denies our whole history to find in the allowance of a requirement to salute our flag on fitting occasions the seeds of sanction for obeisance to a leader.

The wisdom of training children in patriotic impulses by those compulsions which necessarily pervade so much of the educational process is not for our independent judgment. Even were we convinced of the folly of such a measure, such belief would be no proof of its unconstitutionality. For ourselves, we might be tempted to say that the deepest patriotism is best engendered by giving unfettered scope to the most crochety beliefs. Perhaps it is best, even from the standpoint of those interests which ordinances like the one under review seek to promote, to give to the least popular sect leave from conformities like those here in issue. But the court-room is not the arena for debating issues of educational policy. It is not our province to choose among competing considerations in the subtle process of securing effective loyalty to the traditional ideals of democracy, while respecting at the same time individual idiosyncrasies among a people so diversified in racial origins and religious allegiances. So to hold would in effect make us the school board for the country. That authority has not been given to this Court, nor should we assume it.

We are dealing here with the formative period in the development of citizenship. Great diversity of psychological and ethical opinion exists among us concerning the best way to train children for their place in society. Because of these differences and because of reluctance to permit a single, ironcast system of education to be imposed upon a nation compounded of so many strains, we have held that, even though public education is one of our most cherished democratic institutions, the Bill of Rights bars a state from compelling all children to attend the public schools. Pierce v. Society of the Sisters of the Holy Names of Jesus and Mary, 268 U.S. 510. But it is a very different thing for this Court to exercise censorship over the conviction of legislatures that a particular program or exercise will best promote in the minds of children who attend the common schools an attachment to the institutions of their country.

What the school authorities are really asserting is the right to awaken in the child's mind considerations as to the significance of the flag contrary to those implanted by the parent. In such an attempt the state is normally at a disadvantage in competing with the parent's authority, so long—and this is the vital aspect of religious toleration—as parents are unmolested in their right to counteract by their own persuasiveness the wisdom and rightness of those loyalties which the state's educational system is seeking to promote. Except where the transgression of constitutional liberty is too plain for argument, personal freedom is best maintained—so long as the remedial channels of the democratic process remain open and unobstructed—when it is ingrained in a people's habits and not enforced against popular policy by the coercion of adjudicated law. That the flag-salute is an allowable portion of a school program for those who do not invoke conscientious scruples is surely not debatable. But for us to insist that, though the ceremony may be required, exceptional immunity must be given to dissidents, is to maintain that there is no basis for a legislative judgment that such an exemption might introduce elements of difficulty into the school discipline, might cast doubts in the minds of the other children which would themselves weaken the effect of the exercise.

The preciousness of the family relation, the authority and independence which give dignity to parenthood, indeed the enjoyment of all freedom, presuppose the kind of ordered society which is summarized by our flag. A society which is dedicated to the preservation of these ultimate values of civilization may in self-protection utilize the educational process for inculcating those almost unconscious feelings which bind men together in a comprehending loyalty, whatever may be their lesser differences and difficulties. That is to say, the process may be utilized so long as men's right to believe as they please, to win others to their way of belief, and their right to assemble in their chosen places of worship for the devotional ceremonies of their faith, are all fully respected.

Judicial review, itself a limitation on popular government, is a fundamental part of our constitutional scheme. But to the legislature no less than to courts is committed the guardianship of deeply-cherished liberties. Where all the effective means of inducing political changes are left free from interference, education in the abandonment of foolish legislation is itself a training in liberty. To fight out the wise use of legislative authority in the forum of public opinion and before legislative assemblies rather than to transfer such a contest to the judicial arena, serves to vindicate the self-confidence of a free people.

*Reversed.*

## Decision on Mandatory Saluting of the Flag (1943)*

### *Appeal from the U.S. District Court for the Southern District of West Virginia*

*Mr. Justice Jackson Delivered the Opinion of the Court*

Following the decision by this Court on June 3, 1940, in *Minersville School District* v. *Gobitis,* 310 U.S. 586, the West Virginia legislature amended its statutes to require all schools therein to conduct courses of instruction in history, civics, and in the Constitution of the United States and of the State "for the purpose of teaching, fostering and perpetuating the

---

*From *West Virginia State Board of Education* v. *Barnette,* 319 U.S. 624 (1943).

ideals, principles and spirit of Americanism, and increasing the knowledge of the organization and machinery of the government." Appellant Board of Education was directed, with advice of the State Superintendent of Schools, to "prescribe the courses of study covering these subjects" for public schools. The Act made it the duty of private, parochial and denominational schools to prescribe courses of study "similar to those required for the public schools."

The Board of Education on January 9, 1942, adopted a resolution containing recitals taken largely from the Court's *Gobitis* opinion and ordering that the salute to the flag become "a regular part of the program of activities in the public schools," that all teachers and pupils "shall be required to participate in the salute honoring the Nation represented by the Flag; provided, however, that refusal to salute the Flag be regarded as an act of insubordination, and shall be dealt with accordingly."

The resolution originally required the "commonly accepted salute to the Flag" which it defined. Objections to the salute as "being too much like Hitler's were raised by the Parent and Teachers Association, the Boy and Girl Scouts, the Red Cross, and the Federation of Women's Clubs. Some modification appears to have been made in deference to these objections, but no concession was made to Jehovah's Witnesses. What is now required is the "stiff-arm" salute, the saluter to keep the right hand raised with palm turned up while the following is repeated: "I pledge allegiance to the Flag of the United States of America and to the Republic for which it stands; one Nation, indivisible, with liberty and justice for all."

Failure to conform is "insubordination" dealt with by expulsion. Readmission is denied by statute until compliance. Meanwhile the expelled child is "unlawfully, absent" and may be proceeded against as a delinquent. His parents or guardians are liable to prosecution, and if convicted are subject to fine not exceeding $50 and jail term not exceeding thirty days.

Appellees, citizens of the United States and of West Virginia, brought suit in the United States District Court for themselves and others similarly situated asking its injunction to restrain enforcement of these laws and regulations against Jehovah's Witnesses. The Witnesses are an unincorporated body teaching that the obligation imposed by the law of God is superior to that of laws enacted by temporal government. Their religious beliefs include a literal version of Exodus, Chapter 20, verses 4 and 5, which says: "Thou shalt not make unto thee any graven image, or any likeness of anything that is in heaven above, or that is in the earth beneath, or that is in the water under the earth; thou shalt not bow down thyself to them nor serve them." They consider that the flag is an "image" within this command. For this reason they refuse to salute it.

Children of this faith have been expelled from school and are threatened with exclusion for no other cause. Officials threaten to send them to reformatories maintained for criminally inclined juveniles. Parents of such children have been prosecuted and are threatened with prosecutions for causing delinquency.

The Board of Education moved to dismiss the complaint setting forth these facts and alleging that the law and regulations are an unconstitutional denial of religious freedom, and of freedom of speech, and are invalid under the "due process" and "equal protection" clauses of the Fourteenth Amendment to the Federal Constitution. The cause was submitted on the pleadings to a District Court of three judges. It restrained enforcement as to the plaintiffs and those of that class. The Board of Education brought the case here by direct appeal.

This case calls upon us to reconsider a precedent decision, as the Court throughout its history often has been required to do. Before turning to the *Gobitis* case, however, it is desirable to notice certain characteristics by which this controversy is distinguished.

The freedom asserted by these appellees does not bring them into collision with rights asserted by any other individual. It is such conflicts which most frequently require intervention of the State to determine where the rights of one end and those of another begin. But the refusal of these persons to participate in the ceremony does not interfere with or deny rights of others to do so. Nor is there any question in this case that their behavior is peaceable and orderly. The sole conflict is between authority and rights of the individual.

\* \* \*

There is no doubt that, in connection with the pledges, the flag salute is a form of utterance. Symbolism is a primitive but effective way of communicating ideas. The use of an emblem or flag to symbolize some system, idea, institution, or personality, is a short cut from mind to mind. Causes and nations, political parties, lodges and ecclesiastical groups seek to knit the loyalty of their followings to a flag or banner, a color or design.

\* \* \*

It is also to be noted that the compulsory flag salute and pledge requires affirmation of a belief and an attitude of mind. It is not clear whether the regulation contemplates that pupils forego any contrary convictions of their own and become unwilling converts to the prescribed ceremony or whether it will be acceptable if they simulate assent by words without belief and by a gesture barren of meaning. It is now a commonplace that censorship or suppression of expression of opinion is tolerated by our Constitution only when the expression presents a clear and present danger of action of a kind the State is empowered to prevent and punish. It would seem that involuntary affirmation could be commanded only on even more immediate and urgent grounds than silence. But here the power of compulsion is invoked without any allegation that remaining passive during a flag salute ritual creates a clear and present danger that would justify an effort even to muffle expression. To sustain the compulsory flag salute we are required to say that a Bill of Rights which guards the individual's right to speak his own mind, left it open to public authorities to compel him to utter what is not in his mind.

Whether the First Amendment to the Constitution will permit officials to order observance of ritual of this nature does not depend upon whether as a voluntary exercise we would think it to be good, bad or merely innocuous. Any credo of nationalism is likely to include what some disapprove or to omit what others think essential, and to give off different overtones as it takes on different accents or interpretations. If official power exists to coerce acceptance of any patriotic creed, what it shall contain cannot be decided by courts, but must be largely discretionary with the ordaining authority, whose power to prescribe would no doubt include power to amend. Hence validity of the asserted power to force an American citizen publicly to profess any statement of belief or to engage in any ceremony of assent to one, presents questions of power that must be considered independently of any idea we may have as to the utility of the ceremony in question.

Nor does the issue as we see it turn on one's possession of particular religious views or the sincerity with which they are held. While religion supplies appellees' motive for enduring the discomforts of making the issue in this case, many citizens who do not share these religious views hold such a compulsory rite to infringe constitutional liberty of the individual. It is not necessary to inquire whether nonconformist beliefs will exempt from the duty to salute unless we first find power to make the salute a legal duty.

The *Gobitis* decision, however, *assumed,* as did the argument in that case and in this, that power exists in the State to impose the flag salute discipline upon school children in general. The Court only examined and rejected a claim based on religious beliefs of immunity from an unquestioned general rule. The question which underlies the flag salute controversy is whether such a ceremony so touching matters of opinion and political attitude may be imposed upon the individual by official authority under powers committed to any political organization under our Constitution. We examine rather than assume existence of this power and, against this broader definition of issues in this case, reexamine specific grounds assigned for the *Gobitis* decision.

1. It was said that the flag-salute controversy confronted the Court with "the problem which Lincoln cast in memorable dilemma: 'Must a government of necessity be too *strong* for the liberties of its people, or too *weak* to maintain its own existence?'" and that the answer must be in favor of strength....

We think these issues may be examined free of pressure or restraint growing out of such considerations.

It may be doubted whether Mr. Lincoln would have thought that the strength of government to maintain itself would be impressively vindicated by our confirming power of the State to expel a handful of children from school. Such oversimplification, so handy in political debate, often lacks the precision necessary to postulates of judicial reasoning. If validly applied to this problem, the utterance cited would resolve every issue of power in favor of those in authority and would require us to override every liberty thought to weaken or delay execution of their policies.

Government of limited power need not be anemic government. Assurance that rights are secure tends to diminish fear and jealousy of strong government, and by making us feel safe to live under it makes for its better support. Without promise of a limiting Bill of Rights it is doubtful if our Constitution could have mustered enough strength to enable its ratification. To enforce those rights today is not to choose weak government over strong government. It is only to adhere as a means of strength to individual freedom of mind in preference to officialiy disciplined uniformity for which history indicates a disappointing and disastrous end.

The subject now before us exemplifies this principle. Free public education, if faithful to the ideal of secular instruction and political neutrality, will not be partisan or enemy of any class, creed, party, or faction. If it is to impose any ideological discipline, however, each party or denomination must seek to control, or failing that, to weaken the influence of the educational system. Observance of the limitations of the Constitution will not weaken government in the field appropriate for its exercise.

2. It was also considered in the *Gobitis* case that functions of educational officers in States, counties and school districts were such that to interfere with their authority "would in effect make us the school board for the country."

The Fourteenth Amendment, as now applied to the States, protects the citizen against the State itself and all of its creatures—Boards of Education not excepted. These have, of course, important, delicate, and highly discretionary functions, but none that they may not perform within the limits of the Bill of Rights. That they are educating the young for citizenship is reason for scrupulous protection of Constitutional freedoms of the individual, if we are not to strangle the free mind at its source and teach youth to discount important principles of our government as mere platitudes.

Such Boards are numerous and their territorial jurisdiction often small. But small and local authority may feel less sense of responsibility to the Constitution, and agencies of publicity may be less vigilant in calling it to account. The action of Congress in making flag observance voluntary and respecting the conscience of the objector in a matter so vital as raising the Army contrasts sharply with these local regulations in matters relatively trivial to the welfare of the nation. There are village tyrants as well as village Hampdens, but none who acts under color of law is beyond reach of the Constitution.

3. The *Gobitis* opinion reasoned that this is a field "where courts possess no marked and certainly no controlling competence," that it is committed to the legislatures as well as the courts to guard cherished liberties and that it is constitutionally appropriate to "fight out the wise use of legislative authority in the forum of public opinion and before legislative assemblies rather than to transfer such a contest to the judicial arena," since all the "effective means of inducing political changes are left free."

The very purpose of a Bill of Rights was to withdraw certain subjects from the vicissitudes of political controversy, to place them beyond the reach of majorities and officials and to establish them as legal principles to be applied by the courts. One's right to life, liberty, and property, to free speech, a free press, freedom of worship and assembly, and other fundamental rights may not be submitted to vote; they depend on the outcome of no elections.

In weighing arguments of the parties it is important to distinguish between the due process clause of the Fourteenth Amendment as an instrument for transmitting the principles of the First Amendment and those cases in which it is applied for its own sake. The test of legislation which collides with the Fourteenth Amendment, because it also collides with the principles of the First, is much more definite than the test when only the Fourteenth is involved. Much of the vagueness of the due process clause disappears when the specific prohibitions of the First become its standard. The right of a State to regulate, for example, a public utility may well include, so far as the due process test is concerned, power to impose all of the restrictions which a legislature may have a "rational basis" for adopting. But freedoms of speech and of press, of assembly, and of worship may not be infringed on such slender grounds. They are susceptible of restriction only to prevent grave and immediate danger to interests which the State may lawfully protect. It is important to note that while it is the Fourteenth Amendment which bears directly upon the State it is the more specific limiting principles of the First Amendment that finally govern this case.

Nor does our duty to apply the Bill of Rights to assertions of official authority depend upon our possession of marked competence in the field where the invasion of rights occurs. True, the task of translating the majestic generalities of the Bill of Rights, conceived as part of the pattern of liberal government in the eighteenth century, into concrete restraints on officials dealing with the problems of the twentieth century, is one to disturb self-confidence. These principles grew in soil which also produced a philosophy that the individual was the center of society, that his liberty was attainable through mere absence of governmental restraints, and that government should be entrusted with few controls and only the mildest supervision over men's affairs. We must transplant these rights to a soil in which the *laissez-faire* concept or principle of noninterference has withered at least as to economic affairs, and social advancements are increasingly sought through closer integration of society and through expanded and strengthened governmental controls. These changed conditions often deprive precedents of reliability and cast us more than we would choose upon our own judgment. But we act in these matters not by authority of our competence but by force of our commissions. We cannot, because of modest estimates of our competence in such specialties as public education, withhold the judgment that history authenticates as the function of this Court when liberty is infringed.

4. Lastly, and this is the very heart of the *Gobitis* opinion, it reasons that "National unity is the basis of national security," that the authorities have "the right to select appropriate means for its attainment," and hence reaches the conclusion that such compulsory measures toward "national unity" are constitutional. Upon the verity of this assumption depends our answer in this case.

National unity as an end which officials may foster by persuasion and example is not in question. The problem is whether under our Constitution compulsion as here employed is a permissible means for its achievement.

Struggles to coerce uniformity of sentiment in support of some end thought essential to their time and country have been waged by many good as well as by evil men. Nationalism is a relatively recent phenomenon but at other times and places the ends have been racial or territorial security, support of a dynasty or regime, and particular plans for saving souls. As first and moderate methods to attain unity have failed, those bent on its accomplishment must resort to an ever-increasing severity. As governmental pressure toward unity becomes greater, so strife becomes more bitter as to whose unity it shall be. Probably no deeper division of our people could proceed from any provocation than from finding it necessary to choose what doctrine and whose program public educational officials shall compel youth to unite in embracing. Ultimate futility of such attempts to compel coherence is the lesson of every such effort from the Roman drive to stamp out Christianity as a disturber of its pagan unity, the Inquisition, as a means to religious and dynastic unity, the Siberian exiles as a means to Russian unity, down to the last failing efforts of our present totalitarian enemies. Those who begin coercive elimination of dissent soon find themselves exterminating dissenters. Compulsory unification of opinion achieves only the unanimity of the graveyard.

It seems trite but necessary to say that the First Amendment to our Constitution was designed to avoid these ends by avoiding these beginnings. There is no mysticism in the American concept of the State or of the nature or origin of its authority. We set up government by consent of the governed, and the Bill of Rights denies those in power any legal opportunity to coerce that consent. Authority here is to be controlled by public opinion, not public opinion by authority.

The case is made difficult not because the principles of its decision are obscure but because the flag involved is our own. Nevertheless, we apply the limitations of the Constitution with no fear that freedom to be intellectually and spiritually diverse or even contrary will disintegrate the social organization. To believe that patriotism will not flourish if patriotic ceremonies are voluntary and spontaneous instead of a compulsory routine is to make an unflattering estimate of the appeal of our institutions to free minds. We can have intellectual individualism and the rich cultural diversities that we owe to exceptional minds only at the price of occasional eccentricity and abnormal attitudes. When they are so harmless to others or to the State as those we deal with here, the price is not too great. But freedom to differ is not limited to things that do not matter much. That would be a mere shadow of freedom. The test of its substance is the right to differ as to things that touch the heart of the existing order.

If there is any fixed star in our constitutional constellation, it is that no official, high or petty, can prescribe what shall be orthodox in politics, nationalism, religion, or other matters of opinion or force citizens to confess by word or act their faith therein. If there are any circumstances which permit an exception, they do not now occur to us....

The decision of this Court in *Minersville School District* v. *Gobitis* and the holdings of those few *per curiam* decisions which preceded and foreshadowed it are overruled, and the judgment enjoining enforcement of the West Virginia Regulation is *affirmed*.

\* \* \*

One who belongs to the most vilified and persecuted minority in history is not likely to be insensible to the freedoms guaranteed by our Constitution. Were my purely personal attitude relevant I should wholeheartedly associate myself with the general libertarian views in the Court's opinion, representing as they do the thought and action of a lifetime. But as judges we are neither Jew nor Gentile, neither Catholic nor agnostic. We owe equal attachment to the Constitution and are equally bound by our judicial obligations whether we derive our citizenship from the earliest or the latest immigrants to these shores. As a member of this Court I am not justified in writing my private notions of policy into the Constitution, no matter how deeply I may cherish them or how mischievous I may deem their disregard.

# QUESTIONS

1. Describe in your own words the religious aspects of the First Amendment.

2. What does it mean to declare a law unconstitutional? On what basis did the U.S. Supreme Court declare Oregon's 1922 compulsory school law unconstitutional?

3. Is it legal or constitutional for the state to compel children to attend school? If not, why? If yes, on what grounds?

4. Do you think that the 1922 Oregon law reflected a bias toward Roman Catholicism?

5. Based on the *Gobitis* decision, is compulsory flag salute constitutional?

6. Based on the *Barnette* decision, is compulsory flag salute constitutional?

7. Why do these two cases revolve around the free exercise clause of the First Amendment?

8. Distinguish between a "preferred" freedom and a regular freedom.

9. Can you explain why in the midst of World War II, when patriotism was at its peak, the U.S. Supreme Court declared compulsory flag salute unconstitutional?

# 5 Religion and the Schools

## The Establishment Clause

The courts have assisted U.S. public schools in complying with both the free exercise and establishment clauses of the First Amendment. Regarding the role of religion in public schools, the Supreme Court followed Thomas Jefferson's lead in suggesting that the First Amendment "erected a wall between Church and State which must be kept high and impregnable."

In the case *Illinois ex. rel. McCollum Board of Education* (1948), the Supreme Court ruled against allowing religious instruction on a public school campus even though parents had signed permission slips for their children to participate and the classes were conducted by volunteers and/or paid professionals from various denominations and faiths. Students choosing not to participate were asked to leave their classrooms and go to the library or to some other part of the school. The Court ruled against the practice, indicating that it resulted in using the state's compulsory school system to aid or promote the work of religious groups.

Such rulings have been and continue to be controversial, leading critics to blame the courts for making education godless. *Engel v Vitale* (1962) may be the most reviled of these cases. In this case, the Supreme Court denied the right of a public school system to conduct prayer services within school buildings during regular school hours. This case revolved around the New York Board of Regents' approval of a request by a local school district to begin the school day with the following brief prayer: "Almighty God, we acknowledge our dependence upon thee and we beg Thy blessings upon us, our parents, our teachers, and our country." Students were not compelled to recite the prayer if they or their parents objected. The Supreme Court ruled against allowing the district to begin each school day with this prayer, in part, because governmental officials had written the prayer, thus seemingly putting the state in the position of promoting or establishing religion.

The Schempp and Murray cases were equally controversial. In 1959, the Pennsylvania legislature passed a law requiring public schools to begin the day with a public reading of at least ten verses from the Bible. The Schempp family, Unitarians from the Germantown section of Philadelphia, objected to this practice. The Schempp children attended Abington Senior High School, where Bible verses were read over the intercom each morning and students stood in their homeroom and repeated them in unison. Even though students could leave the classroom or choose not to participate, the federal district court ruled that the

Pennsylvania statute violated the First and Fourteenth Amendments. The school district and the state attorney general appealed to the Supreme Court.

At roughly the same time, a similar controversy involving professed atheists Madalyn Murray and her son was working its way through the Maryland courts. Based on a 1905 ruling by the School Commissioners of Baltimore, Maryland, school began each day with reading—without comment—of a chapter in the Bible and/or the recitation of the Lord's Prayer. The Maryland courts initially upheld these practices, but eventually both the Schempp and Murray cases reached the Supreme Court.

Ruling on both cases in one opinion, the Supreme Court declared Bible reading and prayer in the public schools unconstitutional. In rendering its decision, the Court engaged in a comprehensive review of the legal history of the church/state relationship in this country. In announcing its decision, the Court made it clear that legal precedent had consistently taken a position of neutrality toward religion and "while protecting all, it prefers none, and it disparages none." The decision made it clear that religious activities, Bible reading, and prayer are not permissible in the public schools of this nation.

As we begin the new millennium, it remains to be seen if the Puritan/Jeffersonian legacy will continue to manifest itself in the controversy over the role of religion in the public schools. An answer to this question is dependent in part on the resolution of other issues. Will the public or common school that emerged in the nineteenth century and became the dominant form of schooling in the twentieth century survive and prosper? Is common or public education desirable or possible in the world of the twenty-first century? Even though definitive answers will not be forthcoming, our discussion of local versus centralized control of schooling can contribute to a better understanding of the questions about the future of public education in this country.

For more information concerning legal conflicts over religion and the schools, see Louis Fischer and David Schimmel, *The Rights of Student and Teachers* (New York: Harper & Row, Publishers, 1982), pp. 138–169.

# Decision on Released Time for Religious Instruction on School Premises (1948)*

## *Appeal from the Supreme Court of Illinois*

### *Mr. Justice Black Delivered the Opinion of the Court*

This case relates to the power of a state to utilize its tax-supported public school system in aid of religious instruction insofar as that power may be restricted by the First and Fourteenth Amendments to the Federal Constitution.

The appellant, Vashti McCollum, began this action for mandamus against the Champaign Board of Education in the Circuit Court of Champaign County, Illinois. Her asserted interest was that of a resident and taxpayer of Champaign and of a parent whose child was

*From *Illinois ex, rel. McCollum* v. *Board of Education.* 333 U.S. 203 (1948).

then enrolled in the Champaign public schools. Illinois has a compulsory education law which, with exceptions, requires parents to send their children, aged seven to sixteen, to its tax-supported public schools where the children are to remain in attendance during the hours when the schools are regularly in session. Parents who violate this law commit a misdemeanor punishable by fine unless the children attend private or parochial schools which meet educational standards fixed by the State. District boards of education are given general supervisory powers over the use of the public school buildings within the school districts....

Appellant's petition for mandamus alleged that religious teachers, employed by private religious groups, were permitted to come weekly into the school buildings during the regular hours set apart for secular teaching, and then and there for a period of thirty minutes substitute their religious teaching for the secular education provided under the compulsory education law. The petitioner charged that this joint public-school religious-group program violated the First and Fourteenth Amendments to the United States Constitution....

Although there are disputes between the parties as to various inferences that may or may not properly be drawn from the evidence concerning the religious program, the following facts are shown by the record without dispute. In 1940 interested members of the Jewish, Roman Catholic, and a few of the Protestant faiths formed a voluntary association called the Champaign Council on Religious Education. They obtained permission from the Board of Education to offer classes in religious instruction to public school pupils in grades four to nine inclusive. Classes were made up of pupils whose parents signed printed cards requesting that their children be permitted to attend; they were held weekly, thirty minutes for the lower grades, forty-five minutes for the higher. The council employed the religious teachers at no expense to the school authorities, but the instructors were subject to the approval and supervision of the superintendent of schools. The classes were taught in three separate religious groups by Protestant teachers, Catholic priests, and a Jewish rabbi, although for the past several years there have apparently been no classes instructed in the Jewish religion. Classes were conducted in the regular classrooms of the school building. Students who did not choose to take the religious instruction were not released from public school duties; they were required to leave their classrooms and go to some other place in the school building for pursuit of their secular studies. On the other hand, students who were released from secular study for the religious instructions were required to be present at the religious classes. Reports of their presence or absence were to be made to their secular teachers.

The foregoing facts, without reference to others that appear in the record, show the use of tax-supported property for religious instruction and the close cooperation between the school authorities and the religious council in promoting religious education. The operation of the State's compulsory education system thus assists and is integrated with the program of religious instruction carried on by separate religious sects. Pupils compelled by law to go to school for secular education are released in part from their legal duty upon the condition that they attend the religious classes. This is beyond all question a utilization of the tax-established and tax-supported public school system to aid religious groups to spread their faith. And it falls squarely under the ban of the First Amendment (made applicable to the States by the Fourteenth) as we interpreted it in *Everson* v. *Board of Education,* 330 U.S. 1.

* * *

Recognizing that the Illinois program is barred by the First and Fourteenth Amendments if we adhere to the views expressed both by the majority and the minority in the *Everson* case, counsel for the respondents challenge those views as dicta and urge that we reconsider and repudiate them. They argue that historically the First Amendment was intended to forbid only government preference of one religion over another, not an impartial governmental assistance of all religions. In addition they ask that we distinguish or overrule our holding in the *Everson* case that the Fourteenth Amendment made the "establishment of religion" clause of the First Amendment applicable as a prohibition against the States. After giving full consideration to the arguments presented we are unable to accept either of these contentions.

To hold that a state cannot consistently with the First and Fourteenth Amendments utilize its public school system to aid any or all religious faiths or sects in the dissemination of their doctrines and ideals does not, as counsel urge, manifest a governmental hostility to religion or religious teachings. A manifestation of such hostility would be at war with our national tradition as embodied in the First Amendment's guaranty of the free exercise of religion. For the First Amendment rests upon the premise that both religion and government can best work to achieve their lofty aims if each is left free from the other within its respective sphere. Or, as we said in the *Everson* case, the First Amendment has erected a wall between Church and State which must be kept high and impregnable.

Here not only are the State's tax-supported public school buildings used for the dissemination of religious doctrines. The State also affords sectarian groups an invaluable aid in that it helps to provide pupils for their religious classes through use of the State's compulsory public school machinery. This is not separation of Church and State.

The cause is reversed and remanded to the State Supreme Court for proceedings not inconsistent with this opinion.

*Reversed and remanded.*

*Mr. Justice Frankfurter Delivered the Following Opinion, in Which Mr. Justice Jackson, Mr. Justice Rutledge, and Mr. Justice Burton Join*

We dissented in *Everson* v. *Board of Education,* 330 U.S. 1, because in our view the Constitutional principle requiring separation of Church and State compelled invalidation of the ordinance sustained by the majority. Illinois has here authorized the commingling of sectarian with secular instruction in the public schools. The Constitution of the United States forbids this.

This case, in the light of the *Everson* decision, demonstrates anew that the mere formulation of a relevant Constitutional principle is the beginning of the solution of a problem, not its answer. This is so because the meaning of a spacious conception like that of the separation of Church from State is unfolded as appeal is made to the principle from case to case. We are all agreed that the First and the Fourteenth Amendments have a secular reach far more penetrating in the conduct of Government than merely to forbid an "established church." But agreement, in the abstract, that the First Amendment was designed to erect a "wall of separation between church and State," does not preclude a clash of views as to what the wall separates. Involved is not only the Constitutional principle but the implications of judicial review in its enforcement. Accommodation of legislative freedom and Constitutional limitations upon that freedom cannot be achieved by a mere phrase. We cannot illuminatingly apply the "wall-of-separation" metaphor until we have considered the relevant history of religious education in America, the place of the "released time" movement in that history, and its precise manifestation in the case before us.

To understand the particular program now before us as a conscientious attempt to accommodate the allowable functions of Government and the special concerns of the Church within the framework of our Constitution and with due regard to the kind of society for which it was designed, we must put this Champaign program of 1940 in its historic setting. Traditionally, organized education in the Western world was Church education. It could hardly be otherwise when the education of children was primarily study of the Word and the ways of God. Even in the Protestant countries, where there was a less close identification of Church and State, the basis of education was largely the Bible, and its chief purpose inculcation of piety. To the extent that the State intervened, it used its authority to further aims of the Church.

The emigrants who came to these shores brought this view of education with them. Colonial schools certainly started with a religious orientation. When the common problems of the early settlers of the Massachusetts Bay Colony revealed the need for common schools, the object was the defeat of "one chief project of that old deluder, Satan, to keep men from the knowledge of the Scriptures." The Laws and Liberties of Massachusetts, 1648 edition (Cambridge 1929) 47.

The evolution of colonial education, largely in the service of religion, into the public school system of today is the story of changing conceptions regarding the American democratic society, of the functions of State-maintained education in such a society, and of the role therein of the free exercise of religion by the people. The modern public school derived from a philosophy of freedom reflected in the First Amendment....

Separation in the field of education, then, was not imposed upon unwilling States by force of superior law. In this respect the Fourteenth Amendment merely reflected a principle then dominant in our national life. To the extent that the Constitution thus made it binding upon the States, the basis of the restriction is the whole experience of our people. Zealous watchfulness against fusion of secular and religious activities by Government itself, through any of its instruments but especially through its educational agencies, was the democratic response of the American community to the particular needs of a young and growing nation, unique in the composition of its people....

It is pertinent to remind that the establishment of this principle of Separation in the field of education was not due to any decline in the religious beliefs of the people. Horace Mann was a devout Christian, and the deep religious feeling of James Madison is stamped upon the Remonstrance. The secular public school did not imply indifference to the basic role of religion in the life of the people, nor rejection of religious education as a means of fostering it. The claims of religion were not minimized by refusing to make the public schools agencies for their assertion. The nonsectarian or secular public school was the means of reconciling freedom in general with religious freedom. The sharp confinement of the public schools to secular education was a recognition of the need of a democratic society to educate its children, insofar as the State undertook to do so, in an atmosphere free from pressures in a realm in which pressures are most resisted and where conflicts are most easily and most bitterly engendered. Designed to serve as perhaps the most powerful agency for promoting cohesion among a heterogeneous democratic people, the public school must keep scrupulously free from entanglement in the strife of sects. The preservation of the community from divisive conflicts, of Government from irreconcilable pressures by religious groups, of religion from censorship and coercion however subtly exercised, requires strict confinement of the State to instruction other than religious, leaving to the individual's church and home, indoctrination in the faith of his choice....

Mr. Justice Jackson, *concurring.*

# Decision on Recitation of Prayers in Public Schools (1962)*

### *Certiorari to the Court of Appeals of New York*

### *Mr. Justice Black Delivered the Opinion of the Court*

We think that by using its public school system to encourage recitation of the Regents' prayer, the State of New York has adopted a practice wholly inconsistent with the Establishment Clause. There can, of course, be no doubt that New York's program of daily classroom invocation of God's blessings as prescribed in the Regents' prayer is a religious activity. It is a solemn avowal of divine faith and supplication for the blessings of the Almighty. The nature of such a prayer has always been religious, none of the respondents has denied this and the trial court expressly so found....

The petitioners contend among other things that the state laws requiring or permitting use of the Regents' prayer must be struck down as a violation of the Establishment Clause because that prayer was composed by governmental officials as a part of a governmental program to further religious beliefs. For this reason, petitioners argue, the State's use of the Regents' prayer in its public school system breaches the constitutional wall of separation between Church and State. We agree with that contention since we think that the constitutional prohibition against laws respecting an establishment of religion must at least mean that in this country it is no part of the business of government to compose official prayers for any group of the American people to recite as a part of a religious program carried on by government.

It is a matter of history that this very practice of establishing governmentally composed prayers for religious services was one of the reasons which caused many of our early colonists to leave England and seek religious freedom in America. The Book of Common Prayer, which was created under governmental direction and which was approved by Acts of Parliament in 1548 and 1549, set out in minute detail the accepted form and content of prayer and other religious ceremonies to be used in the established, tax-supported Church of

*From *Engel* v. *Vitale,* 370 U.S. 421 (1962).

England. The controversies over the Book and what should be its content repeatedly threat-ened to disrupt the peace of that country as the accepted forms of prayer in the established church changed with the views of the particular ruler that happened to be in control at the time. Powerful groups representing some of the varying religious views of the people strug-gled among themselves to impress their particular views upon the Government and obtain amendments of the Book more suitable to their respective notions of how religious services should be conducted in order that the official religious establishment would advance their particular religious beliefs. Other groups, lacking the necessary political power to influence the Government on the matter, decided to leave England and its established church and seek freedom in America from England's governmentally ordained and supported religion.

It is an unfortunate fact of history that when some of the very groups which had most strenuously opposed the established Church of England found themselves sufficiently in control of colonial governments in this country to write their own prayers into law, they passed laws making their own religion the official religion of their respective colonies. In-deed, as late as the time of the Revolutionary War, there were established churches in at least eight of the thirteen former colonies and established religions in at least four of the other five. But the successful Revolution against English political domination was shortly followed by intense opposition to the practice of establishing religion by law. This opposi-tion crystallized rapidly into an effective political force in Virginia where the minority re-ligious groups such as Presbyterians, Lutherans, Quakers and Baptists had gained such strength that the adherents to the established Episcopal Church were actually a minority themselves. In 1785–1786, those opposed to the established Church, led by James Madi-son and Thomas Jefferson, who, though themselves not members of any of these dissent-ing religious groups, opposed all religious establishments by law on grounds of principle, obtained the enactment of the famous "Virginia Bill for Religious Liberty" by which all re-ligious groups were placed on an equal footing so far as the State was concerned. Similar though less far-reaching legislation was being considered and passed in other States.

By the time of the adoption of the Constitution, our history shows that there was a widespread awareness among many Americans of the dangers of a union of Church and State. These people knew, some of them from bitter personal experience, that one of the greatest dangers to the freedom of the individual to worship in his own way lay in the Gov-ernment's placing its official stamp of approval upon one particular kind of prayer or one particular form of religious services. They knew the anguish, hardship and bitter strife that could come when zealous religious groups struggled with one another to obtain the Gov-ernment's stamp of approval from each King, Queen, or Protector that came to temporary power. The Constitution was intended to avert a part of this danger by leaving the govern-ment of this country in the hands of the people rather than in the hands of any monarch. But this safeguard was not enough. Our Founders were no more willing to let the content of their prayers and their privilege of praying whenever they pleased be influenced by the ballot box than they were to let these vital matters of personal conscience depend upon the succession of monarchs. The First Amendment was added to the Constitution to stand as a guarantee that neither the power nor the prestige of the Federal Government would be used to control, support or influence the kinds of prayer the American people can say—that the people's religions must not be subjected to the pressures of government for change each time a new political administration is elected to office. Under that Amendment's prohibi-tion against governmental establishment of religion, as reinforced by the provisions of the

Fourteenth Amendment, government in this country, be it state or federal, is without power to prescribe by law any particular form of prayer which is to be used as an official prayer in carrying on any program of governmentally sponsored religious activity.

There can be no doubt that New York's state prayer program officially establishes the religious beliefs embodied in the Regents' prayer. The respondents' argument to the contrary, which is largely based upon the contention that the Regents' prayer is "non-denominational" and the fact that the program, as modified and approved by state courts, does not require all pupils to recite the prayer but permits those who wish to do so to remain silent or be excused from the room, ignores the essential nature of the program's constitutional defects. Neither the fact that the prayer may be denominationally neutral nor the fact that its observance on the part of the students is voluntary can serve to free it from the limitations of the Establishment Clause, as it might from the Free Exercise Clause, of the First Amendment, both of which are operative against the States by virtue of the Fourteenth Amendment. Although these two clauses may in certain instances overlap, they forbid two quite different kinds of governmental encroachment upon religious freedom. The Establishment Clause, unlike the Free Exercise Clause, does not depend upon any showing of direct governmental compulsion and is violated by the enactment of laws which establish an official religion whether those laws operate directly to coerce nonob-serving individuals or not. This is not to say, of course, that laws officially prescribing a particular form of religious worship do not involve coercion of such individuals. When the power, prestige and financial support of government is placed behind a particular religious belief, the indirect coercive pressure upon religious minorities to conform to the prevailing officially approved religion is plain. But the purposes underlying the Establishment Clause go much further than that. Its first and most immediate purpose rested on the belief that a union of government and religion tends to destroy government and to degrade religion. The history of governmentally established religion, both in England and in this country, showed that whenever government had allied itself with one particular form of religion, the inevitable result had been that it had incurred the hatred, disrespect and even contempt of those who held contrary beliefs. That same history showed that many people had lost their respect for any religion that had relied upon the support of government to spread its faith. The Establishment Clause thus stands as an expression of principle on the part of the Founders of our Constitution that religion is too personal, too sacred, too holy, to permit its "unhallowed perversion" by a civil magistrate. Another purpose of the Establishment Clause rested upon an awareness of the historical fact that governmentally, established religions and religious persecutions go hand in hand. The Founders knew that only a few years after the Book of Common Prayer became the only accepted form of religious services in the established Church of England, an Act of Uniformity was passed to compel all Englishmen to attend those services and to make it a criminal offense to conduct or attend religious gatherings of any other kind—a law which was consistently flouted by dissenting religious groups in England and which contributed to widespread persecutions of people like John Bunyan who persisted in holding "unlawful [religious] meetings...to the great disturbance and distraction of the good subjects of this kingdom...." And they knew that similar persecutions had received the sanction of law in several of the colonies in this country soon after the establishment of official religions in those colonies. It was in large part to get completely away from this sort of systematic religious persecution that the Founders brought into being our Nation, our Constitution, and our Bill of Rights with its prohibition against any governmental establishment of religion. The New York laws officially prescribing the Regents' prayer are inconsistent with both the purposes of the Establishment Clause and with the Establishment Clause itself.

It has been argued that to apply the Constitution in such a way as to prohibit state laws respecting an establishment of religious services in public schools is to indicate a hositility toward religion or toward prayer. Nothing, of course, could be more wrong. The history of man is inseparable from the history of religion. And perhaps it is not too much to say that since the beginning of that history many people have devoutly believed that "More things are wrought by prayer than this world dreams of." It was doubtless largely due to men who believed this that there grew up a sentiment that caused men to leave the cross-currents of officially established state religions and religious persecution in Europe and come to this country filled with the hope that they could find a place in which they could pray when they pleased to the God of their faith in the language they chose. And there were men of this same faith in the power of prayer who led the fight for adoption of our Constitution and also for our Bill of Rights with the very guarantees of religious freedom that forbid the sort of governmental activity which New York has attempted here. These men knew that the First Amendment, which tried to put an end to governmental control of religion and of prayer, was not written to destroy either. They knew rather that it was written to quiet well-justified fears which nearly all of them felt arising out of an awareness that governments of the past had shackled men's tongues to make them speak only the religious thoughts that government wanted them to speak and to pray only to the God that government wanted them to pray to. It is neither sacrilegious nor antireligious to say that each separate government in this country should stay out of the business of writing or sanctioning official prayers and leave that purely religious function to the people themselves and to those the people choose to look to for religious guidance.

*Reversed and remanded.*

Mr. Justice Frankfurter took no part in the decision of this case.

Mr. Justice White took no part in the consideration or decision of this case.

Mr. Justice Douglas, concurring.

## *Mr. Justice Stewart, Dissenting*

With all respect, I think the Court has misapplied a great constitutional principle. I cannot see how an "official religion" is established by letting those who want to say a prayer say it. On the contrary, I think that to deny the wish of these school children to join in reciting this prayer is to deny them the opportunity of sharing in the spiritual heritage of our Nation.

The Court's historical review of the quarrels over the Book of Common Prayer in England throws no light for me on the issue before us in this case. England had then and has now an established church. Equally unenlightening, I think, is the history of the early establishment and later rejection of an official church in our own States. For we deal here not with the establishment of a state church, which would, of course, be constitutionally impermissible, but with whether school children who want to begin their day by joining in prayer must be prohibited from doing so. Moreover, I think that the Court's task, in this as in all areas of constitutional adjudication, is not responsibly aided by the uncritical invocation of metaphors like the "wall of separation," a phrase nowhere to be found in the Constitution. What is relevant to the issue here is not the history of an established church in sixteenth century England or in eighteenth century America, but the history of the religious traditions of our people, reflected in countless practices of the institutions and officials of our government.

At the opening of each day's Session of this Court we stand, while one of our officials invokes the protection of God. Since the days of John Marshall our Crier has said, "God save the United States and this Honorable Court." Both the Senate and the House of Representatives open their daily Sessions with prayer. Each of our Presidents, from George Washington to John F. Kennedy, has upon assuming his Office asked the protection and help of God.

The Court today says that the state and federal governments are without constitutional power to prescribe any particular form of words to be recited by any group of the American people on any subject touching religion. The third stanza of "The Star-Spangled Banner," made our National Anthem by Act of Congress in 1931, contains these verses:

> *"Blest with victory, and peace, may the heav'n rescued land*
> *Praise the Pow'r that hath made and preserved us a nation!*
> *Then conquer we must, when our cause it is just,*
> *And this be our motto 'In God is our Trust.' "*

In 1954 Congress added a phrase to the Pledge of Allegiance to the Flag so that it now contains the words "one Nation *under* God, indivisible, with liberty and justice for all." In 1952 Congress enacted legislation calling upon the President each year to proclaim a National Day of Prayer. Since 1865 the words "IN GOD WE TRUST" have been impressed on our coins.

Countless similar examples could be listed, but there is no need to belabor the obvious....

I do not believe that this Court, or the Congress, or the President has by the actions and practices I have mentioned established an "official religion" in violation of the Constitution. And I do not believe the State of New York has done so in this case. What each has done has been to recognize and to follow the deeply entrenched and highly cherished spiritual traditions of our Nation—traditions which come down to us from those who almost two hundred years ago avowed their "firm reliance on the Protection of divine Providence" when they proclaimed the freedom and independence of this brave new world.

I dissent.

# Decision on Bible Reading in the Public Schools (1963)*

### *Appeal from U.S. District Court for the Eastern District of Pennsylvania*

#### *Mr. Justice Clark Delivered the Opinion of the Court*

First, this Court has decisively settled that the First Amendment's mandate that "Congress shall make no law respecting an establishment of religion, or prohibiting the free exercise thereof" has been made wholly applicable to the States by the Fourteenth Amendment....

*From *Abington School District* v. *Schempp.* 374 U.S. 203 (1963)

Second, this Court has rejected unequivocally the contention that the Establishment Clause forbids only governmental preference of one religion over another. Almost 20 years ago in *Everson*…the Court said that "[n]either a state nor the Federal Government can set up a church. Neither can pass laws which aid one religion, aid all religions, or prefer one religion over another…."

While none of the parties to either of these cases has questioned these basic conclusions of the Court, both of which have been long established, recognized and consistently reaffirmed, others continue to question their history, logic and efficacy. Such contentions, in the light of the consistent interpretation in cases of this Court, seem entirely untenable and of value only as academic exercises….

The wholesome "neutrality" of which this Court's cases speak thus stems from a recognition of the teachings of history that powerful sects or groups might bring about a fusion of governmental and religious functions or a concert or dependency of one upon the other to the end that official support of the State or Federal Government would be placed behind the tenets of one or of all orthodoxies. This the Establishment Clause prohibits. And a further reason for neutrality is found in the Free Exercise Clause, which recognizes the value of religious training, teaching and observance and, more particularly, the right of every person to freely choose his own course with reference thereto, free of any compulsion from the state. This the Free Exercise Clause guarantees. Thus, as we have seen, the two clauses may overlap. As we have indicated, the Establishment Clause has been directly considered by this Court eight times in the past score of years and, with only one Justice dissenting on the point, it has consistently held that the clause withdrew all legislative power respecting religious belief or the expression thereof. The test may be stated as follows: what are the purpose and the primary effect of the enactment? If either is the advancement or inhibition of religion then the enactment exceeds the scope of legislative power as circumscribed by the Constitution. That is to say that to withstand the strictures of the Establishment Clause there must be a secular legislative purpose and a primary effect that neither advances nor inhibits religion…. The Free Exercise Clause, likewise considered many times here, withdraws from legislative power, state and federal, the exertion of any restraint on the free exercise of religion. Its purpose is to secure religious liberty in the individual by prohibiting any invasions thereof by civil authority. Hence it is necessary in a free exercise case for one to show the coercive effect of the enactment as it operates against him in the practice of his religion. The distinction between the two clauses is apparent—a violation of the Free Exercise Clause is predicated on coercion while the Establishment Clause violation need not be so attended….

…In both cases the laws require religious exercises and such exercises are being conducted in direct violation of the rights of the appellees and petitioners. Nor are these required exercises mitigated by the fact that individual students may absent themselves upon parental request, for that fact furnishes no defense to a claim of unconstitutionality under the Establishment Clause…. Further, it is no defense to urge that the religious practices here may be relatively minor encroachments on the First Amendment. The breach of neutrality that is today a trickling stream may all too soon become a raging torrent and, in the words of Madison, "it is proper to take alarm at the first experiment on our liberties."…

It is insisted that unless these religious exercises are permitted a "religion of secularism" is established in the schools. We agree of course that the State may not establish a "religion of secularism" in the sense of affirmatively opposing or showing hostility to religion, thus "preferring those who believe in no religion over those who do believe." We do not agree, however, that this decision in any sense has that effect. In addition, it might well be said that one's education is not complete without a study of comparative religion or the history of religion and its relationship to the advancement of civilization. It certainly may be said that the Bible is worthy of study for its literary and historic qualities. Nothing we have said here indicates that such study of the Bible or of religion, when presented objectively as part of a secular program of education, may not be effected consistently with the First Amendment. But the exercises here do not fall into those categories. They are religious exercises, required by the States in violation of the command of the First Amendment that the Government maintain strict neutrality, neither aiding nor opposing religion.

Finally. we cannot accept that the concept of neutrality, which does not permit a State to require a religious exercise even with the consent of the majority of those affected, collides with the majority's right to free exercise of religion. While the Free Exercise Clause clearly prohibits the use of state action to deny the rights of free exercise to *anyone,* it has never meant that a majority could use the machinery of the State to practice its beliefs. Such a contention was effectively answered by MR. JUSTICE JACKSON for the Court in *West Virginia State Board of Education* v. Barnette....

"The very purpose of the Bill of Rights was to withdraw certain subjects from the vicissitudes of political controversy, to place them beyond the reach of majorities and officials and to establish them as legal principles to be applied by the courts. One's right to ...freedom of worship...and other fundamental rights may not be submitted to vote; they depend on the outcome of no elections."

The place of religion in our society is an exalted one, achieved through a long tradition of reliance on the home, the church and the inviolable citadel of the individual heart and mind. We have come to recognize through bitter experience that it is not within the power of government to invade that citadel, whether its purpose or effect be to aid or oppose, to advance or retard. In the relationship between man and religion, the State is firmly committed to a position of neutrality. Though the application of that rule requires interpretation of a delicate sort, the rule itself is clearly and concisely stated in the words of the First Amendment....

## QUESTIONS

1. How does the First Amendment's establishment clause erect a wall between church and state?

2. Assuming that all parents or guardians support it, why is it wrong or illegal to allow religious instruction to occur on a public school campus?

3. On what grounds have daily Bible readings and public prayer in the public schools been declared unconstitutional?

4. Explain in your own words the meaning of the phrase "while protecting all, it prefers none and it disparages none."

5. Some suggest that the U.S. Suprme Court decison declaring prayer and Bible reading in public schools unconstitutional is antagonistic toward religion. Is this assertion correct or incorrect? Explain your answer.

6. Are the First and Fourteenth Amendements antithetical to religion? Why or why not?

7. What, if any, are the potential dangers in the union of church and state?

8. Do you agree with the argument presented in *Engel v Vitale* that a "union of government and religion tends to destroy government and to degrade religion"? Why or why not?

9. Was the phrase "one Nation under God, indivisible, with liberty and justice for all" a part of the flag salute during both the *Gobitis* and *Barnette* cases?

10. Summarize in your own words Justice Stewart's dissent in the *Engel v Vitale* decision.

11. Based on the *Abington v Schempp* decision, how important is it for public schools to offer instruction in the history of religion or in religion's role in the advancement of civilization?

## SUGGESTIONS FOR FURTHER READING

Lawrence A. Cremin, *American Education: The Colonial Experience: 1607–1783.* (New York: Harper Touchbooks, 1970).

Louis Fischer and David Schimmel, *The Rights of Students and Teachers.* (New York: Harper & Row Publishers, 1982).

Henry J. Perkinson, *Two Hundred Years of American Educational Thought.* (New York: David McKay, Inc., 1976).

David B. Tyack, editor, *Turning Points in American Educational History.* (New York: John Wiley and Sons, 1967).

Rush Welter, *Popular Education and Democratic Thought in America.* (New York: Columbia University Press, 1962).

# PART TWO

# Local versus Centralized Control of Schooling

## Past and Present

# CHAPTER

# 6

# The District School and Noah Webster's United States

As we discuss in Chapter 2, Thomas Jefferson failed in his effort to develop a statewide system of education. Indeed, even though Jefferson emerged as one of the most influential and highly regarded national leaders, education changed little in the decades following the Revolutionary War. Because the war was fought to conserve the freedoms already afforded Englishmen, educational issues were not paramount. The lack of interest in Jefferson's plan for an expansive statewide system of education or in his plans for reforming education suggests that citizens of the newly established country were generally satisfied with the educational system inherited from the colonial era.

Although the quality of schooling available to children and youth varied greatly from community to community and region to region, the district school emerged as the dominate form of schooling in both the colonial and early national periods of American history. During these years, there was widespread suspicion of any form of centralized control, and the village or neighborhood school often constituted the sole civic or public entity that people were willing—albeit begrudgingly—to support. During this period, towns or townships were established as legal entities for school purposes only. Absent little state or federal involvement in education, these small political entities exercised virtually total control over the school and the education it offered.

In short, these district or village schools are extreme examples of local or community control. These districts levied their own taxes, established committees to hire a schoolmaster, determined the length of the school year, and constructed and maintained a schoolhouse. Because these activities constituted the primary civic and/or political function of these largely rural districts, members of the village or neighborhood took it seriously. Many people participated in the process, and—in the name of fairness and equity—the school had to be placed in the exact geographic center of the district. Sometimes this meant that schoolhouses stood in swamps or were awkwardly placed on high ridges!

Because a schoolhouse usually was the only public building in a district, it became a multipurpose facility, serving as the meeting place for political debates, social events, and even religious services. Both literally and symbolically, the schoolhouse became the community center. In these small communities, a high percentage of the population often participated in overseeing the operation of the district school. Because people were suspicious and wary of centralized government, these district schools as "pure little democracies" represented the pride and identity of these rural communities. Schoolmasters, usually outsiders hired to teach school, often were young men preparing for a more lucrative career. The failure of a schoolmaster to control the children and youth placed in his charge often pleased residents of the district because it suggested that the standards of the community were superior to those of the outside world. The quality of the education afforded the children and youth varied dramatically from district to district, depending on the extent to which each community valued education. Generally, however, the quality of the education provided in these schools was not high.

Schoolmasters ran the gamut from learned individuals skilled and committed to teaching to illiterate scoundrels on the run from the law or other responsibilities. School facilities were often of poor quality and design, with students either roasting or freezing as they huddled around a potbellied stove. Appropriate pedagogical materials were rare. In the absence of any standardized text, students often used whatever book or books were available at home. With the cost of paper prohibitive, students wrote little. Students committed to memory passages from whatever book was available, reciting the passage on demand to the schoolmaster. Though there were exceptions, district schools were boring places where little was taught and learned.

Even though local control—fueled by a fear of centralized government—dominated schooling during the early years of this nation, the newly formed United States also faced a different yet equally significant political and educational problem. Put simply, how could a sense of nationhood be developed for a social order comprised of semi-autonomous units and cultures suspicious of centralization and nationhood? Unlike the Old World countries possessing long traditions of nationhood, the young country needed to create or manufacture its own sense of nationalism.

In what had recently become the United States of America, no one was born with an allegiance to the new country. Inhabitants of the original thirteen colonies were more likely to think of themselves as New Yorkers, Rhode Islanders, or Carolinians, for example, or as belonging to some other indigenous group (such as Cherokees or Iroquois) rather than to consider themselves Americans. The challenge, both political and educational, was to fashion such disparate groups into Americans. Citizens in such countries as France, England, and Spain had inherited their nationalism. People in the United States had to manufacture theirs.

Rejecting the symbols of nationalism associated with the Old World (the monarchy, the church, and the military establishment), Americans turned to education to foster a sense of unity in the new republic. In this regard, Noah Webster stands above other people in recognizing the importance of language for creating a sense of identity and national pride among former colonists and—to a lesser degree—native Americans.

In 1783, Noah Webster published what came to be known as the *Blue Back Speller.* Officially titled *A Grammatical Institute of the English Language, Part I,* this little blue back spelling book met with immediate, if unexpected, success. Spanning both geographic and generation boundaries, Webster's blue back speller became the standard for a uniquely American way of spelling. His speller conquered the land, traveling west in conestoga wagons, leaping the mountains, and invading the South. Generations of young people from Maine to California learned the same words, the same pronunciations, and the same moral lessons from Noah Webster. Webster helped to free Americans from a sense of inferiority about their language. More than anyone else, he helped break down regional differences in background, class, and religion. He provided Americans with something they could all—New Yorkers as well as Carolinians—be proud of: a common speech and language.

In the speller and in his dictionaries, Webster simplified the spelling of many words and explained their meaning by way of American, rather than British, examples. He was the first person to recognize the potential of education for encouraging nationalism. Even though no one, Webster included, anticipated the remarkable success of the blue back spelling book, Webster recognized the importance of education for promoting nationalism. Through first his speller, and later his dictionaries, his impact was both immediate and profound. At a time when many people in the newly formed United States both feared and opposed centralization and nationalism, Webster unified the people by creating a uniquely American version of the English language.

Also worthy of note is Webster's contribution—albeit unwittingly—to dispelling the deadening ethos of the district school. As his speller traversed the countryside, becoming in the process the authority or standard for the correct spelling of words in American English, district schools began conducting spelling "bees" or spelling "downs." Held once or twice a term on Friday afternoon, these spelling bees excited students and adults alike. Similar to corn-husking or quilting bees, spelling bees became major social events as the whole community gathered at the schoolhouse. The young came to court, politicians to preen, and other people to see and be seen. Analogous to the Friday night high school football game in many communities today, the actual bee was often incidental to the overall significance of the event.

Still the bee had its significance. Attractive, in part, because it transformed the drudgery of school work into a contest, the bee appealed to the competitive nature of the country's early national period. In addition, on almost a subliminal level, Americans understood that spelling was intimately connected to our sense of liberty and justice. Sensing that there was something morally and politically superior about our blurring of class differences in the United States, residents in rural communities understood that class and regional differences began to disappear or, at least, no longer mattered.

Because spelling bees emphasized the pronunciation as well as the correct American spelling, they symbolized for many Americans that genuine equality was within our grasp based on the ability to read, write, and speak the same way. In Europe, language was used to separate people, but in the United States—thanks to Webster—it is used to bring people together. The spelling bee was a vehicle for fostering community pride and also for creating a sense of unity around an event that was uniquely American. It accomplished both of these conflicting objectives by making it possible for someone from a remote or rural district to demonstrate by correctly spelling the last word from the last page of Webster's speller that his village or hamlet was equal to any other village or hamlet in the nation, if not the world.

As we embark on the twenty-first century, local control of schooling still represents to many people the best hope for fulfilling our national promise. To other people, the chances of achieving our "manifest destiny" are greatly enhanced by embracing and modernizing the common school. Before discussing the contemporary manifestations of the local-versus-centralized-control debate, we now discuss the development of statewide systems of education, often referred to as the common school crusade.

---

For more information about the district school, see Robert L. Church and Michael W. Sedlak, *Education in the United States: An Interpretive History* (New York: The Free Press, 1976), pp. 3–22.

# Description of a District School in Union County, Pennsylvania (1857)*

Sir: In accordance with the instructions of the Department, I have the honor of submitting the following Report:

## The School-House

The situation of the house is such, that with a little trouble and expense it can be made to look quite beautiful. But, as it is, there is no fence around the house; there is no playground except the highway; and a few old oak trees in the rear (in a field, where, of course, the pupils are not permitted to enter) are all that is near to remind a person of shade trees. There is no house, shed, or any thing of the kind in which to put the wood, coal, etc., used for warming the house. There is no privy, and it is deplorable that that part is nearly always neglected in building schoolhouses. The house is twenty-four feet long and twenty-two wide, with a ceiling eight and a half feet high. It is of brick, and was built about four years ago. There is a small wood stove in the house. In cold weather it is impossible to get the house comfortable, but with a large coal stove this might easily be done. There is no arrangement at all for ventilation, not even a trap-door in the ceiling.

## School Furniture

The number of desks is sufficient to accommodate forty-eight pupils. They are of different heights, the lower are placed nearest the platform occupied bv the teacher, and those that are higher, back farther. They are arranged in tiers, fronting toward the south, with an aisle between each tier. There are five tiers, and two pupils can set at each desk in three of them, but the desks in the tiers along the walls are calculated for one pupil only. The desks intended for the *smaller pupils*, are high enough for the *tallest*. They are made of white pine boards, planed smooth, but they are not painted. They have no lids, but there is a board under them where the scholar can keep his books, &c. The teacher's desk is situated at the south end of the house, on a small platform which is about eight inches high. The blackboard is about ten feet in length, and three in width, and is nailed to the wall behind the teacher's desk. There is not a map, globe, chart, or anything of the kind belonging to the school furniture. At the distance of six feet from the floor there is a strip of board nailed to each wall, in which nails are driven and on these nails the hats, cloaks, shawls, &c., are hung. This is a poor arrangement, for the scholars must always get on the benches with their feet when they wish to hang up their clothes, and then do the same to get them again.

## The School

This is not a graded school, but all lawful scholars are admitted. The whole number of scholars last winter was forty-five, while the average per day was only twenty-one. The scholars are well-classified. The branches taught are, Reading, Writing, Orthography, Spelling, Arithmetic written and mental, English Grammar, Geography, Music and Book-keeping. The books used, are Porter's Rhetorical Reader, Sander's Readers Nos. 1 and 2, Sander's Spelling Book: (one of the scholars had Adam's Arithmetic, and another had Greenleaf's), Davie's

Arithmetic, Colburn's Mental Arithmetic, Smith's English Grammar, Morse's Geography, and Crittenden's Book-keeping.—The New Testament is also used daily, but not as a text book. The punishments are not corporal.—Government is maintained chiefly by appealing to the nobler natures of the pupils, and to their sense of duty. Three intermissions are given each day. First one commencing at 10½ o'clock A.M., and lasting 20 minutes—that is, the boys have ten minutes, and the girls ten; second, there is an intermission at noon of one hour; and third, commencing at 2½ o'clock, P.M., twenty minutes more are given. The attention paid to study by the pupils is not as great as it should be; still some of them made a good degree of advancement, but the degree of advancement of the majority of the pupils is poor, considering what it might have been, had they been more careful to improve their privileges. Their attendance is regular during the latter part of December, the month of January, and part of February, but the rest of the time, it is very irregular.

### *The Teacher*

The teacher of this school is nineteen years of age, and was educated principally at Mifflinburg Academy. He has been teaching school three winters. He does not know yet whether he will be a permanent teacher or not. The School and Schoolmaster, Page's Theory and Practice of Teaching, the Pennsylvania School Journal, and the New York Teacher, are the principal educational books and periodicals he has read. At the close of the term, there was an examination and exhibition, and the number of visitors on that occasion was quite large. The visits of the Directors were not very frequent. During the five months that I taught, only one Director visited the school, and he was there only twice. The President of the Board and the Secretary were on the way to visit the school at one time, but it so happened that there was no school on that day. Most of the parents visited the school once, and some of them twice, but I had to invite some of them pretty often before they did so.

## Noah Webster Urges Reform of Spelling (1789)*

It has been observed by all writers, on the English language, that the orthography or spelling of words is very irregular; the same letters often representing different sounds, and the same sounds often expressed by different letters. For this irregularity, two principal causes may be assigned:

1. The changes to which the pronunciation of a language is liable, from the progress of science and civilization,
2. The mixture of different languages, occasioned by revolutions in England, or by a predilection of the learned, for words of foreign growth and ancient origin.

\* \* \*

The question now occurs; ought the Americans to retain these faults which produce innumerable inconveniencies in the acquisition and use of the language, or ought they at

*From Noah Webster, "An Essay on the Necessity, Advantages, and Practicality of Reforming the Mode of Spelling and of Rendering the Orthography of Words Correspondent to Pronunciation," *Dissertations on the English Language. With Notes, Historical and Critical, to Which Is Added, by Way of Appendix, an Essay on a Reformed Mode of Spelling, with Dr. Franklin's Arguments on That Subject* (Boston, 1789), pp. 391, 393–98, 405–6.

once to reform these abuses, and introduce order and regularity, into the orthography of the AMERICAN TONGUE?

Let us consider this subject with some attention.

Several attempts were formerly made in England to rectify the orthography of the language. But I apprehend their schemes failed to success, rather on account of their intrinsic difficulties, than on account of any necessary impracticability of a reform. It was proposed, in most of these schemes, not merely to throw out superfluous and silent letters, but to introduce a number of new characters. Any attempt on such a plan must undoubtedly prove unsuccessful. It is not to be expected that an orthography, perfectly regular and simple, such as would be formed by a "Synod of Grammarians on principles of science," will ever be substituted for that confused mode of spelling which is now established. But it is apprehended that great improvements may be made, and an orthography almost regular, or such as shall obviate most of the present difficulties which occur in learning our language, may be introduced and established with little trouble and opposition.

The principal alterations, necessary to render our orthography sufficiently regular and easy, are these:

**1.** The omission of all superfluous or silent letters, as *a* in *bread*. Thus *bread, head, give, breast, built, meant, realm, friend,* would be spelt, *bred, hed, giv, brest, bilt, ment, relm, frend.* Would this alteration produce any inconvenience, any embarrassment or expense? By no means. On the other hand, it would lessen the trouble of writing, and much more, of learning the language, it would reduce the true pronunciation to a certainty, and while it would assist foreigners and our own children in acquiring the language, it would render the pronunciation uniform, in different parts of the country, and almost prevent the possibility of changes.

**2.** A substitution of a character that has a certain definite sound, for one that is more vague and indeterminate. Thus by putting *ee* instead of *ea* or *ie,* the words *mean, near, speak, grieve, zeal,* would become *meen, neer, speek, greev, zeel.* This alteration could not occasion a moments trouble; at the same time it would prevent a doubt respecting the pronunciation; whereas the *ea* and *ie* having different sounds, may give a learner much difficulty. Thus *greef* should be substituted for *grief; kee* for *key; beleev* for *believe; laf* for *laugh; dawter* for *daughter; plow* for *plough; tuf* for *tough; proov* for *prove; blud;* for *blood;* and *draft* for *draught.* In this manner *ch* in Greek derivatives, should be changed into *k;* for the English *ch* has a soft sound, as in *cherish;* but *k* always a hard sound. Therefore *character, chorus, cholic, architecture,* should be written *karacter, korus, kolic, arkitecture;* and were they thus written, no person could mistake their true pronunciation.

Thus *ch* in French derivatives should be changed into *sh; machine, chaise, chevalier,* should be written *masheen, shaze, shevaleer,* and *pique, tour, oblique,* should be written *peek, toor, obleek.*

**3.** A trifling alteration in a character, or the addition of a point would distinguish different sounds, without the substitution of a new character. Thus a very small stroke across *th* would distinguish its two sounds. A point over a vowel, in this manner, *ȧ,* or * u̇,* or *ī,* might answer all the purposes of different letters. And for the dipthong *ow,* let the two letters be united by a small stroke, or both engraven on the same piece of metal, with the left hand line of the *w* united to the *o.*

These, with a few other inconsiderable alterations, would answer every purpose, and render the orthography sufficiently correct and regular.

The advantages to be derived from these alterations are numerous, great and permanent.

**1.** The simplicity of the orthography would facilitate the learning of the language. It is now the work of years for children to learn to spell; and after all, the business is rarely accomplished. A few men, who are bred to some business that requires constant exercise in writing, finally learn to spell most words without hesitation: but most people remain, all their lives, imperfect masters of spelling, and liable to make mistakes, whenever they take up a pen to write a short note. Nay, many people, even of education and fashion, never attempt to write a letter, without frequently consulting a dictionary.

But with the proposed orthography, a child would learn to spell, without trouble, in a very short time, and the orthography being very regular, he would ever afterwards find it difficult to make a mistake. It would, in that case, be as difficult to spell *wrong,* as it is now to spell *right.*

Besides this advantage, foreigners would be able to acquire the pronunciation of English, which is now so difficult and embarrassing, that they are either wholly discouraged on the first attempt, or obliged, after many years labor, to rest contented with an imperfect knowledge of the subject.

**2.** A correct orthography would render the pronunciation of the language, as uniform as the spelling in books. A general uniformity thro the United States, would be the event of such a reformation as I am here recommending. All persons, of every rank, would speak with some degree of precision and uniformity. Such a uniformity in these states is very desireable; it would remove prejudice, and conciliate mutual affection and respect.

**3.** Such a reform would diminish the number of letters about one sixteenth or eighteenth. This would save a page in eighteen; and a saving of an eighteenth in the expense of books, is an advantage that should not be overlooked.

**4.** But a capital advantage of this reform in these states would be, that it would make a difference between the English orthography and the American. This will startle those who have not attended to the subject; but I am confident that such an event is an object of vast political consequence. For,

The alteration, however small, would encourage the publication of books in our own country. It would render it, in some measure, necessary that all books should be printed in America. The English would never copy our orthography for their own use; and consequently the same impressions of books would not answer for both countries. The inhabitants of the present generation would read the English impressions; but posterity, being taught a different spelling, would prefer the American orthography.

Besides this, a *national language* is a band of *national union.* Every engine should be employed to render the people of this country *national;* to call their attachments home to their own country; and to inspire them with the pride of national character. However, they may boast of Independence, and the freedom of their government, yet their *opinions* are not sufficiently independent; an astonishing respect for the arts and literature of their parent country, and a blind imitation of its manners, are still prevalent among the Americans.

\* \* \*

Sensible I am how much easier it is to *propose* improvements, than to *introduce* them. Every thing *new* starts the idea of difficulty; and yet it is often mere novelty that excites the appearance; for on a slight examination of the proposal, the difficulty vanishes. When we firmly *believe* a scheme to be practicable, the work is *half* accomplished. We are more frequently deterred by fear from making an attack, than repulsed in the encounter.

Habit also is opposed to changes, for it renders even our errors dear to us. Having surmounted all difficulties in childhood, we forget the labor, the fatigue, and the perplexity we suffered in the attempt, and imagin[e] the progress of our studies to have been smooth and easy. What seems intrinsically right, is so merely thro habit.

Indolence is another obstacle to improvements. The most arduous task a reformer has to execute, is to make people *think,* to rouse them from that lethargy, which, like the mantle of sleep, covers them in repose and contentment.

But America is in a situation the most favorable for great reformations, and the present time is, in a singular degree, auspicious. The minds of men in this country have been awakened. New scenes have been, for many years, presenting new occasions for exertion; unexpected distresses have called forth the powers of invention; and the application of new expedients has demanded every possible exercise of wisdom and talents. Attention is roused; the mind expanded; and the intellectual faculties invigorated. Here men are prepared to receive improvements, which would be rejected by nations, whose habits have not been shaken by similar events.

*Now* is the time, and *this* the country, in which we may expect success, in attempting changes favorable to language, science and government. Delay, in the plan here proposed, may be fatal; under a tranquil general government, the minds of men may again sink into indolence; a national acquiescence in error will follow; and posterity be doomed to struggle with difficulties, which time and accident will perpetually multiply.

Let us then seize the present moment, and establish a *national language,* as well as a national government. Let us remember that there is a certain respect due to the opinions of other nations. As an independent people, our reputation abroad demands that, in all things, we should be federal; be *national,* for if we do not respect *ourselves,* we may be assured that *other nations* will not respect us. In short, let it be impressed upon the mind of every American, that to neglect the means of commanding respect abroad, is treason against the character and dignity of a brave independent people.

# Noah Webster on the Necessity for an American Language (1789)\*

A regular study of language has, in all civilized countries, formed a part of a liberal education. The Greeks, Romans, Italians and French successively improved their native tongues,

\*From Noah Webster, "An Essay on the Necessity, Advantages, and Practicality of Reforming the Mode of Spelling…" *Dissertations on the English Language…* (Boston, 1789), pp. 17–19, 288–90, 393–98.

taught them in Academies at home, and rendered them entertaining and useful to the foreign student.

The English tongue, tho later in its progress towards perfection, has attained to a considerable degree of purity, strength and elegance, and been employed, by an active and scientific nation, to record almost all the events and discoveries of ancient and modern times.

This language is the inheritance which the Americans have received from their British parents. To cultivate and adorn it, is a task reserved for men who shall understand the connection between language and logic, and form an adequate idea of the influence which a uniformity of speech may have on national attachments.

It will be readily admitted that the pleasures of reading and conversing, the advantage of accuracy in business, the necessity of clearness and precision in communicating ideas, require us to be able to speak and write our own tongue with ease and correctness. But there are more important reasons, why the language of this country should be reduced to such fixed principles, as may give its pronunciation and construction all the certainty and uniformity which any living tongue is capable of receiving.

The United States were settled by emigrants from different parts of Europe. But their descendants mostly speak the same tongue; and the intercourse among the learned of the different States, which the revolution has begun, and an American Court will perpetuate, must gradually destroy the differences of dialect which our ancestors brought from their native countries. This approximation of dialects will be certain; but without the operation of other causes than an intercourse at Court, it will be slow and partial. The body of the people, governed by habit, will still retain their respective peculiarities of speaking; and for want of schools and proper books, fall into many inaccuracies, which, incorporating with the language of the state where they live, may imperceptibly corrupt the national language. Nothing but the establishment of schools and some uniformity in the use of books, can annihilate differences in speaking and preserve the purity of the American tongue. A sameness of pronunciation is of considerable consequence in a political view; for provincial accents are disagreeable to strangers and sometimes have an unhappy effect upon the social affections. All men have local attachments, which lead them to believe their own practice to be the least exceptionable. Pride and prejudice incline men to treat the practice of their neighbors with some degree of contempt. Thus small differences in pronunciation at first excite ridicule—a habit of laughing at the singularities of strangers is followed by disrespect—and without respect friendship is a name, and social intercourse a mere ceremony.

These remarks hold equally true, with respect to individuals, to small societies, and to large communities. Small causes, such as a nicknames or a vulgar tone in speaking, have actually created a dissocial spirit between the inhabitants of the different states, which is often discoverable in private business and public deliberations. Our political harmony is therefore concerned in a uniformity of language.

As an independent nation, our honor requires us to have a system of our own, in language as well as government. Great Britain, whose children we are, and whose language we speak, should no longer be our standard; for the taste of her writers is already corrupted, and her language on the decline. But if it were not so, she is at too great a distance to be our model, and to instruct us in the principles of our own tongue.

It must be considered further, that the English is the common root or stock from which our national language will be derived. All others will gradually waste away—and within a century and a half, North America will be peopled with a hundred millions of men, *all speaking the same language.* Place this idea in comparison with the present and possible future bounds of the language in Europe—consider the Eastern Continent as inhabited by nations, whose knowledge and intercourse are embarrassed by differences of language; then anticipate the period when the people of one quarter of the world, will be able to associate and converse together like children of the same family.[1] Compare this prospect, which is not visionary, with the state of the English language in Europe, almost confined to an Island and to a few millions of people; then let reason and reputation decide, how far America should be dependent on a transatlantic nation, for her standard and improvements in language.

Let me add, that whatever predilection the Americans may have for their native European tongues, and particularly, the British descendants for the English, yet several circumstances render a future separation of the American tongue from the English, necessary and unavoidable. The vicinity of the European nations, with the uninterrupted communication in peace, and the changes of dominion in war, are gradually assimilating their respective languages. The English with others is suffering continual alterations. America, placed at a distance from those nations, will feel, in a much less degree, the influence of the assimilating causes; at the same time, numerous local causes, such as a new country, new associations of people, new combinations of ideas in arts and science, and some intercourse with tribes wholly unknown in Europe, will introduce new words into the American tongue. These causes will produce, in a course of time, a language in North America, as different from the future language of England, as the modern Dutch, Danish and Swedish are from the German, or from one another: Like remote branches of a tree springing from the same stock; or rays of light, shot from the same center, and diverging from each other, in proportion to their distance from the point of separation.

Whether the inhabitants of America can be brought to a perfect uniformity in the pronunciation of words, it is not easy to predict; but it is certain that no attempt of the kind has been made, and an experiment, begun and pursued on the right principles, is the only way to decide the question. Schools in Great Britain have gone far towards demolishing local dialects—commerce has also had its influence—and in America these causes, operating more generally, must have a proportional effect.

In many parts of America, people at present attempt to copy the English phrases and pronunciation—an attempt that is favored by their habits, their prepossessions and the intercourse between the two countries. This attempt has, within the period of a few years, produced a multitude of changes in these particulars, especially among the leading classes of people. These changes make a difference between the language of the higher and common ranks, and indeed between the *same* ranks in *different* states; as the rage for copying the English, does not prevail equally in every part of North America.

But besides the reasons already assigned to prove this imitation absurd, there is a difficulty attending it, which will defeat the end proposed by its advocates; which is, that the English themselves have no standard of pronunciation, nor can they ever have one on the

---

[1]Even supposing that a number of republics, kingdoms or empires, should within a century arise and divide this vast territory; still the subjects of all will speak the same language, and the consequence of this uniformity will be an intimacy of social intercourse hitherto unknown, and a boundless diffusion of knowledge.

plan they propose. The Authors, who have attempted to give us a standard, make the practice of the court and stage in London the sole criterion of propriety in speaking. An attempt to establish a standard on this foundation is both *unjust* and *idle*. It is unjust, because it is abridging the nation of its rights: The *general practice* of a nation is the rule of propriety, and this practice should at least be consulted in so important a matter, as that of making laws for speaking. While all men are upon a footing and no singularities are accounted vulgar or ridiculous, every man enjoys perfect liberty. But when a particular set of men, in exalted stations, undertake to say, "we are the standards of propriety and elegance, and if all men do not conform to our practice, they shall be accounted vulgar and ignorant," they take a very great liberty with the rules of the language and the rights of civility.

But an attempt to fix a standard on the practice of any particular class of people is highly absurd: As a friend of mine once observed, it is like fixing a light house on a floating island. It is an attempt to *fix* that which is in itself *variable;* at least it must be variable so long as it is supposed that a local practice has no standard but a *local practice;* that is, no standard but *itself.* While this doctrine is believed, it will be impossible for a nation to follow as fast as the standard changes—for if the gentlemen at court constitute a standard, they are above it themselves, and their practice must shift with their passions and their whims.

But this is not all. If the practice of a few men in the capital is to be the standard, a knowledge of this must be communicated to the whole nation. Who shall do this? An able compiler perhaps attempts to give this practice in a dictionary; but it is probable that the pronunciation, even at court, or on the stage, is not uniform. The compiler therefore must follow his particular friends and patrons; in which case he is sure to be opposed and the authority of his standard called in question; or he must give two pronunciations as the standard, which leaves the student in the same uncertainty as it found him. Both these events have actually taken place in England, with respect to the most approved standards; and of course no one is unevenly followed.

Besides, if language must vary, like fashions at the caprice of a court, we must have our standard dictionaries republished, with the fashionable pronunciation, at least once in five years; otherwise a gentleman in the country will become intolerably vulgar, by not being in a situation to adopt the fashion of the day. The *new* editions of them will supersede the *old* and we shall have our pronunciation to re-learn with the polite alterations, which are generally corruptions.

Such are the consequences of attempting to make a local practice the *standard* of language in a *nation.* The attempt must keep the language in perpetual fluctuation, and the learner in uncertainty.

If a standard therefore cannot be fixed on local and variable custom, on what shall it be fixed? If the most eminent speakers are not to direct our practice, where shall we look for a guide? The answer is extremely easy; the *rules of the language itself,* and the *general practice of the nation,* constitute propriety in speaking. If we examine the structure of any language, we shall find a certain principle of analogy running through the whole. We shall find in English that similar combinations of letters have usually the same pronunciation, and that words, having the same terminating syllable, generally have the accent at the same distance from that termination. These principles of analogy were not the result of design—they must have been the effect of accident, or that tendency which all men feel towards uniformity. But the principles, when established, are productive of great convenience, and become an authority superior to the arbitrary decisions of any man or class of men. There is one exception only to this remark: When a deviation from analogy has become the universal practice of a nation, it then takes place of all rules and becomes the standard of propriety.

The two points therefore, which I conceive to be the basis of a standard in speaking, are these, *universal undisputed practice,* and the *principle of analogy. Universal practice* is generally, perhaps always, a rule of propriety; and in disputed points, where people differ in opinion and practice, *analogy* should always decide the controversy.

# Q U E S T I O N S

1.  Why was there so little interest in a statewide system of education in post-revolutionary war United States?

2.  Why was local or community control of schooling so important to citizens of the United States during the first third of the nineteenth century?

3.  Compare your own elementary school experiences to that offered in an early nineteenth century district school.

4.  What is meant by the suggestion that Americans—citizens of the newly established United States—had to manufacture their nationalism?

5.  What role did Noah Webster's *Blue Back Speller* play in fostering a community and national pride?

6.  To what extent is the contemporary Friday night football game analogous to the spelling bee or spelling down of early nineteenth-century district schools?

7.  Should the schools of tomorrow be controlled by local communities or governed by a centralized state or national entity? Explain your answer.

8.  Explain in your own words why attendance at district schools was very irregular except during the months of December, January, and February.

9.  Imagine yourself as the teacher in a district school. How would you teach the twenty-one to forty-five students of all ages who arrived each day for school?

# 7  Horace Mann and the Common School Crusade

Proclaiming the common school as "the greatest discovery ever made by man," Horace Mann and other common school crusaders provided—during the last two-thirds of the nineteenth century—both a compelling rationale for more centralized, state systems of education and the moral and political will and skill necessary for creating such systems. A politician from the Boston area of Massachusetts, Horace Mann succeeded where Thomas Jefferson failed in creating the first statewide system of schooling in the nation.

Born in 1796, Mann's life spanned a period in which Massachusetts changed dramatically. Throughout his youth and young manhood, more than two-thirds of the population lived in rural communities. Immigration was slow and had little effect on the homogenous nature of the population. As a continuation of the Puritan legacy, schools were created and supported for the common good or wealth of the larger society. The economic base for such communities remained—as it had for generations—rooted in agriculture and commerce.

Mann saw all of this change. During the 1830s and 1840s, Mann observed many immigrants, largely from Ireland, pouring into this pure Yankee commonwealth. In addition, he experienced the transformation of the rural, agrarian nature of Massachusetts into an increasingly urbanized and industrialized region. Within his life span (Mann died in 1859), the agrarian, homogenous Yankee commonwealth of his youth had been transformed into an urbanized, industrial, and more culturally diverse society. This was the context that produced the call for a revival of the common school. Mann and other school reformers campaigned vigorously for a renewed emphasis on free public schooling as an antidote to the evils associated with industrialization, urbanization, and immigration.

Serving as a state senator from the Boston area, Mann chided his colleagues for failing to provide moral guidance to the masses. Already concerned with the moral decay of the society, Mann was especially alarmed when he witnessed a spontaneous and senseless riot in the streets. Such events reinforced his conviction that "the educated, the wealthy, the intelligent" had abdicated their roles as the moral stewards of society. As many of his colleagues and other members of the upper classes abandoned the public or common schools in favor of private education, Mann viewed such developments as dangerous because segregating education by classes could only increase prejudice and hatred. To Mann and other school reformers, elevating the common or public school to provide the best education available anywhere was the solution to the unraveling of the social fabric and the moral decline of U.S. society.

In 1837, the Massachusetts legislature passed a bill establishing a state board of education. Appointed by the governor and intended to be an advisory board rather than a board of control, the legislation charged the board with gathering and disseminating information about education statewide. In asking Horace Mann to serve as the executive secretary for the first state board of education in the nation, the governor made a wise choice. Mann's friends thought he was committing political suicide in accepting the appointment. Frustrated by his inability to change the ideas of his colleagues, Mann embraced this new position as an opportunity for changing future generations. Stating "men are cast iron, but children are wax," Mann enthusiastically embarked on his new mission.

Embracing Daniel Webster's notion of education as "a wise and liberal system of police," Mann championed the virtues of common schooling to audiences big and small throughout the commonwealth. His position as executive secretary had no formal power, but through the force of his own will and political acumen, Mann wielded tremendous influence. For more than a decade as the executive to the first state board of education in the nation, Mann recommended and the legislature passed a number of statutes that in effect established in Massachusetts the first state system of public education in the country.

Not everyone agreed with Mann's vision. People clamoring for local or community control of schools—the champions of the district schools as "pure little democracies"—opposed Mann's attempt to dictate educational policy from the state capitol. A skilled politician, Mann softened their opposition by convincing these people that an improved common school would provide all children with the knowledge and skills necessary for success in this new, industrialized world of the nineteenth-century United States.

In a sense, Horace Mann began what became a national crusade for the revival of the common school spirit in the United States. Even though the country does not have a national or federal system of education, Horace Mann and other school reformers achieved a remarkable consensus from Massachusetts's to California regarding the nature and purpose of schooling. Following Massachusetts's lead, virtually every state had a Mann-like figure championing the virtues of the common or public school. By 1848, twenty-four of the thirty states in the union had named a chief state school officer and had followed the Massachusetts lead in establishing statewide systems of education. As a group, these were men of prominence whose successes in multiple careers would serve them well in their roles as chief state school officers. As David Tyack explains,

> lacking formal power, the reformer needed the eloquence and craft of a trial lawyer, the sophistication of a politician, the zeal and supernatural sanctions of a preacher, the sharp pen of a journalist, and learning of a professor. Taken as a group, the chief reformers has all these skills.[1]

Through their skill, vision, and commitment, these common school crusaders fashioned a new U.S. institution. Known as the common or public school, it was to be free (supported by public tax dollars) and open and attractive to all people. The curriculum emphasized basic skills (the three R's) and, purportedly, the values common to all Americans. In reality, this common school crusade embraced a nonsectarian Protestant morality and a nonpartisan republicanism. As we discuss in Chapters 9, 11, 12, and 13, reality rarely corresponded with this vision, but a remarkable majority of people in this country embraced and/or aspired to this uniquely U.S. educational creed.

---

[1] David B. Tyack, ed., *Turning Points in American Educational History* (New York: John Wiley & Sons, 1967) p. 125. For more information about Horace Mann and the common school crusade, see Henry J. Perkinson, *Two Hundred Years of American Educational Thought* (New York: David McKay Company, 1976), pp. 59–102.

## Senator Daniel Webster on the Schools as a "Wise and Liberal System of Police" (1820)*

I must yet advert to another most interesting topic,—the Free Schools. In this particular, New England may be allowed to claim, I think, a merit of a preculiar character. She early adopted, and has constantly maintained the principle, that it is the undoubted right and the bounden duty of government to provide for the instruction of all youth. That which is elsewhere left to chance or to charity, we secure by law. For the purpose of public instruction, we hold every man subject to taxation in proportion to his property, and we look not to the question, whether he himself have, or have not, children to be benefited by the education for which he pays. We regard it as a wise and liberal system of police, by which property, and life, and the peace of society are secured. We seek to prevent in some measure the extension of the penal code, by inspiring a salutary and conservative principle of virtue and of knowledge in an early age. We strive to excite a feeling of respectability, and a sense of character, by enlarging the capacity and increasing the sphere of intellectual enjoyment. By general instruction, we seek, as far as possible, to purify the whole moral atmosphere; to keep good sentiments uppermost, and to turn the strong current of feeling and opinion as well as the censures of the law and the denunciations of religion, against immorality and crime. We hope for a security beyond the law, and above the law, in the prevalence of an enlightened and well-principled moral sentiment. We hope to continue and prolong the time, when, in the villages and farmhouses of New England, there may be undisturbed sleep within unbarred doors, and knowing that our government rests directly on the public will, in order that we may preserve it we endeavor to give a safe and proper direction to that public will. We do not, indeed, expect all men to be philosophers or statesmen; but we confidently trust, and our expectation of the duration of our system of government rests on that trust, that, by the diffusion of general knowledge and good and virtuous sentiments, the political fabric may be secure, as well against open violence and overthrow, as against the slow, but sure, undermining of licentiousness.

*From Edward Everett, ed., *Works of Daniel Webster* (Boston, 1854), vol. I, pp. 41–42.

## Horace Mann's Thoughts on Being Chosen Secretary of the Massachusetts Board of Education (1837)*

*June 28.* This morning, received a call from Mr. Dwight on the subject of the Secretaryship; and as the meeting of the Board is appointed for to-morrow, and as he did not seem to have arrived at any certain conclusions in his own mind, I thought the time had already come when points should be stated explicitly. I therefore wrote to Mr. Dwight, saying that it would be better for the cause if the candidate who should be selected should appear to have been the first choice of the Board; that I therefore should feel it to be a duty to decline the

*From Mary Peabody Mann, *Life of Horace Mann* (Boston, 1865), pp. 79–81, 82–83, 86–87, 90.

honor of being voted for, unless it was *bonâ fide* my intention to accept; that I would accordingly, regard the subject in its business aspects alone, and place the matter in a point of view not liable to be mistaken. I then stated, that, as I should have some professional business to close up, it had all along been my intention not to receive more than twenty-five hundred dollars for the first year, that as to subsequent years, if the Legislature should add any thing to the one thousand they have now appropriated as the salary of the Secretary, half of that addition should be added to the sum of twenty-five hundred until it became three thousand, but should not go beyond the latter sum, that by this it would become the interest of the Secretary so to discharge his duties as to gain the favor of the public, and that it was quite well in all cases, and with regard to all, to make their interest and their duty draw in the same direction, if possible. This was the substance of my letter; though it had the proper amount of interlardings and lubrifications. I tremble, however, at the idea of the task that possibly now lies before me. Yet, I can now conscientiously say that here stands my purpose, ready to undergo the hardships and privations to which I must be subject, and to encounter the jealousy, the misrepresentation, and the prejudice almost certain to arise; here stands my mind, ready to meet them in the spirit of a martyr. To-morrow will probably prescribe for me a course of life. Let it come! I know one thing,—if I stand by the principles of truth and duty, nothing can inflict upon me any permanent harm.

*June 29.* I cannot say that this day is one to which I have not looked forward with deep anxiety. The chance of being offered a station which would change the whole course of my action, and consequently of my duties, through life, was not to be regarded with indifference. The deep feeling of interest was heightened by the reflection, that, in case of my receiving the appointment of Secretary of the Board of Education, my sphere of *possible* usefulness would be indefinitely enlarged, and that my failure would forever force into contrast the noble duty and the inadequate discharge of it. The day is past. I have received the offer. The path of usefulness is opened before me. My present purpose is to enter into it. Few undertakings, according to my appreciation of it, have been greater. I know of none which may be more fruitful in beneficent results.

God grant me an annihilation of selfishness, a mind of wisdom, a heart of benevolence! How many men I shall meet who are accessible only through a single motive, or who are incased in prejudice and jealousy, and need, not to be subdued, butt to be remodelled! how many who will vociferate their devotion to the public, but whose thoughts will be intent on themselves! There is but one spirit in which these impediments can be met with success: it is the spirit of self-abandonment, the spirit of martyrdom. To this, I believe, there are but few, of all those who wear the form of humanity, who will not yield. I must not irritate, I must not humble, I must not degrade any one in his own eyes. I must not present myself as a solid body to oppose an iron barrier to any. I must be a fluid sort of a man, adapting myself to tastes, opinions, habits, manners, so far as this can be done without hypocrisy or insincerity, or a compromise of principle. In all this, there must be a higher object than to win personal esteem, or favor, or worldly applause. A new fountain may now be opened. Let me strive to direct its current in such a manner, that if, when I have departed from life, I may still be permitted to witness its course, I may behold it broadening and deepening in an everlasting progression of virtue and happiness.

*June 30.* This morning I communicated my acceptance of the Secretaryship of the Board of Education. Afterwards I sat with the Board until they adjourned without day. I then handed to the Governor the resignation of my membership of the Board. I now stand in a new relation to them; nor to them only: I stand in a new relation to the world. Obligations to labor in the former mode are removed; but a more elevated and weighty obligation to toil supplies the place of the former. Henceforth, so long as I hold this office, I devote myself to the supremest welfare of mankind upon earth. An inconceivably greater labor is undertaken. With the highest degree of prosperity, results will manifest themselves but slowly. The harvest is far distant from the seed-time. *Faith* is the only sustainer. I have faith in the improvability of the race,—in their accelerating improvability. This effort may do, apparently, but little. But mere beginning in a good cause is never little. If we can get this vast wheel into any perceptible motion, we shall have accomplished much. And more and higher qualities than mere labor and perseverance will be requisite. Art for applying will be no less necessary th—— —— nd deducing. No object ever gave scope for cious use of them. At first, it will be better When walking over quagmires, we should advice which all the sages who ever lived ger, and in favor of success, as to undertake rit. Men can resist the influence of talent; w will combat goodness for any length of se is a certain conqueror. Love is a univer- st persecution, torture, death, but will be ympathy. Here is a clew given by God to

Boston, July 2, 1837.

light of your pen visited me! It really is e mean time, what a change in externals , counsellor, or lawyer. My lawbooks are r my forum. My jurisdiction is changed. I myself to the larger sphere of mind and morals. avin, posed of materials almost unmalleable, I am about ansf— en are cast-iron; but children are wax. Strength ex- pende— ual, which would make no impression upon the former.

But you will ask what is the interpretation of this oracular ambiguity. A law was passed last winter, constituting a Board of Education "consisting of the Governor and Lieut.–Govemor, *ex officiis,* and eight other persons to be appointed by the Governor and Council;" which Board was authorized to appoint a Secretary, whose duty it should be "to collect information of the actual condition and efficiency of the common schools and other means of popular education, and to diffuse as widely as possible, throughout every part of the Commonwealth, information of the most approved and successful modes of instruction." I have accepted that office. If I do not succeed in it, I will lay claim at least to the benefit of the saying, that in great attempts it is glorious even to fail.

\* \* \*

Boston, July 16, 1837.

My Dear Sister,—You will be not a little surprised to learn how great a change has come over my course of business-life since I last saw you. I have quitted the profession of the law. I hope that no necessity will ever compel me to resume it again. But why, you would ask, and for what object? I will tell you.... I have accepted the office of Secretary of the Board; and, as it will occupy all my time (and is sufficient to occupy me in ten places at once if that were possible), I necessarily leave my profession in order to bestow upon it my undivided attention. Could I be assured that my efforts in this new field of labor would be crowned with success, I know of no occupation that would be more agreeable to me,— more congenial to my tastes and feelings. It presents duties entirely accordant with principle.... Some persons think it not wise to leave my profession, which has hitherto treated me quite as well as I have deserved: others profess to think that my prospects in political life were not to be bartered for a post whose returns for effort and privation must be postponed to another generation; and that my present position in the Senate would be far preferable to being a post-rider from county to county looking after the welfare of children who will never know whence benefits may come, and encountering the jealousy and prejudice and misrepresentation of ignorant parents. But is it not better to do good than to be commended for having done it? If no seed were ever to be sown save that which would promise the requital of a full harvest before we die, how soon would mankind revert to barbarism! If I can be the means of ascertaining what is the best construction of houses, what are the best books, what is the best arrangement of studies, what are the best modes of instructions if I can discover by what appliance of means a non-thinking, non-reflecting, non-speaking child can most surely be trained into a noble citizen ready to contend for the right and to die for the right,—if I can only obtain and diffuse throughout this State a few good ideas on these and similar subjects, may I not flatter myself that my ministry, has not been wholly in vain?...

* * *

*Nov. 3....* Have been engaged all the week at court in Dedham, arguing causes. The interests of a client are small, compared with the interests of the next generation. Let the next generation, then, be my client....

# Henry Barnard on the Needs of the Connecticut Common Schools (1839)*

**1.** The first great want of our system of public schools, is a more decided, active, generous public sentiment enlisted in its support. That there is at this time a wide spread and paralizing apathy over the public mind, in relation to the whole subject—a want of proper appreciation of the immense, the inconceivable importance of good common schools to our individual, social and national well-being, is manifest, from the alarming number of children of the teachable age who are in no schools whatever, the still larger number who are in expensive private schools, the irregular attendance of those who are enrolled as

*From *First Annual Report of the Board of Commissioners of Common Schools in Connecticut...1839,* pp. 52–54.

pupils in the public schools, the thinly attended school meetings, both of the society and the district, and the unwillingness, not only of the public generally, but of that large class who are foremost in promoting other benevolent, patriotic and religious enterprizes, to make personal or pecuniary sacrifices to promote the increasing prosperity of common schools. The system will continue to move on in feeble and irregular action, so long as its various parts are not animated with a more vigorous principle of life. The late demonstration of increasing public interest, and the consequent activity imparted to the administration of the school system, show conclusively that the right beginning of this work of school improvement is in awakening, correcting, and elevating public sentiment in relation to it. To accomplish this, the measure recommended by the Board, the agency of the public press, the living voice, voluntary associations, seem to me as judicious and efficient, as can under present circumstances be devised. They have been found successful elsewhere. They have in some degree, it is hoped, been of service here. But all this is not enough. Public opinion will not long remain in advance of the law. Every advance, if it is of a general character, must be secured, and if proper steps are taken will very naturally be secured, by being embodied into the law.

**2.**  A revision of our school law, with a few amendments, so as to remove obstacles in the way of improvement, seems to me indispensable. In consequence of these obstacles in the law itself, efforts to introduce a gradation of schools, to employ two or more teachers in the same district, to build more commodious school houses, have failed, at least for the present. An amendment of the law so as to authorize districts which are prepared for it, to introduce these and other improvements, and especially the city and populous districts, cannot be objected to, because no district would be compelled to avail themselves of its provision.

To give greater efficacy to the examination of teachers, and indeed to the whole department of school superintendence, I would suggest the propriety of recommending to the Legislature, a modification of the section requiring the appointment of school visiters, so as to authorize the choice of a Board not to exceed one for a district, with power to delegate the execution of their rules and regulations to two persons who should receive a small compensation for their services. The duties are arduous, delicate, and necessary, and require both time and talent for their faithful discharge. The experience of some fifteen or twenty societies where the practice of appointing a smaller number and paying them has been adopted, is such as to satisfy me that the work will be better done all over the State, as soon as the practice is made general. The duties, too, of this class of officers should be made more specific, and a failure on their part should incur some penalty.

To secure the more general and punctual attendance of all the children enumerated, at the public schools, I think it very desirable to alter, in some respects, the present mode of sustaining them. The expense of the school, so far as those who are unable to bear it are concerned, should fall, not upon those who patronize the public school, but upon the property of the school society or town. The present mode makes it the interest of those who have property, to abandon the public school, for in so doing they avoid all the expense of supporting the schools beyond the avails of the public money. In addition to this, if the public money was distributed to the districts according to the actual attendance at the school, and not the enumeration, it would make it the interest of the district, and of every parent in it, to see that the attendance was general and punctual.

## Q U E S T I O N S

1. Describe in your own words how the evils associated with industrialization, urbanization, and immigration persuaded Horace Mann and other people to campaign for a revival of the common school.

2. Explain the meaning of the phrase "men are cast iron, but children are wax."

3. What do you think is meant by the characterization of education as "a wise and liberal system of police"?

4. What are the characteristics of a common school? Why is it called or identified as common?

5. Is the argument that the common school "lessen[ed] the distance and weaken[ed] the jealousies, which generally subsist between the educated and uneducated" as valid today as it was in Horace Mann's time? Why or why not?

6. Assess Mann's motivation for abandoning the profession of the law and assuming the position of Secretaryship of the Board of Education. Why does he speak of this new task as a ministry?

7. In what way or ways is Henry Barnard like Horace Mann? How is he different? Explain your answer.

# CHAPTER

# 8

# The "One Best System" and the Feminization of the Teaching Profession

As we discuss in the previous chapter, the common school crusade emerged, at least in part, to combat the fragmentation and degradation of U.S. society resulting from the triple threat of industrialization, urbanization, and immigration. As the common school crusade caught on across the nation and as state after state began establishing a state system of education, the issue became how to organize or structure a more centralized system of schooling open and attractive to all. Assuming consensus on the values and skills everyone needs to know, how can these be taught effectively and efficiently.

Just as Horace Mann and other school reformers believed in the power of the common school as an antidote to the evils of modern life, their successors believed that standardization and uniformity—crucial components of the industrialized world—were essential characteristics of civilization itself. School reformers argued that modern civilization is characterized by uniformity and unity. There is a best way, and once discovered that way is the best for everyone. It is ironic, if not surprising, that the champions of the common or public school as the antidote for the evils associated with our industrialized and urbanized modern world considered the factory or industrial model as the "one best system" for school organization.

In emulating this "one best system," school reformers struggled throughout the last half of the nineteenth century to establish urban school systems in which trained professional educators, rather than a group of laymen, controlled the school from the top downward. Their goal was to create new controls over pupils, teachers, principals, and other subordinates such that the superintendent or system head could efficiently direct all aspects of the educational system. The intent was to replace village or district schools in which laymen participated in decentralized decision-making with a new bureaucratic model of a closed, top-down, nonpolitical system.

Crucial to any bureaucratic system is the objective and efficient classification of students. As an integral part of this "one best system," school reformers advocated replacing the heterogeneous groupings of students with a graded school similar to that found in Prussia. Such a graded model required a new kind of structure and resulted in the building of egg-crate schools. Much like egg crates stacked on top of each other, these new schools were multistoried, with compartments or classrooms on top of one another. Such schools had one or more classrooms for each grade with—ideally—a specially trained teacher covering a standardized curriculum for each grade. The Quincy School in Boston, Massachusetts, was the first of these egg-crate schools built in the United States. Opening its doors in 1848, it could accommodate 700 students in its four stories and twelve classrooms. In a very real sense, schools resembled factories. Students constituted the raw materials, fashioned—as they progressed through a series of compartments and treatments—into finished educational products.

In this factorylike school, the curriculum was prescribed and standardized. As such, creativity and independence in teachers—though ideally trained to teach a specific grade level or field—were not valued. In the "one best system," teaching was considered women's work because women were thought to be more passive and less intelligent than men. Hiring women to teach was also more economical because women typically were paid less than men. Further indication of the gender bias inherent in this "one best system" is the preponderance of male principals and other leaders, with women almost always assuming more subordinate roles.

The "one best system" emerged as the dominant educational model during the latter half of the nineteenth century, because—in part—its hierarchical structure and the male chauvinism of the larger society fit together. Combining the assumptions that organization implies subordination and that men are naturally superior to women, this second generation of educational reformers created a school system in which women teachers were treated not as professionals but as idealized daughters who needed and accepted the fatherly advice of their male principals and superintendents. Such chauvinism permeated the entire structure, but it is most apparent in the divergent pay scales for men and women teachers and administrators. By 1902, this feminization of the teaching profession was largely complete, with women comprising 98 percent of all urban elementary teachers and being paid less than half that of their male counterparts.

The legacy of this hierarchical and chauvinistic "one best system" survives and even prospers as we enter the twenty-first century. Even though Gerald Grant and Christine E. Murray suggest that "Teaching in America" is gradually evolving into a more equitable and genuine profession, the "one best system" of school organization maintains a powerful presence in the culture of schooling in our nation.

For a more comprehensive discussion of this topic, see David B. Tyack, *The One Best System: A History of American Urban Education* (Cambridge, MA: Harvard University Press, 1974).

# Horace Mann's Twelfth Annual Report (1848)*

*The Capacities of Our Present School System to
Improve the Pecuniary Condition,
and to Elevate the Intellectual and Moral Character,
of the Commonwealth*

Under the Providence of God, our means of education are the grand machinery by which the "raw material" of human nature can be worked up into inventors and discoverers, into

*From Massachusetts Board of Education, *Twelfth Annual Report of the Secretary of the Board* (Boston, 1849), pp. 32, 37, 42, 45, 48–49, 52–53, 58–60, 76, 84–86, 89, 93–97, 98, 116–117, 121, 124, 139–140.

skilled artisans and scientific farmers, into scholars and jurists, into the founders of benevolent institutions, and the great expounders of ethical and theological science. By means of early education, those embryos of talent may be quickened, which will solve the difficult problems of political and economical law, and by them, too, the genius may be kindled which will blaze forth in the Poets of Humanity. Our schools, far more than they have done, may supply the Presidents and Professors of Colleges, and Superintendents of Public Instruction, all over the land;

\* \* \*

Without undervaluing any other human agency, it may be safely affirmed that the Common School, improved and energized, as it can easily be, may become the most effective and benignant of all the forces of civilization. Two reasons sustain this position. In the first place, there is a universality in its operation, which can be affirmed of no other institution whatever. If administered in the spirit of justice and conciliation, all the rising generation may be brought within the circle of its reformatory and elevating influences. And, in the second place, the materials upon which it operates are so pliant and ductile as to be susceptible of assuming a greater variety of forms than any other earthly work of the Creator. The inflexibility and ruggedness of the oak, when compared with the lithe sapling or the tender germ, are but feeble emblems to typify the docility of childhood, when contrasted with the obduracy and intractableness of man. It is these inherent advantages of the Common School, which, in our own State, have produced results so striking, from a system so imperfect, and an administration so feeble. In teaching the blind, and deaf and dumb, in kindling the latent spark of intelligence that lurks in an idiot's mind, and in the more holy work of reforming abandoned and outcast children, education has proved what it can do, by glorious experiments. These wonders it has done in its infancy, and with the lights of a limited experience, but, when its faculties shall be fully developed, when it shall be trained to wield its mighty energies for the protection of society against the giant vices which now invade and torment it,—against intemperance, avarice, war, slavery, bigotry, the woes of want and the wickedness of waste,—then, there will not be a height to which these enemies of the race can escape, which it will not scale, nor a Titan among them all, whom it will not slay.

\* \* \*

### *Physical Education*

In the worldy prosperity of mankind, Health and Strength are indispensable ingredients.

Looking to the various disorders and disabilities, which, as every one's experience or observation shows him, do invade and prostrate the human frame, some may be slow to believe that all men, or even the majority of them, will ever be able to administer to those which fall to their share. But, in the first place, it may be asked that a judicious course of physical training, faithfully observed through all the years of infancy, childhood, and adolescence, will avert a vast proportion of the pains and distempers, that now besiege and subdue the human system, or some of its vital organs, and hence, that one may safely be ignorant of symptoms and of remedies which he will never have occasion to recognize or to use;—as one who seeks a residence remote from wild beasts has no practical occasion to know how they are hunted;—and, in the next place, that, if every one does not know, in all cases, how it can against the wastings of ill health, and the havoc of unnecessary death, and it is bound to use equal vigilance, whether these calamities invade us from abroad, or are born of homebred ignorance and folly. And, as has been before intimated, who does not know that the aggregate suffering and loss from general and diffused causes of ill health are indefinitely greater than from the sudden irruption or outbreak of all the contagions and epidemics with which we are ever afflicted? For this greater evil, then, society is bound to provide,—not a remedy, but something better than a remedy,—a preventive. Intelligence and obedience would be an antidote, sovereign in its efficacy, and universal in its applicability.

Now it is beyond all question, that, with the rarest exceptions, every child in the Commonwealth may be indued with this intelligence; and what is equally important, trained to conforming personal habits. Enlightened by knowledge, and impelled by the force of early and long-continued habit, he would not only see the reasonableness adapting his regimen to his condition in the varying circumstances of life but he would feel a personal interest in doing so, as men now feel a personal interest in procuring the gratifications of money or of power. Habit and knowledge will coincide; they will draw in the same direction; they will not be antagonists, as is now so generally the case with those adult men who acquire sound knowledge after bad habits have been enthroned,—the blind force of the latter spurning all the arguments and warnings of the former. This work may be mainly done, during the period of non-age, or before children are emancipated from parental control. Let a child wash himself all over every morning, for sixteen years, and he will as soon go without his breakfast as his bath. This is but a specimen of the effect of a long-continued observance of Nature's "Health Regulations."

Not only will a general knowledge of Human Physiology, or the Laws of Health, do much to supersede the necessity of a knowledge of Pathology, or the Laws of Disease, but the former is as much better than the latter as prevention is better than remedy,—as much better as all the comforts and securities of an unburnt dwelling are than two thirds of its value in money from the insurance office. A general diffusion of physiological knowledge will save millions annually to the State. It will gradually revolutionize many of the absurd customs and usages of society,— conforming them more and more to the rules of reason and true enjoyment, and withdrawing them more and more from the equally vicious extremes of barbarism and of artificial life. It will restrain the caprices and follies of Fashion, in regard to dress and amusement, and subordinate its ridiculous excesses to the laws of health and decency. It will reproduce the obliterated lines that once divided day and night. It will secure cleanliness and purity, more intimate and personal than any the laundress can supply. It will teach men "to eat that they may live, instead of living that they may eat." When Satan approaches in that form, in which he has hitherto been most seductive and successful,—the form of intoxicating beverages,—those who wear the talisman of this science will have an antidote against his temptations. It is a lesson of unspeakable importance, to learn that nourishment and not pleasure is the primary object of food. God, indeed, in his benevolence, has made the reception of this food not only reparative but pleasant. But to lose sight of the first object, in a brutish desire for the second, is voluntarily to alter our position in the scale of being; and, from the rank of men, to descend to the order of the beasts. Physiology would reverse the ancient fable, and transform into men the swine who now sit at epicurean tables, and drink of the Circean cup.

\* \* \*

My general conclusion, then, under this head, is, that it is the duty of all the governing minds in society,—whether in office or out of it,—to diffuse a knowledge of these beautiful and beneficent laws of health and life, throughout the length and breadth of the State;—to popularize them; to make them, in the first place, the common acquisition of all, and, through education and custom, the common inheritance of all; so that the healthful habits naturally growing out of their observance, shall be inbred in the people; exemplified in the personal regimen of each individual; incorporated into the economy of every household; observable in all private dwellings, and in all public edifices, especially in those buildings which are erected by capital for the residence of their work-people, or for renting to the poorer classes; obeyed, by supplying cities with pure water; by providing public baths, public walks, and public squares; by rural cemeteries; by the drainage and sewage of populous towns, and in whatever else may promote the general salubrity of the atmosphere;—in fine, by a religious observance of all those sanitary regulations with which modern science has blessed the world.

For this thorough diffusion of sanitary intelligence, the Common School is the only agency. It is, however, an adequate agency. Let Human Physiology be introduced as an indispensable branch of study into our Public Schools; let no teacher be approved who is not master of its leading principles, and of their applications to the varying circumstances of life; let all the older classes in the schools be regularly and rigidly examined upon this study by the school committees, and a speedy change would come over our personal habits, over our domestic usages, and over the public arrangements of society. Temperance and moderation would not be such strangers at the table. Fashion, like European sovereigns, if not compelled to abdicate and fly, would be forced to compromise for the continued possession of her throne, by the surrender to her subjects of many of their natural rights. A sixth order of architecture would be invented,—the Hygienic,—which, without subtracting at all from the beauty of any order, would add a new element of utility to them all. The "Health Regulations" of cities would be issued in a revised code,—a code that would bear the scrutiny of science. And, as the result and reward of all, a race of men and women, loftier in stature, firmer in structure, fairer in form, and better able to perform the duties and bear the burdens of life, would revisit the earth. The minikin specimens of the race, who now go on dwindling and tapering from parent to child, would reascend to manhood and womanhood. Just in proportion as the laws of health and life were discovered and obeyed would pain, disease, insanity, and untimely death, cease from among men. Consumption would remain, but it would be consumption in the active sense.

### *Intellectual Education, as a Means of Removing Poverty, and Securing Abundance*

\* \* \*

Now two or three things will doubtless be admitted to be true, beyond all controversy, in regard to Massachusetts. By its industrial condition, and its business operations, it is exposed, far beyond any other state in the Union, to the fatal extremes of overgrown wealth and desperate poverty. Its population is far more dense than that of any other state. It is four or five times more dense than the average of all the other states, taken together, and density of population has always been one of the proximate causes of social inequality. According to population and territorial extent, there is far more capital in Massachusetts,—capital which is moveable, and instantaneously available,—than in any other state in the Union; and probably both these qualifications respecting population and territory could be omitted without endangering the truth of the assertion. It has been recently stated, in a very respectable public journal, on the authority of a writer conversant with the subject, that, from the last of June, 1846, to the lst of August, 1848, the amount of money invested, by the citizens of Massachusetts, "in manufacturing cities, railroads and other improvements," is "fifty-seven millions of dollars, of which more than fifty has been paid in and expended." The dividends to be received by citizens of Massachusetts from June, 1846, to April, 1849, are estimated, by the same writer, at ten millions, and the annual increase of capital at "little short of twenty-two millions." If this be so, are we not in danger of naturalizing and domesticating among ourselves those hideous evils which are always engendered between Capital and Labor, when all the capital is in the hands of one class, and all the labor is thrown upon another?

Now, surely, nothing but Universal Education can counterwork this tendency to the domination of capital and servility of labor. If one class possesses all the wealth and the education, while the residue of society is ignorant and poor, it matters not by what name the relation between them may be called; the latter, in fact and in truth, will be the servile dependents and subjects of the former. But if education be equally diffused, it will draw property after it, by the strongest of all attractions; for such a thing never did happen, and never can happen, that an intelligent and practical body of men should be permanently poor. Property and labor, in different classes, are essentially antagonistic; but property and labor, in the same class, are essentially fraternal. The people of Massachusetts have, in some degree, appreciated the truth that the unexampled prosperity of the State,—its comfort, its competence, its general intelligence and virtue,—is attributable to the education, more or less perfect, which all its people have received; but are then sensible of a fact equally important?—namely, that it is to this same education that two thirds of the people are indebted for not being, to-day, the vassals of as severe a tyranny, in the form of capital, the lower classes of Europe are bound to in the form of brute force.

Education, then, beyond all other devices of human origin, is the great equalizer of the conditions of men—the balance-wheel of the social machinery. I do not here mean that it so elevates the moral nature as to make men disdain and abhor the oppression of their fellow-men. This idea pertains to another of its attributes. But I mean that it gives each man the independence and the means, by which he can resist the selfishness of other men. It does better than to disarm the poor of their hostility towards the rich; it prevents being poor. Agrarianism is the revenge of poverty against wealth. The wanton destruction of the property of others,—the burning of hay-ricks and corn-ricks, the demolition of machinery, because it supersedes hand-labor, the sprinkling of vitriol on rich dresses,—is only agrarianism run mad. Education prevents both the revenge and the madness. On the other hand, a fellow-feeling for one's class or caste is the common instinct of hearts not wholly sunk in selfish regards for person, or for family. The spread of education, by enlarging the cultivated class or caste, will open a wider area over which the social feelings will expand and, if this education should be universal and complete, it would do more than all things else to obliterate factitious distinctions in society.

\* \* \*

## *Political Education*

The necessity of general intelligence,—that is, of education (for I use the terms as substantially synonymous, because general intelligence can never exist without general education, and general education will be sure to produce general intelligence,)—the necessity of general intelligence, under a republican form of government, like most other very important truths, has become a very trite one. It is so trite, indeed, as to have lost much of its force by its familiarity. Almost all the champions of education seize upon this argument, first of all; because it is so simple as to be understood by the ignorant, and so strong as to convince the skeptical. Nothing would be easier than to follow in the train of so many writers, and to demonstrate, by logic, by history, and by the nature of the case, that a republican form of government, without intelligence in the people, must be, on a vast scale, what a madhouse, without superintendent or keepers, would be, on a small one;— the despotism of a few succeeded by universal anarchy, and anarchy by despotism, with no change but from bad to worse. Want of space and time alike forbid me to attempt any full development of the merits of this theme; but yet, in the closing one of a series of reports, partaking somewhat of the nature of a summary of former arguments, an omission of this topic would suggest to the comprehensive mind the idea of incompleteness.

I have now given a hasty review of a single class of errors, those pertaining to the collection of revenue,—into which governments have fallen, through a want of intelligence;— through a want of such intelligence, it may be added, as any discreet and reflecting man would exercise in the management of his own affairs. And when will rulers be wiser than they have been? Never, until the people, to whom they are responsible, shall permit it and demand it. Never will wisdom preside in the halls of legislation and its profound utterances be recorded on the pages of the statute book, until Common Schools,—or some other agency of equal power, not yet discovered,—shall create a more far-seeing intelligence and a purer morality than has ever yet existed among communities of men. Legislators, in the execution of their high guardianship over public interests, will never secure to the State even the greatest amount of wealth, while they seek to obtain it at the price of morality. It is only when the virtue of the people is supremely cared for, that they will discover the comprehensive meaning of the Scripture, that Godliness is profitable unto all things.

However elevated the moral character of a constituency may be; however well informed in matters of general science or history, yet they must, if citizens of a Republic, understand something of the true nature and functions of the government under which they live. That any one who is to participate in the government of a country when he becomes a man, should receive no instruction respecting the nature and functions of the government he is afterwards to administer, is a political solecism. In all nations, hardly excepting the most rude and barbarous, the future sovereign receives some training which is supposed to fit him for the exercise of the powers and duties of his anticipated station. Where, by force of law, the government devolves upon the heir, while yet in a state of legal infancy, some regency or other substitute, is appointed, to act in his stead, until his arrival at mature age; and, in the meantime, he is subjected to such a course of study and discipline, as will tend to prepare him, according to the political theory of the time and the place, to assume the reins of authority at the appointed age. If, in England, or in the most enlightened European monarchies, it would be a proof of restored barbarism, to permit the future sovereign to grow up without any knowledge of his duties,—and who can doubt that it would be such a proof,—then, surely, it would be not less a proof of restored, or of never-removed barbarism, amongst us, to empower any individual to use the elective franchise, without preparing him for so momentous a trust. Hence, the constitution of the United States, and of our own State, should be made a study in our Public Schools. The partition of the powers of government into the three co-ordinate branches,—legislative, judicial, and executive,—with the duties appropriately devolving upon each; the mode of electing or of appointing all officers, with the reasons on which it was founded; and, especially, the duty of every citizen, in a government of laws, to appeal to the courts for redress in all cases of alleged wrong, instead of undertaking to vindicate his own rights by his own arm; and, in a government where the people are the acknowledged sources of power, the duty of changing laws and rulers by an appeal to the ballot, and not by rebellion, should be taught to all the children until they are fully understood.

Had the obligations of the future citizen been sedulously inculcated upon all the children of this Republic, would the patriot have had to mourn over so many instances, where the voter, not being able to accomplish his purpose by voting, has proceeded to accomplish it by violence where, agreeing with his fellow-citizens, to use the machinery of the ballot, he makes a tacit reservation, that, if that machinery not move according to his pleasure, he will wrest or break it? If the responsibleness and value of the elective franchise were duly appreciated, the day of our State and National elections would be among the most solemn and religious days on the calendar. Men would approach them, not only with preparation and solicitude, but with the sobriety and solemnity, with which discreet and religious-minded men meet the great crises of life. No man would throw away his vote, through caprice or wantonness, any more than he would throw away his estate, or sell his family, into bondage. No man would cast his vote through malice or revenge any more than a good surgeon would amputate a limb, or a good navigator sail through perilous straits, under the same criminal passions.

But, perhaps, it will be objected, that the constitution is subject to different readings or that the policy of different administrations has become the subject of party strife; and, therefore, if any thing of constitutional or political law is introduced into our schools, there is danger that teachers will be chosen on account of their affinities to this or that political party or that teachers will feign affinities which they do not feel, in order that they may be chosen and so each schoolroom will at length become a miniature political club-room, exploding with political resolves, or flaming out with political addresses, prepared, by beardless boys, in scarcely legible hand-writing, and in worse grammar.

With the most limited exercise of discretion, all apprehensions of this kind are wholly groundless. There are different readings of the constitution, it is true; and there are partisan topics which agitate the country from side to side; but the controverted points, compared with those about which there is no dispute, do not bear the proportion of one to a hundred. And what is more, no man is qualified, or can be qualified, to discuss the disputable questions, unless previously and thoroughly versed in those questions, about which there is no dispute. In the terms and principles common to all, and recognized by all, is to be found the only common medium of language and of idea, by which the parties can become intelligible to each other; and there, too, is the only common ground, whence the arguments of the disputants can be drawn.

It is obvious, on the other hand, that if the tempest of political strife were to be let loose upon our Common Schools, they would be overwhelmed with sudden ruin. Let it be once understood, that the schoolroom is a legitimate theatre for party politics, and with what violence will hostile partisans struggle to gain possession of the stage, and to play their parts upon it!

\* \* \*

But to avoid such a catastrophe, shall all teaching, relative to the nature of our government, be banished from our schools; and shall our children be permitted to grow up in entire ignorance of the political history of their country? In the schools of a republic, shall the children be left without any distinct knowledge of the nature of a republican government; or only with such knowledge as they may pick up from angry political discussions, or from party newspapers; from caucus speeches, or Fourth of July orations,—the Apocrypha of Apocrypha?

Surely, between these extremes, there must be a medium not difficult to be found. And is not this the middle course, which all sensible and judicious men, all patriots, and all genuine republicans, must approve?—namely, that those articles in the creed of republicanism, which are accepted by all, believed in by all, and which form the common basis of our political faith, shall be taught to all. But when the teacher, in the course of his lessons or lectures on the fundamental law, arrives at a controverted text, he is either to read it without comment or remark; or, at most, he is only to say that the passage is the subject of disputation and that the schoolroom is neither the tribunal to adjudicate, nor the forum to discuss it.

Such being the rule established by common consent, and such the practice, observed with fidelity under it, it will come to be universally understood that political proselytism is no function of the school; but that all indoctrination into matters of controversy between hostile political parties is to be elsewhere sought for, and elsewhere imparted. Thus, may all the children of the Commonwealth receive instruction in the great essentials of political knowledge,—in those elementary ideas without which they will never be able to investigate more recondite and debatable questions;

\* \* \*

…Indeed, so decisive is the effect of early training upon adult habits and character, that numbers of the most able and experienced teachers,—those who have had the best opportunities to become acquainted with the errors and the excellences of children, their waywardness and their docility,—have unanimously declared it to be their belief, that, if all the children in the community, from the age of four years to that of sixteen, could be brought within the reformatory and elevating influences of schools, the dark host of private vices and public crimes, which now embitter domestic peace and stain the civilization of the age, might, in ninety-nine cases in every hundred, be banished from the world. When Christ taught his disciples to pray, "Thy kingdom come, thy will be done, *on earth* as it is done in heaven," did he teach them to pray for what shall never come to pass! And if this consummation is ever to be realized, is it to be by some mighty, sudden, instantaneous revolution, effected by a miracle; or is it to be produced gradually by that Providence which uses human agents as its instruments?

Were we to hear that some far-off land had been discovered, over which the tempest of war had never swept; where institutions of learning and religion were reverenced and their ministers held in the foremost rank of honor; where falsehood, detraction, and perjury were never uttered; where neither intemperance, nor the guilty knowledge how to prepare its means, nor the guilty agents to diffuse them, were ever known; where all the obligations, growing out of the domestic relations, were sacredly kept; where office always sought the wisest and best men for incumbents, and never failed to find them; where witnesses were true, and jurors just (for we can hardly conceive of a state of society upon earth so perfect as to exclude all differences of opinion about rights;) in fine, where all men were honest in their dealings, and exemplary in their lives,—with the exception of here and there an individual, who, from the rareness of his appearance, would be regarded almost as a monster;— were we to hear of such a realm, who, that loves peace and the happiness that comes from security and order, would not wish to escape from the turmoil and the violence, the rancor and the mean ambitions, of our present sphere, and go there to dwell and to die? And yet, it is the opinion of our most intelligent, dispassionate, and experienced teachers, that we can, in the course of two or three generations, and through the instrumentality of good teachers and good schools, superinduce, substantially, such a state of society upon the present one; and this, too, without any miracle, without any extraordinary sacrifices, or costly effort; but only by working our existing Common School system with such a degree of vigor as can easily be put forth, and at such an expense as even the poorest community can easily bear. If the leaders of society,—those whose law-giving eloquence determines what statutes,—shall be enacted by the Legislature, or those who speak for the common heart in self-constituted assemblies, or those who shape popular opinion through the public press, or in the private intercourse of life,—if these are not yet prepared to have faith in the reformatory power of an early and wise training for the young, the fact only shows and measures the extent of the work which teachers and educationists have yet to perform. If men decline to cooperate with us, because uninspired by our living faith, then the arguments, the labors, and the results, which will create this faith, are a preliminary step in our noble work.

\* \* \*

### Religious Education

But, it will be said that this grand result, in Practical Morals, is a consummation of blessedness that can never be attained without Religion; and that no community will ever be religious, without a Religious Education. Both these propositions, I regard as eternal and immutable truths. Devoid of religious principles and religious affections, the race can never fall so low but that it may sink still lower; animated and sanctified by them, it can never rise so high but that it may ascend still higher. And is it not at least as presumptuous to expect that mankind will attain to the knowledge of truth, without being instructed in truth, and without that general expansion and development of faculty which will enable them to recognize and comprehend truth, in any other department of human interest, as in the department of religion? No creature of God, of whom we have any knowledge, has such a range of moral oscillation as a human being. He may despise privileges, and turn a deaf ear to warnings and instructions, such as evil spirits may never have known, and therefore be more guilty than they; or, ascending through temptation and conflict, along the radiant pathway of duty, he may reach the sublimest heights of happiness, and may there experience the joys of a contrast, such as ever-perfect beings can never feel. And can it be that our nature, in this respect, is taken out of the law that governs it in every other respect;—the law, namely, that the teachings which supply it with new views, and the training that leads it to act in conformity with those views, are ineffective and nugatory?

* * *

After years of endurance, after suffering under misconstructions of conduct, and the imputation of motives, whose edge is sharper than a knife, it was, at my suggestion and by making use of materials which I had laboriously collected, that the Board made its Eighth Annual Report;—a document said to be the ablest argument in favor of the use of the Bible in Schools, any where to be found. This Report had my full concurrence. Since its appearance, I have always referred to it, as explanatory of the views of the Board, and as setting forth the law of a wise Commonwealth and the policy of a Christian people. Officially and unofficially, publicly and privately, in theory and in practice, my course has always been in conformity with its doctrines. And I avail myself of this, the last opportunity which I may ever have, to say, in regard to all affirmations or intimations, that I have ever attempted to exclude religious instruction from school, or to exclude the Bible from school, or to impair the force of that volume, arising out of itself, are now, and always have been, without substance or semblance of truth.

But it may still be said, and it is said, that, however sincere, or however religiously disposed, the advocates of our school system may be, still the character of the system is not to be determined by the number, nor by the sincerity of its defenders, but by its own inherent attributes; and that, if judged by these attributes, it is, in fact and in truth, an irreligious, an un-Christian, and an anti-Christian system. Having devoted the best part of my life to the promotion of this system, and believing it to be the only system which ought to prevail, or can permanently prevail, in any free country; I am not content to see it suffer, unrelieved, beneath the weight of amputations so grievous; nor is it right that any hostile system should be built up by so gross a misrepresentation of ours. That our Public Schools are not Theological Seminaries, is admitted. That they are debarred by law from inculcating the peculiar and distinctive doctrines or any one religious denomination amongst us, is claimed and that they are also prohibited from ever teaching that what they do teach is the whole of religion, or all that is essential to religion or to salvation, is equally certain. But our system earnestly inculcates all Christian morals; it founds its morals on the basis of religion; it welcomes the religion of the Bible; and, in recieving the Bible, it allows it to do what it is allowed to do in no other system,—*to speak for itself.* But here it stops, not because it claims to have compassed all truth, but because it disclaims to act as an umpire between hostile religious opinions.

The very terms, *Public School,* and *Common School,* bear upon their face, that they are schools which the children of the entire community may attend. Every man, not on the pauper list, is taxed for their support. But he is not taxed to support them as special religious institutions; if he were, it would satisfy, at once, the largest definition of a Religious Establishment. But he is taxed to support them, as a *preventive* means against dishonesty, against fraud, and against violence; on the same principle that he is taxed to support criminal courts as a *punitive* means against the same offences. He is taxed to support schools, on the same principle that he is taxed to support paupers, because a child without education is poorer and more wretched than a man without bread. He is taxed to support schools, on the same principle that he would be taxed to defend the nation against foreign invasion, or against rapine committed by a foreign foe; because the general prevalence of ignorance, superstition, and vice, will breed Goth and Vandal at home, more fatal to the public well-being, than any Goth or Vandal from abroad. And, finally, he is taxed to support schools, because they are the most effective means of developing and training those powers and faculties in a child, by which, when he becomes a man, he may understand what his highest interests and his highest duties are and may be, in fact, and not in name only, a free agent. The elements of a political education are not bestowed upon any school child, for the purpose of making him vote with this or that political party when he becomes of age; but for the purpose of enabling him to choose for himself, with which party he will vote. So the religious education which a child receives at school, is not imparted to him, for the purpose of making him join this or that denomination, when he arrives at years of discretion, for for the purpose of enabling him to judge for himself, according to the dictates of his on reason and conscience....

This topic invites far more extended exposition; but this must suffice. In bidding an official Farewell to a system, with which I have been so long connected, to which I have devotd my means, my strength, my health, twelve years of time, and, doubtless, twice that number of years from what might otherwise have been my term of life, I have felt bound to submit these brief views in its defence. In justice to my own name and memory; in justice to the Board of which I was originally a member, and from which I have always sought counsel and guidance; and in justice to thousands of the most wise, upright, and religious-minded men in Massachusetts, who have been fellow-laborers in advancing the great cause of Popular Education, under the auspices of this system, I have felt bound to vindicate it from the aspersions cast upon it, and to show its consonance with the eternal principles of equity and justice. I have felt bound to show, that, so far from its being an irreligious, an anti-Christian, or an un-Christian system, it is a system which recognizes religious obligations in their fullest extent; that it is a system which invokes a religious spirit, and can never be fitly administered without such a spirit; that it inculcates great commands, upon which hang all the law and the prophets; that it welcomes the Bible, and therefore welcomes all the doctrines which the Bible really contains, and that it listens to these doctrines so reverently, that, for the time being, it will not suffer any rash mortal to thrust in his interpolations of their meaning, or overlay the text with any of the "many inventions" which the heart of man has sought out. It is a system, however, which leaves open all other means of instruction,—the pulpits, the Sunday schools, the Bible classes, the catechisms, of all denominations,—to be employed according to the preferences of individual parents. It is a system which restrains itself from teaching, that what it does teach is all that needs to be taught or that should be taught; but leaves this to be decided by each man for himself, according to the light of his reason and consciences and on his responsibility to that Great Being, who, in holding him to an account for the things done in the body, will hold him to the strictest account for the manner in which he has "trained up" his children.

\* \* \*

Such, then, in a religious point of view, is the Massachusetts system of Common Schools. Reverently, it recognizes and affirms the sovereign rights of the Creator; sedulously and sacredly it guards the religious rights of the creature; while it seeks to remove all hindrances, and to supply all furtherances to a filial and paternal communion between man and his Maker. In a social and political sense, it is a *Free* school system. It knows no distinction of rich and poor, of bond and free, or between those who, in the imperfect light of this world, are seeking, through different avenues, to reach the gate of heaven. Without money and without price, it throws open its doors, and spreads the table of its bounty, for all the children of the State. Like the sun, it shines, not only upon the good, but upon the evil, that they may become good; and, like the rain, its blessings descend, not only upon the just, but upon the unjust, that their injustice may depart from them and be known no more.

# The Superiority of Women as Teachers (1846)*

Now, without expressing any opinion as to the influence, on health and morals, of taking women away from domestic habits and pursuits, to labor with men in shops and mills, I simply ask if it would not be *better* to put the thousands of men who are keeping school for young children into the mills, and employ the women to train the children?

Wherever education is most prosperous, there woman is employed more than man. In Massachusetts, where education is highest, five out of seven of the teachers are women; while in Kentucky, where education is so much lower, five out of six of the teachers are men.

Another cause of depression to our sex is found in the fact that there is no profession for women of education and high position, which, like law, medicine, and theology, opens the way to competence, influence, and honor, and presents motives for exertion. Woman ought never to be led to married life except under the promptings of pure affection. To marry for an establishment, for a position, or for something to do, is a deplorable wrong. But how many women, for want of a high and honorable profession to engage their time, are led to this melancholy course? This is not so because Providence has not provided an ample place for such a profession for woman, but because custom or prejudice, or a low estimate of its honorable character, prevents her from entering it. *The education of children, that* is the true and noble profession of a woman—*that* is what is worthy the noblest powers and affections of the noblest minds.

Another cause which deeply affects the best interests of our sex is the contempt, or utter neglect and indifference, which has befallen this only noble profession open to woman. There is no employment, however disagreeable or however wicked, which custom and fashion cannot render elegant, interesting, and enthusiastically sought. A striking proof of this is seen in the military profession. This is the profession of *killing our fellow-creatures,* and is attended with everything low, brutal, unchristian, and disgusting; and yet what halos of glory have been hung around it, and how the young, generous, and enthusi-

*From Catherine E. Beecher. *The Evils Suffered by American Women and American Children: The Causes and the Remedy* (New York, 1846), pp. 9–10.

astic have been drawn into it! If one-half the poetry, fiction, oratory, and taste thus misemployed had been used to embellish and elevate the employment of training the mind of childhood, in what an altered position should we find this noblest of all professions!

As it is, the employment of teaching children is regarded as the most wearying drudgery, and few resort to it except from necessity, and one very reasonable cause of this aversion is the utter neglect of any arrangements for preparing teachers for this arduous and difficult profession. The mind of a young child is like a curious instrument, capable of exquisite harmony when touched by a skillful hand, but sending forth only annoying harshness when unskillfully addressed. To a teacher is committed a collection of these delicate contrivances; and, without experience, without instruction, it is required not only that each one should be tuned aright, but that all be combined in excellent harmony: as if a young girl were sent into a splendid orchestra, all ignorant and unskillful, and required to draw melody from each instrument, and then to combine the whole in faultless harmony. And in each case there are, here and there, individual minds, who, without instruction, are gifted by nature with aptness and skill in managing the music either of matter or of mind; but that does not lessen the folly, in either case, of expecting the whole profession, either of music or of teaching, to be pursued without preparatory training.

## Q U E S T I O N S

1. Describe in your own words what is meant by the "one best system."

2. Visualize the blueprint or floor plan of the elementary, middle, and/or high school you attended. How is it similar to and different from the egg-crate school?

3. What is the relationship between the emergence of the "one best system" of schooling and the feminization of the teaching profession? To what extent is teaching still considered to be woman's work?

4. Based on your own experience, to what extent does the "one best system" still dominate our public schools?

5. Explain what Horace Mann means when he suggested that the common school—through the appropriate curriculum and instruction—would "reverse the ancient fable; and transform swine into men."

6. Evaluate Mann's argument that education is the great equalizer of the conditions of men—the balance-wheel of social machinery in his day. Is his argument relevant today? Explain your answer.

7. Compare Mann's position on the relationship of education and general intelligence in a republic to that of Thomas Jefferson. Are Mann's views still relevant in this new century?

8. Describe in your own words the religious point of view—according to Mann—of the Massachusetts system of common schools. How would his views of Bible reading in the schools be viewed today? Do you think it was a cause for concern for any groups during his time?

# CHAPTER

# 9 U.S. Textbooks in the Nineteenth Century

The "one best system" sought to make schooling scientific and professional, but what did children actually learn in the classroom? As noted in the previous chapter, the ultimate goal of this more scientific approach to schooling was to develop a curriculum standardized by grade level and developed by trained educational experts. Even though this vision was apparent by midcentury, the actual materials available for use in U.S. classrooms were neither scientific nor developed by professional educators. In many schools, the Bible remained the most common text, often supplemented by whatever books students might have at home. For much of the century, rote recitation remained the most common form of teaching. In a world without computers, television, or the radio, textbooks were often a child's only contact with the world beyond the boundaries of his or her immediate community. Schools, in addition to emphasizing the three R's, were expected to mold the character of children and youth.

The most popular textbook writers of the nineteenth century succeeded in teaching what they believed to be a moral and religious common denominator. Nineteenth-century textbooks were decidedly moral and religious and purposely created larger-than-life American heroes of the highest moral character. The story of George Washington's inability to tell a lie when asked by his father if he had chopped down the cherry tree is a prime example of the moral vignettes found in these textbooks.

Offering both a more tempered version of the moral absolutism bequeathed to us by the Puritans and a patriotic vision of America that would make Noah Webster proud, the textbooks of the nineteenth century suggested that prosperity and salvation result from hard work, truthfulness, obedience, sobriety, and kindness. Although supposedly nonsectarian and nonpartisan, these works advocated both Protestant religious beliefs and a conservative political ideology. Presenting what they believed to be commonly held values, these textbooks emphasized that parents, teachers, and ministers were the appropriate interpreters of God's moral law. In an attempt to put the fear of God into the mind of young people, these authors sometimes taught by horrible example. More frequently, they provided morality tales about wayward youths seeing the light and returning to the fold before it was too late. In one such vignette, young Jack Halyard obtained some rum on the sly. Becoming a bit tipsy from it, Jack insulted an old man and abused his own mother. By showing remorse and confessing all to his father, Jack avoided the fate of a drunkard who exploded as he tried to light his pipe.

Textbook authors were not professional educators but usually men of conservative persuasion wishing to convey a message or seeking to supplement their income.[1] Many authors came from New England and were teachers, printers, journalists, lawyers, and professors. The most famous was William Holmes McGuffey. Through characters such as Honest George Ellet and through the five million copies sold before his death in 1873, McGuffey impressed the virtues of the Puritan ethic on the minds of schoolage children and youth throughout the United States of the nineteenth century.

These textbook authors succeeded to a remarkable degree in foisting on each new generation a vision of American life and society at odds with the experiences of most nineteenth-century Americans. In a society becoming increasingly urbanized, these authors presented an idealized agrarian society as the norm. On the positive side, many of the texts included selections of excellent literature. As a whole, however, the texts presented a highly romanticized version of nineteenth-century U.S. society that minimized or ignored controversial or problematic aspects of life. In a world experiencing dramatic intellectual, social, economic, and political changes, these textbooks selected themes and content designed to disguise rather than reveal the real world. The quintessential American was presented as the White Anglo-Saxon Protestant farmer or merchant who earned his worldly prosperity and—at the appropriate time—his place in heaven through thrift, perseverance, and hard work. In turn, the texts' use of less than flattering stereotypes of the Black person (called Negro), the Catholic, the Jew, and of most foreigners conveyed the message that the United States belonged to the White, middle-class, Protestant, native-born citizen. As Richard Elson suggests, these textbooks succeeded in transforming the real world into a fantasy constructed by the privileged class "as a guide for each new generation but inhabited by no one outside the pages of school books."[2]

[1]Nineteenth century women educators—such as Emma Willard and Catherine Beecher—also published textbooks during this period focused largely on the art and craft of teaching and on improving female education. See Willystine Goodsell, ed., *Pioneers of Women's Education in the United States* (New York: McGraw-Hill Book Company, Inc., 1931).

[2]David B. Tyack, ed., *Turning Points in American Educational History* (New York: John Wiley & Sons, 1967), p. 184.

# Good Pronunciation with Moral Lessons
# from the American Spelling Book (1831)*

### Table XIII

LESSONS OF EASY WORDS, TO TEACH CHILDREN TO READ, AND TO KNOW THEIR DUTY

### Lesson I

*No man may put off the law of God:*
*My joy is in his law all the day.*
*O may I not go in the way of sin!*
*Let me not go in the way of ill men.*

*From Noah Webster, *The American Spelling Book* (Middletown, Conn., 1831), pp. 53–57.

### II

*A bad man is a foe to the law:*
*It is his joy to do ill.*
*All men go out of the way.*
*Who can say he has no sin?*

### III

*The way of man is ill.*
*My son, do as you are bid:*
*But if you are bid, do no ill.*
*See not my sin, and let me not go to the pit.*

### IV

*Rest in the Lord, and mind his word.*
*My son, hold fast the law that is good.*
*You must not tell a lie, nor do hurt.*
*We must let no man hurt us.*

### V

*Do as well as you can, and do no harm.*
*Mark the man that doth well, and do so too.*
*Help such as want help, and be kind.*
*Let your sins past put you in mind to mend.*

### VI

*I will not walk with bad men, that I may not be cast off with them.*
*I will love the law and keep it.*
*I will walk with the just and do good.*

### VII

*This life is not long; but the life to come has no end.*
*We must pray for them that hate us.*
*We must love them that love not us.*
*We must do as we like to be done to.*

### VIII

*A bad life will make a bad end.*
*He must live well that will die well.*
*He doth live ill that doth not mend.*
*In time to come we must do no ill.*

### IX

*No man can say that he has done no ill.*
*For all men have gone out of the way.*

*There is none that doeth good; no, not one.*
*If I have done harm, I must do it no more.*

### X

*Sin will lead us to pain and wo.*
*Love that which is good, and shun vice.*
*Hate no man, but love both friends and foes.*
*A bad man can take no rest, day nor night.*

### XI

*He who came to save us, will wash us from all sin; I will be glad in his name.*
*A good boy will do all that is just; he will flee from vice; he will do good, and walk in the*
*    way of life.*
*Love not the world, nor the things that are in the world; for they are sin.*
*I will not fear what flesh can do to me; for my trust is in him who made the world.*
*He is nigh to them that pray to him, and praise his name.*

### XII

*Be a good child; mind your book; love your school, and strive to learn.*
*Tell no tales; call no ill names; you must not lie, nor swear, nor cheat, nor steal.*
*Play not with bad boys; use no ill words at play; spend your time well; live in peace, and shun*
*    all strife. This is the way to make good men love you, and save your soul from pain and woe.*

### XIII

*A good child will not lie, swear, nor steal.—He will be good at home, and ask to read his*
*    book, when he gets up he will wash his hands and face clean; he will comb his hair, and*
*    make haste to school; he will not play by the way, as bad boys do.*

### XVI

*When good boys and girls are at school, they will mind their books, and try to learn to spell*
*    and read well, and not play in the time of school.*

# Selection from McGuffey's First Eclectic Reader (1853)*

* * *

### *The Bro-ken Win-dow*

George El-let had a fine New Year's gift. What do you think it was? A bright sil-ver dol-lar! A mer-ry boy was George, when he thought of all the fine things he might buy with it.

*From William Holmes McGuffey's *Eclectic First Reader* (Cincinnati: Winthrop B. Smith & Co., 1853), 100–104.

As soon as the sun be-gan to make the air feel a lit-tle warm, he put on his cap and gloves, and ran in-to the street.

The ground was cov-er-ed with snow, but the sun shone out, and ev-er-y thing look-ed bright. As George went skipping a-long, he met some boys who were throw-ing snow-balls. This is fine sport, and George pull-ed off his gloves, and was soon as bu-sy as the rest. See, how he gath-ers up the snow, and press-es it be-tween his hands.

Now he has hit James Ma-son. But the ball was soft, and James is not hurt. Now he has made an-oth-er ball, and if James does not dodge, George will hit him a-gain. A-way goes the ball! But it miss-ed James, and broke a win-dow on the oth-er side of the street. George was a-fraid that some one would come out of the house and whip him; so he ran off, as fast as he could.

As soon as he got round the next cor-ner, he stop-ped, be-cause he was ver-y sor-ry for what he had done. Just then he saw a man car-ry-ing a box with glass doors, full of pret-ty toys; and as George was on-ly eight years old, he for-got the bro-ken win-dow and ran aft-er the man.

As George was a-bout to buy a lit-tle house with doors and chim-neys, and put his hand in his pock-et for the money, he thought of the bro-ken window. Then he said to him-self, "I have no right to spend this dol-lar for a toy-house. I ought to go back, and pay, for the glass I broke with my snow-ball."

So he gave back the house to the toy-man and turn-ed round. But he was a-fraid of be-ing scold-ed or beat-en, and did not know what to do. He went up and down the street, and felt ver-y bad-ly. He wish-ed to buy some-thing nice with his mon-ey and he al-so wished to pay for the glass he had bro-ken.

At last he said to him-self, "It was wrong to break the win-dow, al-though I did not mean to do it. I will go and pay the man for it at once. If it takes all my mon-ey, I will try not to be sor-ry; and I do not think the man will hurt me, if I of-fer to pay for the mis-chief I have done." He then start-ed off, and felt much hap-pi-er for hav-ing made up his mind to do what was right.

He rang the door bell; and when the man came out, George said, "Sir, I threw a snow-ball through your win-dow. But I did not in-tend to do it, and am ver-y sor-ry, and I wish to pay you. Here is the dol-lar my fa-ther gave me as a New Year's gift, this morn-ing."

The man took the dol-lar, and ask-ed George if he had a-ny more mon-ey. George said he had not. "Well," said the man, "this will be e-nough." So aft-er ask-ing George where he liv-ed, and what was his name, he call-ed him an hon-est lad, and shut the door.

When George had paid the man, he ran a-way, and felt ver-y hap-py, be-cause he had done what he knew to be right. He play-ed ver-y mer- ri-ly all the fore-noon, al-though he had no mon-ey to spend; and went home at din-ner time, with a face as ro-sy, and eyes as bright, as if noth-ing had gone wrong.

At din-ner, Mr. El-let ask-ed George what he had bought with his mon-ey. George ver-y hon-est-ly told him all a-bout the bro-ken win-dow, and said he felt ver-y well, with-out a-ny mon-ey to spend. When din-ner was o-ver, Mr. El-let told George to go and look in his hat.

He did so, and found *two* sil-ver dol-lars. The man, whose win-dow had been bro-ken, had been there, and told George's fa-ther a-bout it. He al-so gave back the dol-lar which George had paid him, and *an-oth-er one* with it.

A few months aft-er that, the man came and told Mr. El-let that he want-ed a good boy to stay in his store, and would like to have George, as soon as he left school, for he was sure that George was an *hon-est boy*. George went to live with this man, who was a rich mer-chant. In a few years he be-came the mer-chant's partner, and is now rich. George oft-en thinks of the *bro-ken win-dow*.

# Lesson from McGuffey's Third Eclectic Reader (1848)*

### *Lesson V*

*Words to be Spelled and Defined*

A-light'-ed, got off, descended
   from.
O-ver-take', to come up with.
Clev'-er-ly, handsomely, skillfully.
Shel'-ter, that which protects.

O-bli -ging, kind, ready to assist.
Phi-los'-o-pher, a man learned in science, *here used figuratively for* a contented person.
Con-tent -ed, quiet, satisfied.

### *The Little Philosopher*

RULE.—This kind of composition is called *Dialogue*. It should be read with the same tone, and in the same manner, that we use in conversation.

Mr. Lenox was one morning riding by himself; he alighted from his horse to look at something on the roadside; the horse got loose and ran away from him. Mr. Lenox ran after him, but could not overtake him. A little boy, at work in a field, heard the horse; and, as soon as he saw him running from his master, ran very quickly to the middle of the road, and catching him by the bridle, stopped him, till Mr. Lenox came up.

MR. LENOX.  Thank you, my good boy, you have caught my horse very cleverly. What shall I give you for your trouble?

BOY.  I want nothing, sir.

MR. L.  Do you want nothing? So much the better for you. Few men can say as much. But what were you doing in the field?

B.  I was rooting up weeds, and tending the sheep that were feeding on turnips.

MR. L.  Do you like to work?

B.  Yes, sir, very well, this fine weather.

MR. L.  But would you not rather play?

*From William Holmes McGuffey, *McGuffey's Newly Revised Third Eclectic Reader* (Cincinnati, 1848), pp. 32–34.

B.  This is not hard work; it is almost as good as play.

MR. L.  Who set you to work?

B.  My father, sir.

MR. L.  What is your name?

B.  Peter Hurdle, sir.

MR. L.  How old are you?

B.  Eight years old, next June.

MR. L.  How long have you been out in this field?

B.  Ever since six o'clock this morning.

MR. L.  Are you not hungry?

B.  Yes, sir, but I shall go to dinner soon.

MR. L.  If you had sixpence now, what would you do with it?

B.  I do not know, sir. I never had so much in my life.

MR. L.  Have you no play things?

B.  Play things? what are they?

MR. L.  Such as nine-pins, marbles, tops, and wooden horses.

B.  No, sir. Tom and I play at foot-ball in winter, and I have a jumping-rope. I had a hoop, but it is broken.

MR. L.  Do you want nothing else?

B.  I have hardly time to play with what I have. I have to drive the cows, and to run of errands, and to ride the horses to the fields, and that is as good as play.

MR. L.  You could get apples and cakes, if you had money, you know.

B.  I can have apples at home. As for cake, I do not want that; my mother makes me a pie now and then, which is as good.

MR. L.  Would you not like a knife to cut sticks?

B.  I have one; here it is; brother Tom gave it to me.

MR. L.  Your shoes are full of holes. Don't you want a new pair?

B.  I have a better pair for Sundays.

MR. L.  But these let in water.

B.  I don't mind that, sir.

MR. L.  Your hat is all torn, too.

B.  I have a better hat at home.

MR. L.  What do you do when it rains?

B.  If it rains very hard when I am in the field, I get under the tree for shelter.

**MR. L.**   What do you do, if you are hungry before it is time to go home?

**B.**   I sometimes eat a raw turnip.

**MR. L.**   But if there are none?

**B.**   Then I do as well as I can without. I work on, and never think of it.

**MR. L.**   Why, my little fellow, you are quite a *philosopher*, but I am sure you do not know what that means.

**B.**   No, sir. I hope it means no harm.

**MR. L.**   No, no! Were you ever at school?

**B.**   No, sir; but father means to send me next winter.

**MR. L.**   You will want books then.

**B.**   Yes, sir, the boys all have an Eclectic spelling book and Reader, and a Testament.

**MR. L.**   Then I will give them to you; tell your father so, and that it is because you are an obliging, contented little boy.

**B.**   I will, sir, Thank you.

**MR. L.**   Good by, Peter.

**B.**   Good moming, sir.

### Questions

What service did this little boy perform for the gentleman? Would he take any pay for it? What did the gentleman think of the boy? What do you suppose made him so contented with his condition? Why should we always be contented with such things as we have? What note is that which is placed after all the questions in this lesson? What stop is that after the last word "sir?"

What nouns are there in the first sentence of this lesson? In what number is each? What is the plural number of each?

### Articulation

Be careful to utter *g* distinctly. Morn-ing, not *morn-in:* ri-ding not *ri-din:* run-ning, not *run-nin:* catch-ing, not *catch-in:* noth-ing, not *noth-in:* root-ing, not *root-in:* tend-ing, not *tend-in:* feed-ing, not *feed-in:* spelling, not *spell-in.*

### To Teachers

The amount of instruction derived from reading exercises, may be increased by introducing, occasionally, questions upon *grammatical construction.* These will assist the pupil in understanding the lesson, and afford valuable *practice* in parsing, and will add interest and variety to the recitation. A few questions are appended to some of the lessons in this book, as specimens of the kind of examination which, it is believed, will be found interesting and instructive.

# Selection from McGuffey's Fifth
# Eclectic Reader (1879)*

### *I. The Good Reader*

**1.** It is told of Frederick the Great, King of Prussia, that, as he was seated one day in his private room, a written petition was brought to him with the request that it should be immediately read. The King had just returned from hunting, and the glare of the sun, or some other cause, had so dazzled his eyes that he found it difficult to make out a single word of the writing.

**2.** His private secretary happened to be absent; and the soldier who brought the petition could not read. There was a page, or favorite boy-servant, waiting in the hall, and upon him the king called. The page was a son of one of the noblemen of the court, but proved to be a very poor reader.

**3.** In the first place, he did not articulate distinctly. He huddled his words together in the utterance, as if they were syllables of one long word, which he must get through with as speedily as possible. His pronunciation was bad, and he did not modulate his voice so as to bring out the meaning of what he read. Every sentence was uttered with a dismal monotony of voice, as if it did not differ in any respect from that which preceded it.

**4.** "Stop!" said the King, impatiently. "Is it an auctioneer's list of goods to be sold that you are hurrying over? Send your companion to me." Another page who stood at the door now entered, and to him the King gave the petition. The second page began by hemming and clearing his throat in such an affected manner that the King jokingly asked him if he had not slept in the public garden with the gate open, the night before.

**5.** The second page had a good share of self-conceit, however, and so was not greatly confused by the King's jest. He determined that he would avoid the mistake which his comrade had made. So he commenced reading the petition slowly and with great formality, emphasizing every word, and prolonging the articulation of every syllable. But his manner was so tedious that the King cried out, "Stop! are you reciting a lesson in the elementary sounds? Out of the room! But no: stay! Send me that little girl who is sitting there by the fountain."

**6.** The girl thus pointed out by the King was a daughter of one of the laborers employed by the royal gardener: and she had come to help her father weed the flower-beds. It chanced that, like many of the poor people in Prussia, she had received a good education. She was somewhat alarmed when she found herself in the King's presence, but took courage when the King told her that he only wanted her to read for him, as his eyes were weak.

**7.** Now, Ernestine (for this was the name of the little girl) was fond of reading aloud, and often many of the neighbors would assemble at her father's house to hear her; those who could not read themselves would come to her, also, with their letters from distant friends or children, and she thus formed the habit of reading various sorts of hand-writing promptly and well.

*From William Holmes McGuffey, *McGuffey's Fifth Eclectic Reader, Revised* (Cincinnati, 1879), pp. 51–55.

**8.** The King gave her the petition, and she rapidly glanced through the opening lines to get some idea of what it was about. As she read, her eyes began to glisten, and her breast to heave. "What is the matter?" asked the King; "don't you know how to read?" "Oh, yes! sire," she replied, addressing him with the title usually applied to him: "I will now read it, if you please."

**9.** The two pages were about to leave the room. "Remain," said the King. The little girl began to read the petition. It was from a poor widow, whose only son had been drafted to serve in the army, although his health was delicate and his pursuits had been such as to unfit him for military life. His father had been killed in battle, and the son had a strong desire to become a portrait-painter.

**10.** The writer told her story in a simple, concise manner, that carried to the heart a belief of its truth, and Ernestine read it with so much feeling, and with an articulation so just, in tones so pure and distinct, that when she had finished, the King, into whose eyes the tears had started, exclaimed, "Oh! now I understand what it is all about; but I might never have known, certainly I never should have felt, its meaning had I trusted to these young gentlemen, whom I now dismiss from my service for one year, advising them to occupy the time in learning to read."

**11.** "As for you, my young lady," continued the King, "I know you will ask no better reward for your trouble than the pleasure of carrying to this poor widow my order for her son's immediate discharge. Let me see if you can write as well as you can read. Take this pen, and write as I dictate." He then dictated an order, which Ernestine wrote, and he signed. Calling one of his guards, he bade him go with the girl and see that the order was obeyed.

**12.** How much happiness was Ernestine the means of bestowing through her good elocution, united to the happy circumstance that brought it to the knowledge of the King! First, there were her poor neighbors, to whom she could give instruction and entertainment. Then, there was the poor widow who sent the petition, and who not only regained her son, but received through Ernestine an order for him to paint the King's likeness, so that the poor boy soon rose to great distinction, and had more orders than he could attend to. Words could not express his gratitude, and that of his mother, to the little girl.

**13.** And Ernestine had, moreover, the satisfaction of aiding her father to rise in the world, so that he became the King's chief gardener. The King did not forget her, but had her well educated at his own expense. As for the two pages, she was indirectly the means of doing them good, also; for, ashamed of their bad reading, they commenced studying in earnest, till they overcame the faults that had offended the King. Both finally rose to distinction, one as a lawyer, and the other as a statesman; and they owed their advancement in life chiefly to their good elocution.

### *Definitions*

1. Pe-tĭ tion, *a formal request.* 3. Ar-tĭć -ū-lāte, *to utter the elementary sounds.* Mŏd′-ū-lāte, *to vary or inflect.* Mo-nŏt′ o-ny, *lack of variety.* 4. Af-fĕct′ ed, *unnatural and silly.* 9. Draft′ed, *selected by lot.* 10. Con-çisé′, *brief and full of meaning.* 11. Dis-chȧrġé, *re-*

*lease.* Dĭc′-tāte, *to utter so that another may write down.* 12.  Dis-tĭnc′tion, *honorable and notable position.* Ex-prĕss′, *to make known the feelings of.*

### *Notes*

Frederick II. of Prussia (*b.* 1712, *d.* 1786), or Frederick the Great, as he was called, was one of the greatest of German rulers. He was distinguished for his military exploits, for his wise and just government, and for his literary attainments. He wrote many able works in the French language. Many pleasant anecdotes are told of this king, of which the one given in the lesson is a fair sample.

## The Lesson of American History (1859)*

I have tried to recount how a few straggling bands of poor wanderers, seeking a scanty living on the wild sea-coast of America, have grown to be one of the greatest nations of the earth. It is a beautiful and a wonderful subject to write about, and I wish, for your sake, that I had written the story with more skill.

No other people, since the world began, ever grew out of so small a beginning to so towering a height of power and prosperity in so short a time. If you seek to know why your countrymen have outstripped all the nations of the earth in this respect, the reason is easily found. The founders of this nation were honest, true men. They were sincere in all they said, upright in all their acts. They feared God and obeyed the laws. They wrought constantly and vigorously at the work they had to do, and strove to live at peace with their neighbors. When they were attacked they fought like men, and, defeated or victorious, would not have peace till their point was gained. Above all, they insisted, from the very first, on being free themselves, and securing freedom for you, their children.

If you follow the example they set, and love truth, honor, religion, and freedom as deeply, and, if need be, defend them as stoutly as they did, the time is not far distant when this country will as far excel other countries in power, wealth, numbers, intelligence, and every good thing, as other countries excelled it before Columbus sailed away from Spain to discover the New World.

## QUESTIONS

1. Describe in your own words the consensus religious view and political conservatism fostered by most nineteenth-century textbooks.

2. From the excerpts included here, identify at least three examples demonstrating both the Puritan ethic of thrift, perseverance, and hard work and a conservative political ideology.

*From John Bonner, *A Child's History of the United States* (New York, 1859), vol. II, pp. 319–20.

3. Would you use "The Broken Window" or "The Good Reader" in an elementary school classroom? Explain your answer.

4. Do these vignettes educate or indoctrinate?

5. How are these texts similar to and different from textbooks used in contemporary elementary classrooms?

6. Is it ever appropriate to indoctrinate our children and youth? Explain your answer.

# CHAPTER

# 10 Educational Vouchers

## Parental versus Societal Control Revisited

Theoretically, an educational voucher system operates as a market place in which the suppliers of educational services are available to people seeking to purchase them. Described as the *enfant terrible* of recent school reform, the idea of educational vouchers has a long history and refuses to die. Voucher advocates claim that educational voucher blends together the best of public and private education. Simply put, the idea is to empower all families with the ability to choose the school their children will attend. In its simplest form, public funds would be distributed to each family in the form of vouchers to be redeemed for educational services at the school of their choice. Voucher advocates argue that such a system extends the prerogatives and priviliges heretofore associated with private education and available only to the rich or well-to-do to the middle and lower classes. Taking advantage of the apparent gap between the promise of public schooling and its performance and giddy with the success of the worldwide market economy, voucher advocates are convinced that education in the twenty-first century must operate like any other economic market.

Educational vouchers and their companion—the charter school movement—represent popular challenges to the public school system in this country. The origin of this challenge has its roots in the nineteenth century, when two prominent statesmen on opposite sides of the Atlantic offered competing views of education. Rather than serving as the safeguard of liberty, as suggested by Thomas Jefferson (see Chapter 2), British philosopher John Stuart Mill warns that a state system of education is likely to become an instrument of indoctrination for fashioning a passive citizenry. As discussed in Chapter 7, Horace Mann and other nineteenth-century school reformers viewed the public school as the vehicle for building community based on common knowledge and common values. Even though the active involvement of parents in the education is a good that is common to all of us, champions of public education fear that privatism will prevail if educational vouchers triumph. They fear that such privatization will destroy the institution that Mann and other reformers believed to be the "great equalizer of the human condition—the balance-wheel of the social machinery." If we abandon our public or common schools for a voucher system, how do we sustain and support the common values and the commitment to the public good fostered by these public schools?

# On Education Vouchers (1971)*

Ever since Adam Smith first proposed that the government finance education by giving parents money to hire teachers, the idea has enjoyed recurrent popularity. Smith's ideal of consumer sovereignty is built into a number of government programs for financing higher education, notably the G.I. Bill and the various state scholarship programs. Similarly a number of foreign countries have recognized the principle that parents who are dissatisfied with their local public school should be given money to establish alternatives.[1] In America, however, public financing for elementary and secondary education has been largely confined to publicly managed schools. Parents who preferred a private alternative have had to pay the full cost out of their own pockets. As a result, we have almost no evidence on which to judge the merit of Smith's basic principle, namely, that if all parents are given the chance, they will look after their children's interest more effectively than will the state.

During the late 1960's, a series of developments in both public and nonpublic education led to a revival of interest in this approach to financing education. In December, 1969, the United States Office of Economic Opportunity made a grant to the Center for the Study of Public Policy to support a detailed study of "education vouchers." This article will summarize the major findings of that report and outline briefly the voucher plan proposed by the Center.[2]

## *The Case of Choice*

Conservatives, liberals, and radicals all have complained at one time or another that the political mechanisms which supposedly make public schools accountable to their clients work clumsily and ineffectively.[3] Parents who think their children are getting inferior schooling, can, it is true, take their grievances to the local school board or state legislature. If legislators and school boards are unresponsive to the complaints of enough citizens, they may eventually be unseated. But mounting an effective campaign to change local public schools takes an enormous investment of time, energy, and money. Dissatisfied though

[1]Estelle Fuchs, "The Free Schools of Denmark," *Saturday Review,* August 16, 1969.

[2]For a complete description of the Center proposal *see Education Vouchers: A Report on Financing Education by Payments to Parents.* Prepared by the Center for the Study of Public Policy, Cambridge, Massachusetts, December, 1970.

[3]For other discussions of the need to encourage alternatives to the present public schools, *see* Kenneth Clark, "Alternative Public School Systems," *Equal Educational Opportunity.* Cambridge: Harvard University Press, 1969; James S. Coleman, "Toward Open Schools," *The Public Interest,* Fall, 1967; Anthony Downs, "Competition and Community Schools," written for a Brookings Institution Conference on the Community School held in Washington, D.C., December 12–13, 1968, Chicago, Illinois, revised version, January, 1969; Milton Friedman, "The Role of Government in Education," *Capitalism and Freedom.* Chicago: University of Chicago Press, 1962; Christopher Jencks, "Is the Public School Obsolete?" *The Public Interest,* Winter, 1966; Robert Krughoff, "Private Schools for the Public," *Education and Urban Society,* Vol. II, November, 1969; Henry M. Levin, "The Failure of the Public Schools and the Free Market," *The Urban Review,* June 6, 1968; Theodore Sizer and Phillip Whitten, "A Proposal for a Poor Children's Bill of Rights," *Psychology Today,* August, 1968; E. G. West, *Education and the State.* London: Institute of Economic Affairs, 1965.

*From Judith Areen and Christopher Jencks, "Education Vouchers: A Proposal for Diversity and Choice." *Teachers College Record,* vol. LXXII, pp. 327–335. Reprinted by permission.

they may be, few parents have the political skill or commitment to solve their problems this way. As a result, effective control over the character of the public schools is largely vested in legislators, school boards, and educators, not parents.[4]

If parents are to take genuine responsibility for their children's education, they cannot rely exclusively on political processes. They must also be able to take individual action on behalf of their own children. At present, only relatively affluent parents retain any effective control over the education of their children. Only they are free to move to areas with "good" public schools, where housing is usually expensive (and often unavailable to black families at any price). Only they can afford nonsectarian, private schooling. The average parent has no alternative to his local public school unless he happens to belong to one of the few denominations that maintain low-tuition schools.

Not only does today's public school have a captive clientele, but it in turn has become the captive of a political process designed to protect the interests of its clientele. Because attendance at a local public school is nearly compulsory, its activities have been subjected to extremely close political control. The state, the local board, and the school administration have established regulations to ensure that no school will do anything to offend anyone of political consequence. Virtually everything of consequence is either forbidden or compulsory. By trying to please everyone, however, the schools have often ended up pleasing no one.

A voucher system seeks to free schools from the restrictions which inevitably accompany their present monopolistic privileges. The idea of the system is relatively simple. A publicly accountable agency would issue a voucher to parents. The parents could take this voucher to any school which agreed to abide by the rules of the voucher system. Each school would turn its vouchers in for cash. Thus parents would no longer be forced to send their children to the school around the corner simply because it was around the corner.

Even if no new schools were established under a voucher system, the responsiveness of existing public schools would probably increase. We believe that one of the most important advantages of a voucher system is that it would encourage diversity and choice *within the public system*. Indeed, if the public system were to begin matching students and schools on the basis of interest, rather than residence, one of the major objectives of a voucher system would be met without even involving the private sector. Popular public schools would get more applicants, and they would also have incentives to accommodate them, since extra students would bring extra funds. Unpopular schools would have few students, and would either have to change their ways or close up and reopen under new management.

As this last possibility suggests, however, there are great advantages to involving the private sector in a voucher system if it is property regulated. Only in this way is the overall

---

[4]School management has been increasingly concentrated in the hands of fewer educators and school boards. The number of school districts, for example, declined from 127,531 in 1930, to less than 20,440 in 1968. The number of public elementary schools dropped from 238,000 to less than 73,000 in the same period. The concentration is particularly striking in urban areas. The New York City School Board alone is responsible for the education of more students than are found in the majority of individual states. Los Angeles has as many students as the state of South Carolina; Chicago as many as Kansas; Detroit as many as Maine. Nearly half of all the students in public schools are under the control of less than 4 percent of the school boards. *See* Department of Health, Education, and Welfare, Digest of Educational Statistics (1969).

system likely to make room for fundamentally new initiatives that come from the bottom instead of the top. And only if private initiative is possible will the public sector feel real pressure to make room for kinds of education that are politically awkward but have a substantial constituency. If the private sector is involved, for example, parents can get together to create schools reflecting their special perspectives or their children's special needs. This should mean that the public schools will be more willing to do the same thing—though they will never be willing or able to accommodate all parental preferences. Similarly, if the private sector is involved, educators with new ideas—or old ideas that are now out of fashion in the public schools—would also be able to set up their own schools. Entrepreneurs who thought they could teach children better and more inexpensively than the public schools would have an opportunity to do so. None of this ensures that every child would get the education he needs, but it would make such a result somewhat more likely than at present.

Beyond this, however, differences of opinion begin. Who would be eligible for vouchers? How would their value be determined? Would parents be allowed to supplement the vouchers from their own funds? What requirements would schools have to meet before cashing vouchers? What arrangements would be made for the children whom no school wanted to educate? Would church schools be eligible? Would schools promoting unorthodox political views be eligible? Once the advocates of vouchers begin to answer such questions, it becomes clear that the catch phrase around which they have united stands not for a single panacea, but for a multitude of controversial programs, many of which have little in common.

### *Revised Vocabulary*

To understand the voucher plan recommended by the Center, it is useful to begin by reconsidering traditional notions about "public" and "private" education. Since the nineteenth century, we have classified schools as "public" if they were owned and operated by a governmental body. We go right on calling colleges "public," even when they charge tuition that many people cannot afford. We also call academically exclusive high schools "public," even they have admissions requirements that only a handful of students can meet. We call neighborhood schools public despite the fact that nobody outside the neighborhood can attend them, and nobody can move into the neighborhood unless he has white skin and a down payment on a $30,000 home. And we call whole school systems "public," even though they refuse to give anyone information about what they are doing, how well they are doing it, and whether children are getting what their parents want. Conversely, we have always called schools "private" if they were owned and operated by private organizations. We have gone on calling these schools "private," even when, as sometimes happens, they are open to every applicant on a nondiscriminatory basis, charge no tuition, and make whatever information they have about themselves available to anyone who asks.

Definitions of this kind conceal as much as they reveal, for they classify schools entirely in terms of who runs them, not how they are run. If we want to describe what is really going on in education, there is much to be said for reversing this emphasis. We would then call a school "public" if it were open to everyone on a nondiscriminatory basis, if it charged no tuition, and if it provided full information about itself to anyone interested. Conversely, we would call any school "private" if it excluded applicants in a discriminatory way, charged tuition, or withheld information about itself. Admittedly, the question of who governs a school cannot be ignored entirely when categorizing the school, but it seems considerably less important than the question of how the school is governed. Adopting this revised vocabulary, we propose a regulatory system with two underlying principles:

—No public money should be used to support "private" schools.

—Any group that operates a "public" school should be eligible for public subsidies.

### *The Proposal*

Specifically, the Center has proposed an education voucher system (for *elementary* education) which would work in the following manner:

**1.** An Educational Voucher Agency (EVA) would be established to administer the vouchers. Its governing board might be elected or appointed, but in either case it should be structured so as to represent minority as well as majority interests. The EVA might be an existing local board of education, or it might be an agency with a larger or smaller geographic jurisdiction. The EVA would receive all federal, state, and local education funds for which children in its areas were eligible. It would pay this money to schools only in return for vouchers. (In addition, it would pay parents for children's transportation costs to the school of their choice.)

**2.** The EVA would issue a voucher to every family in its district with children of elementary school age. The value of the basic voucher would initially equal the per pupil expenditure of the public schools in the area. Schools which took children from families with below-average incomes would receive additional incentive payments. These "compensatory payments" might, for example, make the maximum payment for the poorest child worth double the basic voucher.

**3.** To become an "approved voucher school," eligible to cash vouchers, a school would have to:

    **a.** Accept each voucher as full payment for a child's education, charging no additional tuition.

    **b.** Accept any applicant so long as it had vacant places.

    **c.** If it had more applicants than places, fill at least half these places by picking applicants randomly and fill the other half in such a way as not to discriminate against ethnic minorities.

    **d.** Accept uniform standards established bv the EVA regarding suspension and expulsion of students.

    **e.** Agree to make a wide variety of information about its facilities, teachers, program, and students available to the EVA and to the public.

    **f.** Maintain accounts of money received and disbursed in a form that would allow both parents and the EVA to determine where the money was going. Thus a school operated by the local board of education (a "public" school) would have to show how much of the money to which it was entitled on the basis of its vouchers was actually spent in that school. A school operated by a profit-making corporation would have to show how much of its income was going to the stockholders.

    **g.** Meet existing state requirements for private schools regarding curriculum staffing, and the like.

Control over policy in an approved voucher school might be vested in an existing local school board, a PTA, or any private group. Hopefully, no government restrictions would be placed on curriculum, staffing and the like, except those already established for all private schools in a state.

**4.** Just as at present, the local board of education (which might or might not be the EVA) would be responsible for ensuring that there were enough places in publicly managed schools to accommodate every elementary school age child who did not want to attend a privately managed school. If a shortage of places developed for some reason, the board of education would have to open new schools or create more places in existing schools. (Alternatively, it might find ways to encourage privately managed schools to expand, presumably by getting the EVA to raise the value of the voucher.)

**5.** Every spring each family would submit to the EVA the name of the school to which it wanted to send each of its elementary school age children next fall. Any children already enrolled in a voucher school would be guaranteed a place, as would any sibling of a child enrolled in a voucher school. So long as it had room, a voucher school would be required to admit all students who listed it as a first choice. If it did not have room for all applicants, a school could fill half its places in whatever way it wanted, choosing among those who listed it as a first choice. It could not, however, select these applicants in such a way as to discriminate against racial minorities. It would then have to fill its remaining places by a lottery among the remaining applicants. All schools with unfilled places would report these to the EVA. All families whose children had not been admitted to their first-choice school would then choose an alternative school which still had vacancies. Vacancies would then be filled in the same manner as in the first round. This procedure would continue until every child had been admitted to a school.

**6.** Having enrolled their children in a school, parents would give their vouchers to the school. The school would send the vouchers to the EVA and would receive a check in return.

### *Some Caveats*

The voucher system outlined above is quite different from other systems now being advocated; it contains far more safeguards for the interests of disadvantaged children. A voucher system which does not include these or equally effective safeguards would be worse than no voucher system at all. Indeed, an unregulated voucher system could be the most serious setback for the education of disadvantaged children in the history of the United States. A properly regulated system, on the other hand, may have the potential to inaugurate a new era of innovation and reform in American schools.

One common objection to a voucher system of this kind is that many parents are too ignorant to make intelligent choices among schools. Giving parents a choice will, according to this argument, simply set in motion an educational equivalent of Gresham's Law, in which hucksterism and mediocre schooling drive out high quality institutions. This argument seems especially plausible to those who envisage the entry of large numbers of profit-oriented firms into the educational marketplace. The argument is not, however, supported by much evidence. Existing private schools are sometimes mere diploma mills, but on the average their claims about themselves seem no more misleading, and the quality of the services they offer no lower, than in the public schools. And while some private schools are run by hucksters interested only in profit this is the exception rather than the rule. There is no obvious reason to suppose that vouchers would change all this.

A second common objection to vouchers is that they would "destroy the public schools." Again, this seems far-fetched. If you look at the educational choices made by wealthy parents who can already afford whatever schooling they want for their children, you find that most still prefer their local public schools if these are at all adequate. Furthermore, most of those who now leave the public system do so in order to attend high-cost, exclusive private schools. While some wealthy parents would doubtless continue to patronize such schools, they would receive no subsidy under the proposed system.

Nonetheless, if you are willing to call every school "public" that is ultimately responsible to a public board of education, then there is little doubt that a voucher svstem would result in some shrinkage of the public sector and some growth of the "private" sector. If, on the other hand, you confine the label "public" to schools which are equally open to everyone within commuting distance, you discover that the so-called public sector includes relatively few public schools. Instead, racially exclusive suburbs and economically exclusive neighborhoods serve to ration access to good "public" schools in precisely the same way that admissions committees and tuition charges ration access to good "private" schools. If you begin to look at the distinction between public and private schooling in these terms, emphasizing accessibility rather than control, you are likely to conclude that a voucher svstem, far from destroying the public sector, would greatly expand it, since it would force large numbers of schools, public and private, to open their doors to outsiders.

A third objection to vouchers is that they would be available to children attending Catholic schools. This is not, of course, a necessary feature of a voucher system. The courts, a state legislature, or a local EVA could easily restrict participation to nonsectarian schools. Indeed, some state constitutions clearly require that this be done. The federal Constitution may also require such a restriction, but neither the language of the First Amendment nor the legal precedent is clear on this issue. The First Amendment's prohibition against an "establishment of religion" can be construed as barring payments to church schools, but the "free exercise of religion" clause can also be construed as requiring the state to treat church schools in precisely the same way as other private schools. The Supreme Court has never ruled on a case of this type (e.g., G.I. Bill payments to Catholic colleges or Medicare payments to Catholic hospitals). Until it does, the issue ought to be resolved on policy grounds. And since the available evidence indicates that Catholic schools have served their children no worse than public schools,[5] and perhaps slightly better, there seems no compelling reason to deny them the same financial support given other schools.

The most worrisome objection to a voucher system is that its success would depend on the EVA's willingness to regulate the marketplace vigorously. If vouchers were used on a large scale, state and local regulatory efforts might be uneven or even nonexistent. The regulations designed to prevent racial and economic discrimination seem especially likely to get watered down at the state and local level, or else to remain unenforced. This argument applies, however, to any educational reform, and it also applies to the existing system. If you

[5]Andrew Greeley and Peter Rossi. *The Education of Catholic Americans.* Chicago: Aldine, 1966.

assume any given EVA will be controlled by overt or covert segregationists, you must also assume that this will be true of the local board of education. A board of education that wants to keep racist parents happy hardly needs vouchers to do so. It only needs to maintain the neighborhood school system. White parents who want their children to attend white schools will then find it quite simple to move to a white neighborhood where their children will be suitably segregated. Except perhaps in the South, neither the federal government, the state government, nor the judiciary is likely to prevent this traditional practice.

If, on the other hand, you assume a board which is anxious to eliminate segregation, either for legal, financial, or political reasons, you must also assume that the EVA would be subject to the same pressures. And if an EVA is anxious to eliminate segregation, it will have no difficulty devising regulations to achieve this end. Furthermore, the legal precedents to date suggest that the federal courts will be more stringent in applying the Fourteenth Amendment to voucher systems than to neighborhood school systems. The courts have repeatedly thrown out voucher systems designed to maintain segregation, whereas they have shown no such general willingness to ban the neighborhood school. Outside the South, then, those who believe in integration may actually have an easier time achieving this goal with voucher systems than they will with the existing public schools system. Certainly, the average black parent's access to integrated schools would be increased under a voucher system of the kind proposed by the Center. Black parents could apply to any school in the system, and the proportion of blacks admitted would have to be at least equal to the proportion who applied. This gives the average black parents a far better chance of having their children attend an integrated school than at present. There is, of course, no way to compel black parents to take advantage of this opportunity by actually applying to schools that enroll whites. But the opportunity would be there for all.

### The Proposed Demonstration

The voucher plan described above could in theory be adopted by any local or state jurisdiction interested in increasing diversity in schools and parental choice in selection of schools. In the long run it is not much more expensive than the present system. But the Center has recommended to OEO that a demonstration project be financed first, carefully regulated to ensure that the proposed rules are followed, and carefully monitored to test the effects of dispensing public education funds in the form of vouchers. The Center has recommended that at least 10,000 elementary school students be included in the demonstration site, and that the demonstration city (or part of a city) should contain a population which is racially and economically heterogeneous. Ideally some alternative schools should already exist in the selected area, and the prospects for beginning other new schools should be reasonable.

In March, 1970, staff and consultants of the Center embarked on an extensive investigation of the feasibility of conducting a demonstration project. Superintendents of schools in all cities with a population in excess of 150,000 in the 1960 census, which were not under court or administrative order to desegregate their school systems, were contacted by mail. Expressions of interest were followed up. Meetings were held in interested cities around the country. Local and state school administrators were contacted, as were interested school officials, teachers' groups, parents' organizations, and nonpublic schools.

As of November 1, 1970, five communities had decided to apply for preliminary planning funds. If one or more of these cities decides to conduct a demonstration of the voucher program, we may have a chance at last to test what contributions a voucher program could make to improving the quality of education available to children in this country. If, on the other hand, the National Education Association and the American Federation of Teachers have their way, we shall have no test at all.

## QUESTIONS

1. Do you think that the Puritans and/or Thomas Jefferson would favor or oppose educational vouchers. Why do you think so?

2. Pretend that you are Horace Mann submitting an annual report to the Massachusetts State Board of Education. Develop, as part of the report, Mann's argument favoring or opposing educational vouchers.

3. If parents use educational vouchers (public funds) to send their child to a religious school, does this create a conflict with the establishment clause of the First Amendment?

4. What are the similarities and differences between the current educational voucher proposals and the G. I. Bill?

5. Does the regulated voucher system proposed by Areen and Jencks sufficiently respond to the concerns of Mann, perhaps of Jefferson, and of their contemporary followers?

## SUGGESTIONS FOR FURTHER READING

Robert L. Church and Michael W. Sedlak, *Education in the United States: An Interpretive History*. (New York: The Free Press, 1976).

Barbara Finkelstein, *Governing the Young: Teacher Behavior in Popular Primary Schools in Nineteenth Century United States*. (New York: Teachers College Press, 1997).

Frances Fitzgerald, *American Revised: History Schoolbooks in the Twentieth Century*. (New York: Vintage Books, 1979).

Willystine Goodsell, ed., *Pioneers of Women's Education in the United States*. (New York: McGraw-Hill Book Company, Inc., 1931).

Madeline Grumet, *Bitter Milk: Women and Teaching* (Amherst: The University of Massachusetts Press, 1988).

Nancy Hoffman, *Woman's "True" Profession: Voices from the History of Teaching*. (New York; McGraw-Hill, 1981).

Carl F. Kaestle, *The Evolution of an Urban School System: New York City, 1750–1850*. (Cambridge, MA: Harvard University Press, 1973).

Michael B. Katz, *The Irony of Early School Reform: Education in Mid-Nineteenth Century Massachusetts*. (Boston: Beacon Press, 1968).

Michael B. Katz, *Restructuring American Education*. (Cambridge, MA: Harvard University Press, 1987).

Henry J. Perkinson, *Two Hundred Years of Educational Thought*. (New York: David McKay, Inc., 1976).

Kate Rousmaniere, *City Teachers: Teaching and School Reform in Historical Perspective*. (New York: Teacher's College Press, 1997).

David B. Tyack, *The One Best System: A History of American Urban Education*. (Cambridge, MA: Harvard University Press, 1974).

David B. Tyack, *Turning Points in American Educational History*. (New York: John Wiley & Sons, 1967).

Kathleen Weiler, *Country School Women: Teaching in Rural California, 1850–1950*. (Palo Alto, CA: Stanford University Press, 1998).

# PART THREE

# Retreat from Commonality
## Education of the "Child Races"

# CHAPTER

# 11 Booker T. Washington and Industrial Education

As noted in Chapter 7, the common school crusade originated in New England, spread rapidly through the Mid-Atlantic and Midwestern states, and even established a foothold on the West Coast before the Civil War. As the Civil War came to an end, some northern school reformers suggested that the common school movement could peacefully heal the wounds produced by this conflict and could help reunite the wayward South back into the fold of the United States of America. Some reformers suggested that the war itself might have been prevented had the common school spirit taken root in the Southern states as it had in the North and West.

Such an inflated sense of the power of the common school movement produced a flurry of activity in the aftermath of the war as common school teachers flocked to the South to imbue both newly freed slaves and other uneducated southerners with the common values and knowledge that had been so successful throughout much of the North and West. Although achieving some initial successes in establishing integrated schools in a few southern communities, this missionary effort failed miserably. These naive, albeit good-intentioned school teachers soon realized that South Carolina was different than Massachusetts. Rather than recognizing that their goal was beyond the means of common schooling to achieve, these enthusiastic reformers began to accept the idea that the former slave was not capable of learning and benefiting from the kind of schooling that worked so well in the North and West.

With the inevitable failure of this effort to transform the South into clones of the North and West, reformers lost faith in the efficacy of the common school for all children. Based on their experiences in the post–Civil War South, school reformers concluded that Black people were inferior. For this reason, reformers embraced industrial training as the appropriate education for the so-called child races inhabiting the nation.[1]

Booker T. Washington emerged in the late nineteenth and early twentieth centuries as the most famous advocate of industrial training. Born a slave in Virginia, Washington encountered the roots or foundation of industrial training as an adolescent in Malden, West Virginia. Working as a house boy for Mrs. Viola Ruffner, a Vermont-bred Yankee woman, young Booker T. Washington experienced and embraced as his own the Puritan ethic. According to this ethic, the good Christian merited salvation, and—as secularized by Benjamin Franklin and others—this also meant that material or worldly success came only to those people who merited it. In short, God rewards industry, perseverance, and thrift with material wealth.

Applying this Puritan ethic to himself and his race, Washington believed that through industry, hard work, and perseverance, the Negro could achieve salvation, worldly success, and acceptance as an equal to members of the White race. Like the religious and secularized Puritans preceding him, Washington considered the universe to be a just order. Just as the good Christian merited salvation and the good capitalist merited wealth, the good Negro merited the status of a full-fledged human being.

Entering the Hampton Normal and Agricultural Institute in 1872, Washington encountered a curriculum grounded in these principles. Designed primarily to prepare Negro elementary teachers for the South, the Hampton Institute emphasized the Puritan virtues. According to Samuel Chapman Armstrong, the head of Hampton, the successful Negro teacher must serve as a model of moral character for his or her students. From this perspective industrial education is the salvation of the Negro race. It roots out their supposed natural tendencies to laziness, improvidence, and sensuality.

Washington became Armstrong's most famous student and the most influential advocate of industrial training for Negroes. In 1881, Washington became principal of the newly established Tuskegee Institute in Alabama. As the head of the leading Black industrial training school in the nation, Washington's voice became increasingly influential in both the White and Black communities. Aware of the repression of Negroes sweeping the country in the closing decades of the nineteenth century, Washington argued that industrial education kills "two birds with one stone." It ensured the survival of the Blacks, and it secured the cooperation of the Whites.[2]

Washington is perhaps best known for his speech to a largely White audience at the Atlanta Exposition in 1895. In suggesting that a racially segregated, caste society is compatible with the economic well being of both races, Washington—arguably the most prominent Black leader in the nation—seemed to sanction the Jim Crow practices and policies (*Jim Crow* is the term associated with segregated facilities for the White and "colored" races). This so-called Atlanta Compromise was well received throughout the nation, especially among the White population. Partly due to the impact of this speech, Booker T. Washington had clearly arrived. Increasingly, leaders in the White power structure consulted him regarding appointing Black people to political offices ranging from post office clerks to undersecretaries in the president's cabinet. Due, at least in part, to his acceptance of the White power structure, Booker T. Washington was the Black Horatio Alger, rising higher and farther than any other Black person in the nation.

Washington's accomodationist tendencies had it critics. Foremost among them was William E. B. Du Bois. Raised a free man in Great Barrington, Massachusetts, Du Bois received an education second to none, including a classical course in high school, baccalaureate and Ph.D. degrees from Fish and Harvard Universities, plus study abroad at the University of Berlin. Initially favorably disposed toward Washington and his commitment to improving the conditions of Negroes in America, Du Bois grew increasingly critical of Washington's acquiescence to the White power structure. According to Du Bois, Washington asked the Negro to give up, at least for the present, three things: political power, insistence on civil rights, and the opportunity for genuine higher education. With Washington championing industrial training as the education most appropriate for Negroes, monies that might have gone to support genuine college education for Negro youth went instead to industrial training institutes like Hampton and Tuskegee.

According to Du Bois, all races had a talented tenth that could and should become doctors, lawyers, ministers, businessmen, and community leaders. With the majority of the resources targeted toward industrial training institutes, the talented tenth of the Negro race were being denied the opportunity to achieve their potential and to serve as role models for future generations. Even though Du Bois was recognized for his role in founding the National Association for the Advancement of Colored People (NAACP), his haughty, arrogant demeanor eventually alienated many of his own race as well as members of the White power structure. Though recognized as the leading Black intellectual of his day, Du Bois never achieved the stature or influence of Booker T. Washington.

[1]For more information about the "retreat from commonality," see Robert L. Church and Michael Sedlak, *Education in the United States: An Interpretive History* (New York: The Free Press, 1976), pp. 117–227.

[2]For more information on the educational ideas of Booker T. Washington, see Henry J. Perkinson, *Two Hundred Years of American Educational Thought* (New York: David McKay Company, Inc., 1976), pp. 173–199.

# "Up from Slavery": The Story of Booker T. Washington*

Of my ancestry I know almost nothing. In the slave quarters, and even later, I heard whispered conversations among the coloured people of the tortures which the slaves, including, no doubt, my ancestors on my mother's side, suffered in the middle passage of the slave ship while being conveyed from Africa to America. I have been unsuccessful in securing any information that would throw any accurate light upon the history of my family beyond my mother. She, I remember, had a half-brother and a half-sister. In the days of slavery not very much attention was given to family history and family records—that is, black family records. My mother, I suppose, attracted the attention of a purchaser who was afterward my owner and hers. Her addition to the slave family attracted about as much attention as the purchase of a new horse or cow. Of my father I know even less than of my mother. I do not even know his name. I have heard reports to the effect that he was a white man who lived on one of the near-by plantations. Whoever he was, I never heard of his taking the least interest in me or providing in any way for my rearing. But I do not find especial fault with him. He was simply another unfortunate victim of the institution which the Nation unhappily had engrafted upon it at that time....

After the coming of freedom there were two points upon which practically all the people on our place were agreed, and I find that this was generally true throughout the South: that they must change their names, and that they must leave the old plantation for at least a few days or weeks in order that they might really feel sure that they were free....

In the midst of my struggles and longing for an education, a young coloured boy who had learned to read in the state of Ohio came to Malden. As soon as the coloured people

*Booker T. Washington, *Up from Slavery* (Garden City, New York: Doubleday & Company, Inc., 1901), pp. 2–3, 23, 28–29, 51–53, 80–81.

found out that he could read, a newspaper was secured, and at the close of nearly every day's work this young man would be surrounded by a group of men and women who were anxious to hear him read the news contained in the papers. How I used to envy this man! He seemed to me to be the one young man in all the world who ought to be satisfied with his attainments.

About this time the question of having some kind of a school opened for the coloured children in the village began to be discussed by members of the race. As it would be the first school for Negro children that had ever been opened in that part of Virginia, it was, of course, to be a great event, and the discussion excited the widest interest. The most perplexing question was where to find a teacher. The young man from Ohio who had learned to read the papers was considered, but his age was against him. In the midst of the discussion about a teacher, another young coloured man from Ohio, who had been a soldier, in some way found his way into town. It was soon learned that he possessed considerable education, and he was engaged by the coloured people to teach their first school. As yet no free schools had been started for coloured people in that section, hence each family agreed to pay a certain amount per month, with the understanding that the teacher was to "board 'round"—that is, spend a day with each family. This was not bad for the teacher, for each family tried to provide the very best on the day the teacher was to be its guest. I recall that I looked forward with an anxious appetite to the "teacher's day" at our little cabin.

This experience of a whole race beginning to go to school for the first time, presents one of the most interesting studies that has ever occurred in connection with the development of any race....

As soon as possible after reaching the grounds of the Hampton Institute, I presented myself before the head teacher for assignment to a class. Having been so long without proper food, a bath, and change of clothing, I did not, of course, make a very favourable impression upon her, and I could see at once that there were doubts in her mind about the wisdom of admitting me as a student. I felt that I could hardly blame her if she got the idea that I was a worthless loafer or tramp. For some time she did not refuse to admit me; neither did she decide in my favour, and I continued to linger about her, and to impress her in all the ways I could with my worthiness. In the meantime I saw her admitting other students, and that added greatly to my discomfort, for I felt, deep down in my heart, that I could do as well as they, if I could only get a chance to show what was in me.

After some hours had passed, the head teacher said to me: "The adjoining recitation-room needs sweeping. Take the broom and sweep it."

It occurred to me at once that here was my chance. Never did I receive an order with more delight. I knew that I could sweep, for Mrs. Ruffner had thoroughly taught me how to do that when I lived with her.

I swept the recitation-room three times. Then I got a dusting-cloth and I dusted it four times. All the woodwork around the walls, every bench, table, and desk, I went over four times with my dusting-cloth. Besides, every piece of furniture had been moved and every closet and corner in the room had been thoroughly cleaned. I had the feeling that in a large measure my future depended upon the impression I made upon the teacher in the cleaning of that room. When I was through, I reported to the head teacher. She was a "Yankee" woman who knew just where to look for dirt. She went into the room and inspected the floor and closets; then she took her handkerchief and rubbed it on the woodwork about the walls, and over the table and benches. When she was unable to find one bit of dirt on the floor, or a particle of dust on any of the furniture, she quietly remarked, "I guess you will do to enter this institution."...

The years from 1867 to 1878 I think may be called the period of Reconstruction. This included the time that I spent as a student at Hampton and as a teacher in West Virginia. During the whole of the Reconstruction period two ideas were constantly agitating the minds of the coloured people, or, at least, the minds of a large part of the race. One of these was the craze for Greek and Latin learning, and the other was a desire to hold office.

It could not have been expected that a people who had spent generations in slavery, and before that generations in the darkest heathenism, could at first form any proper conception of what an education meant. In every part of the South, during the Reconstruction period, schools, both day and night, were filled to overflowing with people of all ages and conditions, some being as far along in age as sixty and seventy years. The ambition to secure an education was most praiseworthy and encouraging. The idea, however, was too prevalent that, as soon as one secured a little education, in some unexplainable way he would be free from most of the hardships of the world, and, at any rate, could live without manual labour. There was a further feeling that a knowledge, however little, of the Greek and Latin languages would make one a very superior human being something bordering almost on the supernatural. I remember that the first coloured man whom I saw who knew something about foreign languages impressed me at that time as being a man of all others to be envied.

Naturally, most of our people who received some little education became teachers or preachers. While among these two classes there were many capable, earnest, godly men and women, still a large proportion took up teaching or preaching as an easy way to make a living. Many became teachers who could do little more than write their names. I remember there came into our neighbourhood one of this class, who was in search of a school to teach, and the question arose while he was there as to the shape of the earth and how he would teach the children concerning this subject. He explained his position in the matter by saying that he was prepared to teach that the earth was either flat or round, according to the preference of a majority of his patrons.

# Booker T. Washington on the Educational Outlook
# for Negroes in the South (1885)*

Fourteen years ago it is said that Northern teachers in the South for the purpose of teaching colored schools were frightened away by the whites from the town of Tuskegee, Alabama. Four years ago the democratic members of the Alabama Legislature from Tuskegee voluntarily offered and had passed by the General Assembly a bill, appropriating $2000 annually to pay the salaries of teachers in a colored normal school to be located at Tuskegee. At

*From Booker T. Washington, "The Educational Outlook in the South," National Education Association *Journal of Proceedings and Addresses,* 1884 (Boston, 1885), pp. 125–30.

the end of the first session of the school the legislature almost unanimously passed a second bill appropriating an additional $1000 annually, for the same purpose. About one month ago one of the white citizens of Tuskegee who had at first looked on the school in a cold, distant kind of way said to me, "I have just been telling the white people that the negroes are more interested in education than we, and are making more sacrifices to educate themselves." At the end of the first year's work, some of the whites said, "We are glad that the Normal School is here because it draws people and makes labor plentiful." At the close of the second year, several said that the Normal School was beneficial because it increased trade, and at the close of the last session more than one has said that the Normal School is a good institution, it is making the colored people in this State better citizens. From the opening of the school to the present, the white citizens of Tuskegee have been among its warmest friends. They have not only given of their money but they are ever ready to suggest and devise plans to build up the institution. When the school was making an effort to start a brick-yard, but was without means, one of the merchants donated an outfit of tools. Every white minister in the town has visited the school and given encouraging remarks. When the school was raising money to build our present hall, it occurred to one of the teachers that it would be a good idea to call on the white ladies for contributions in the way of cakes, etc., toward a fair. The result was that almost every lady, called on, gave something and the fair was made up almost entirely of articles given by these friends. A former slave-holder working on a negro normal school building under a negro master-carpenter is a picture that the last few years have made possible.

Any movement for the elevation of the Southern negro in order to be successful, must have to a certain extent the co-operation of the Southern whites. They control government and own the property—whatever benefits the black man benefits the white man. The proper education of all the whites will benefit the negro as much as the education of the negro will benefit the whites. The Governor of Alabama would probably count it no disgrace to ride in the same railroad coach with a colored man, but the ignorant white man who curries the Governor's horse would turn up his nose in disgust. The president of a white college in Tuskegee makes a special effort to furnish our young men work that they may be able to remain in school, while the miserable unlettered "brother in white" would say "you can't learn a nigger anything." Brains, property, and character for the Negro will settle the question of civil right. The best course to pursue in regard to the civil rights bill in the South is to let it alone; let it alone and it will settle itself. Good school teachers and plenty of money to pay them will be more potent in settling the race question than many civil rights bills and investigating committees. A young colored physician went into the city of Montgomery, Alabama, a few months ago to practice his profession—he was the first to professionally enter the ex-confederate capital. When his white brother physicians found out by a six days' examination that he had brains enough to pass a better examination, as one of them said, than many of the whites had passed, they gave him a hearty welcome and offered their services to aid him in consultation or in any other way possible— and they are standing manfully up to their promise. Let there be in a community a negro who by virtue of his superior knowledge of the chemistry of the soil, his acquaintance with the most improved tools and best breeds of stock, can raise fifty bushels of corn to the acre while his white neighbor only raise thirty, and the white man will come to the black man to learn. Further, they will sit down on the same train, in the same coach and on the same seat to talk about it. Harmony will come in proportion as the black man gets something that the white man wants, whether it be of brains or of material. Some of the county whites looked at first with disfavor on the establishing of a normal school in Tuskegee. It turned out that there was no brick-yard in the county; merchants and farmers wanted to build, but bricks must be brought from a distance or they must wait for one house to burn down before building another. The normal school with student labor started a brick-yard. Several kilns of bricks were burned; the whites came [for] miles around for bricks. From examining bricks they were led to examine the workings of the school. From the discussion of the brick-yard came the discussion of negro education—and thus many of the "old masters" have been led to see and become interested in negro education. In Tuskegee a negro mechanic manufactures the best tin ware, the best harness, the best boots and shoes, and it is common to see his store crowded with white customers from all over the county. His word or note goes as far as that of the whitest man.

I repeat for emphasis that any work looking towards the permanent improvement of the negro South, must have for one of its aims the fitting of him to live friendly and peaceably with his white neighbors both socially and politically. In spite of all talk of exodus, the negro's home is permanently in the South: for coming to the bread-and-meat side of the question, the white man needs the negro, and the negro needs the white man. His home being permanently in the South it is our duty to help him prepare himself to live there an independent, educated citizen.

In order that there may be the broadest development of the colored man and that he may have an unbounded field in which to labor, the two races must be brought to have faith in each other. The teachings of the negro in various ways for the last twenty years have been rather too much to array him against his white brother than to put the two races in co-operation with each other. Thus, Massachusetts supports the Republican party, because the Republican party supports Massachusetts with a protective tariff, but the negro supports the Republican party simply because Massachusetts does. When the colored man is educated up to the point of reasoning that Massachusetts and Alabama are a long ways apart and the conditions of life are very different and if free trade enables my white neighbor across the street to buy his plows at a cheaper rate it will enable me to so the same thing, then will he be consulted in governmental questions. More than once have I noticed that when the whites were in favor of prohibition the blacks led even by sober upright ministers voted against it simply because the whites were in favor of it and for that reason the blacks said that they knew it was a "Democratic trick." If the whites vote to levy a tax to build a school-house it is a signal for the blacks to oppose the measure, simply because the whites favor it. I venture the assertion that the sooner the colored man South learns that one political party is not composed of all angels and the other of all devils, and that all his enemies do not live in his town or neighborhood and all his friends in some distant section of the country, the sooner will his educational advantages be enhanced many fold. But matters are gradually changing in this respect. The black man is beginning to find out that there are those even among the Southern whites who desire his elevation. The negro's new faith in the white man is being reciprocated in proportion as the negro is rightly educated. The white brother is beginning to learn by degrees that all negroes are not liars and chicken thieves. A former owner of seventy-five or one hundred slaves and now a large planter and merchant said to me a few days ago, "I can see every day the change that is coming about.

I have on one of my plantations a colored man who can read and write and he is the most valuable man on the farm. In the first place I can trust him to keep the time on the others or with any thing else. If a new style of plow or cotton planters is taken on the place he can understand its construction in half the time that any of the others can."

My faith is that reforms in the South are to come from within. Southern people have a good deal of human nature. They like to receive praise of doing good deeds and they don't like to obey orders that come from Washington telling them they must lay aside at once customs that they have followed for centuries, and henceforth there must be but one railroad coach, one hotel, and one school-house for ex-master and ex-slave. In proof of my first assertion, the railroads in Alabama required colored passengers to pay the same fare as the whites, and then compelled the colored to ride in the smoking-car. A committee of leading colored people laid the injustice of the matter before the railroad commissioners of Alabama, who at once ordered that within thirty days every railroad in the State should provide equal, but separate accommodations for both races. Every prominent newspaper in the State pronounced it a just decision. Alabama gives $9000 annually towards the support of colored normal schools. The last legislature increased the annual appropriation for free schools by $100,000, making the total annual appropriation over $500,000, and nearly half of this amount goes to colored schools, and I have the first time to hear of any distinction being made between the races by any State officer in the distribution of this fund. Why, my friends, more pippins are growing in the South than crab-apples, more roses than thorns.

Now, in regard to what I have said about the relations of the two races, there should be no unmanly cowering, or stooping to satisfy unreasonable whims of Southern white men, but it is charity and wisdom to keep in mind the two hundred years' schooling in prejudice against the negro, which ex-slave-holders are called upon to conquer. A certain class of whites South object to the general education of the colored man, on the ground that when he is educated he ceases to do manual labor, and there is no evading the fact that much aid is withheld from negro education in the South, by the States, on these grounds. Just here the great mission of INDUSTRIAL EDUCATION, coupled with the mental comes in. "It kills two birds with one stone," viz.: secures the co-operation of the whites and does the best possible thing for the black man. An old colored man in a cotton-field in the middle of July, lifted his eyes towards heaven and said, "De cotton is so grassy, de work is so hard, and de sun am so hot, I believe dis darkey am called to preach." This old man, no doubt, stated the true reason why not a few enter school. Educate the black man, mentally and industrially, and there will be no doubt of his prosperity; for a race who have lived at all, and paid for the last twenty years, twenty-five and thirty per cent interest on the dollar advanced for food with almost no education, can certainly take care of themselves when educated mentally and industrially.

The Tuskegee Normal School, located in the black belt of Alabama, with an ignorant, degraded negro population of twenty-five thousand within a radius of twenty miles, has a good chance to see the direct needs of the people; and to get a correct idea of their condition one must leave the towns and go far out into the country, miles from any railroad, where the majority of the people live. They need teachers with not only trained heads and hearts, but with trained hands. School-houses are needed in every township and country. The present wrecks of log-cabins and bush harbors, where many of the schools are now taught, must be replaced by comfortable, decent houses. In many school-houses rails are used for seats, and often the fire is on the outside of the house, while teacher and scholars are on the inside. Add to this a teacher who can scarcely write his name, and who is as weak mentally as morally, and you have but a faint idea of the educational condition of many parts of the South. It is the work of Tuskegee to send into these places, teachers who will not stand off and tell the people what to do, or what ought to be done, but to send those who can take hold and show the people *how* to do. The blacksmiths, carpenters, brickmasons, and tinners, who learned their trades in slavery, are dying out, and slavery having taught the colored boy that labor is a disgrace few of their places are being filled. The negro now has a monopoly of the trades in the South, but he can't hold it unless the young men are taught trades while in school. The large number of educated loafers to be seen around the streets of our large cities furnishes another reason in favor of industrial education. Then the proud fop with his beaver hat, kid gloves, and walking cane, who has done no little to injure the cause of education South, by industrial training, would be brought down to something practical and useful. The Tuskegee Normal School, with a farm of 500 acres, carpenter's shop, printing-office, blacksmith shop and brick-yard for boys, and a sewing department, laundry, flower gardening, and practical housekeeping for girls, is trying to do its part towards furnishing industrial training. We ask help for nothing that we can do for ourselves; nothing is bought that the students can produce. The boys raise the vegetables, have done the painting, made the brick, the chairs, the tables, the desks; have built a stable, a carpenter's shop, and a blacksmith's shop. The girls do the entire housekeeping, including the mending, ironing, and washing of the boys' clothes; besides they make many garments to sell.

The majority of the students are poor and able to pay but little cash for board; consequently, the school keeps three points before it. First, to give the student the best mental training; secondly, to furnish him with labor that will be valuable to the school, and that will enable the student to learn something from the labor *per se;* thirdly, to teach the dignity of labor.

# Booker T. Washington's Atlanta Exposition Address (1895)*

*Mr. President and Gentlemen of the Board of Directors and Citizens:*
One third of the population of the South is of the Negro race. No enterprise seeking the material, civil, or moral welfare of this section can disregard this element of our population and reach the highest success. I but convey to you, Mr. President and Directors, the sentiment of the masses of my race when I say that in no way have the value and manhood of the American Negro been more fittingly and generously recognized than by the managers of this magnificent Exposition at every stage of its progress. It is a recognition that will do more to cement the friendship of the two races than any occurrence since the dawn of our freedom.

*From *The Story of My Life and Work. An Autobiography* (Atlanta, 1901), pp. 137–143.

Not only this, but the opportunity here afforded will awaken among us a new era of industrial progress. Ignorant and inexperienced, it is not strange that in the first years of our new life we began at the top instead of at the bottom; that a seat in Congress or the State Legislature was more sought than real estate or industrial skill; that the political convention or stump speaking had more attractions than starting a dairy farm or truck garden.

A ship lost at sea for many days suddenly sighted a friendly vessel. From the mast of the unfortunate vessel was seen a signal: 'Water, water; we die of thirst!' The answer from the friendly vessel at once came back: 'Cast down your bucket where you are.' A second time the signal, 'Water, water; send us water!' ran up from the distressed vessel, and was answered: 'Cast down your bucket where you are.' And a third and fourth signal for water was answered: 'Cast down your bucket where you are.' The captain of the distressed vessel, at last heeding the injunction, cast down his bucket, and it came up full of fresh, sparkling water from the mouth of the Amazon River. To those of my race who depend on bettering their condition in a foreign land, or who underestimate the importance of cultivating friendly relations with the Southern white man, who is their next door neighbor, I would say: 'Cast down your bucket where you are'—cast it down making friends in every manly way of the people of all races by whom we are surrounded.

Cast it down in agriculture, mechanics, in commerce, in domestic service, and in the professions. And in this condition it is well to bear in mind that whatever other sins the South may be called to bear, when it comes to business, pure and simple, it is in the South that the Negro is given a man's chance in the commercial world, and in nothing is this Exposition more eloquent than in emphasizing this chance. Our greatest danger is, that in the great leap from slavery to freedom we may overlook the fact that the masses of us are to live by the productions of our hands, and fail to keep in mind that we shall prosper in proportion as we learn to dignify and glorify common labor, and put brains and skill into the common occupations of life; shall prosper in proportion as we learn to draw the line between the superficial and the substantial, the ornamental gewgaws of life and the useful. No race can prosper till it learns that there is as much dignity in tilling a field as in writing a poem. It is at the bottom of life we must begin, and not at the top. Nor should we permit our grievances to overshadow our opportunities.

To those of the white race who look to the incoming of those of foreign birth and strange tongue and habits for the prosperity of the South, were I permitted, I would repeat what I say to my own race, 'Cast down your bucket where you are. Cast it down among the 8,000,000 Negroes whose habits you know, whose fidelity and love you have tested in days when to have proved treacherous meant the ruin of your firesides. Cast down your bucket among these people who have, without strikes and labor wars, tilled your fields, cleared your forests, builded your railroads and cities, and brought forth treasures from the bowels of the earth, and helped make possible this magnificent representation of the progress of the South. Casting down your bucket among my people, helping and encouraging them as you are doing on these grounds, and, with education of head, hand and heart, you will find that they will buy your surplus land, make blossom the waste places in your fields, and run your factories. While doing this, you can be sure in the future, as in the past, that you and your families will be surrounded by the most patient, faithful, law-abiding, and unresentful people that the world has seen. As we have proved our loyalty to you in the past, in nursing your children, watching by the sick bed of your mothers and fathers, and often following them with tear-dimmed eyes to their graves, so in the future, in our humble way, we shall stand by you with a devotion that no foreigner can approach, ready to lay down lives, if need be, in defense of yours, interlacing our industrial, commercial, civil, and religious life with yours in a way that shall make the interests of both races one. In all things that are purely social we can be as separate as the fingers, yet one as the hand in all things essential to mutual progress.

There is no defense or security for any of us except in the highest intelligence and development of all. If anywhere there are efforts tending to curtail the fullest growth of the Negro, let these efforts be turned into stimulating, encouraging, and making him the most useful and intelligent citizen. Efforts or means so invested will pay a thousand per cent interest. These efforts will be twice blessed—'Blessing him that gives and him that takes.'
There is no escape through law of man or God from the inevitable:

'The laws of changeless justice bind
Oppressor with oppressed;
And close as sin and suffering joined
We march to fate abreast.'

Nearly sixteen millions of hands will aid you in pulling the load upward, or they will pull against you the load downwards. We shall constitute one-third and more of the ignorance and crime of the South, or one-third its intelligence and progress; we shall contribute one-third to the business and industrial prosperity of the South, or we shall prove a veritable body of death, stagnating, depressing, retarding every effort to advance the body politic.

Gentlemen of the Exposition, as we present to you our humble effort at an exhibition of our progress, you must not expect overmuch. Starting thirty years ago with ownership here and there in a few quilts and pumpkins and chickens (gathered from miscellaneous sources), remember the path that has led from these to the invention and production of agricultural implements, buggies, steam engines, newspapers, books, statuary, carving, painting, the management of drug stores and banks, has not been trodden without contact with thorns and thistles. While we take pride in what we exhibit as a result of our independent efforts, we do not for a moment forget that our part in this exhibition would fall far short of your expectations but for the constant help that has come to our educational life, not only from the Southern States, but especially from Northern philanthropists, who have made their gifts a constant stream of blessing and encouragement.

The wisest among my race understand that the agitation of questions of social equality is the extremest folly, and that progress in the enjoyment of all the privileges that will come to us must be the result of severe and constant struggle rather than of artificial forcing. No race that has anything to contribute to the markets of the world is long in any degree ostracized. It is important and right that all privileges of the law be ours, but it is vastly more important that we be prepared for the exercise of those privileges. The opportunity to earn a dollar in a factory just now is worth infinitely more than the opportunity to spend a dollar in an opera house.

In conclusion, may I repeat that nothing in thirty years has given us more hope and encouragement, and drawn us so near to you of the white race, as this opportunity offered by the Exposition; and here bending, as it were, over the altar that represents the results of the struggles of your race and mine, both starting practically empty-handed three decades ago, I pledge that, in your effort to work out the great and intricate problem which God has laid at the doors of the South, you shall have at all times the patient, sympathetic help of my race; only let this be constantly in mind that, while from representations in these buildings of the product of field, of forest, of mine, of factory, letters, and art, much good will come, yet far and beyond material benefits will be the higher good, that let us pray God will come, in a blotting out of sectional differences and racial animosities and suspicions, in a determination to administer absolute justice, in a willing obedience among all classes to the mandates of law. This, coupled with our material prosperity, will bring into our beloved South a new heaven and a new earth.

# W. E. B. Du Bois on Booker T. Washington (1903)*

Mr. Washington represents in Negro thought the old attitude of adjustment and submission; but adjustments at such a peculiar time as to make his programme unique. This is an age of unusual economic development, and Mr. Washington's programme naturally takes an economic cast, becoming a gospel of Work and Money to such an extent as apparently almost completely to overshadow the higher aims of life. Moreover, this is an age when the more advanced races are coming in closer contact with the less developed races, and the race-feeling is therefore intensified; and Mr. Washington's programme practically accepts the alleged inferiority of the Negro races. Again, in our own land, the reaction from the sentiment of war time has given impetus to race-prejudice against Negroes, and Mr. Washington withdraws many of the high demands of Negroes as men and American citizens. In other periods of intensified prejudice all the Negro's tendency to self-assertion has been called forth; at this period a policy of submission is advocated. In the history of nearly all other races and peoples the doctrine preached at such crises has been that manly self-respect is worth more than lands and houses, and that a people who voluntarily surrender such respect, or cease striving for it, are not worth civilizing.

In answer to this, it has been claimed that the Negro can survive only through submission. Mr. Washington distinctly asks that black people give up, at least for the present, three things,—

First, political power.

Second, insistence on civil rights,

Third, higher education of Negro youth,—

and concentrate all their energies on industrial education, the accumulation of wealth, and the conciliation of the South. This policy has been courageously and insistently advocated

---

*From W. E. B. Du Bois. *The Souls of Black Folk: Essays and Sketches* (Chicago, 1903), pp. 49–59.

for over fifteen years, and has been triumphant for perhaps ten years. As a result of this tender of the palm-branch, what has been the return? In these years there have occurred:

1. The disfranchisement of the Negro.
2. The legal creation of a distinct status of civil inferiority for the Negro.
3. The steady withdrawal of aid from institutions for the higher training of the Negro.

These movements are not, to be sure, direct results of Mr. Washington's teachings; but his propaganda has, without a shadow of doubt, helped their speedier accomplishment. The question then comes: Is it possible, and probable, that nine millions of men can make effective progress in economic lines if they are deprived of political rights, made a servile caste, and allowed only the most meagre chance for developing their exceptional men? If history and reason give any distinct answer to these questions, it is an emphatic *No*. And Mr. Washington thus faces the triple paradox of his career:

1. He is striving nobly to make Negro artisans business men and property-owners, but it is utterly impossible; under modern competitive methods, for workingmen and property-owners to defend their rights and exist without the right of suffrage.

2. He insists on thrift and self-respect, but at the same time counsels a silent submission to civic inferiority such as is bound to sap the manhood of any race in the long run.

3. He advocates common-school and industrial training, and deprecates institutions of higher learning; but neither the Negro common-schools, nor Tuskegee itself, could remain open a day were it not for teachers trained in Negro colleges, or trained by their graduates.

This triple paradox in Mr. Washington's position is the object of criticism by two classes of colored Americans. One class is spiritually descended from Toussaint the Savior, through Gabriel, Vesey, and Turner, and they represent the attitude of revolt and revenge; they hate the white South blindly and distrust the white race generally, and so far as they agree on definite action, think that the Negro's only hope lies in emigration beyond the borders of the United States. And yet, by the irony of fate, nothing has more effectually made this programme seem hopeless than the recent course of the United States toward weaker and darker peoples in the West Indies, Hawaii, and the Philippines,—for where in the world may we go and be safe from lying and brute force?

The other class of Negroes who cannot agree with Mr. Washington has hitherto said little aloud. They deprecate the sight of scattered counsels, of internal disagreement; and especially they dislike making their just criticism of a useful and earnest man an excuse for a general discharge of venom from small-minded opponents. Nevertheless, the questions involved are so fundamental and serious that it is difficult to see how men like the Grimkes, Kelly Miller, J. W. E. Bowen, and other representatives of this group, can much longer be silent. Such men feel in conscience bound to ask of this nation three things:

1. The right to vote.
2. Civic equality.
3. The education of youth according to ability.

They acknowledge Mr. Washington's invaluable service in counseling patience and courtesy in such demands; they do not ask that ignorant black men vote when ignorant whites are debarred, or that any reasonable restrictions in the suffrage should not be applied; they know that the low social level of the mass of the race is responsible for much discrimination against it, but they also know, and the nation knows, that relentless color-prejudice is more often a cause than a result of the Negro's degradation; they seek the abatement of this relic of barbarism, and not its systematic encouragement and pampering by all agencies of social power from the Associated Press to the Church of Christ. They advocate, with Mr. Washington, a broad system of Negro common schools supplemented by thorough industrial training; but they are surprised that a man of Mr. Washington's insight cannot see that no such educational system ever has rested or can rest on any other basis than that of the well-equipped college and university, and they insist that there is a demand for a few such institutions throughout the South to train the best of the Negro youth as teachers, professional men, and leaders.

This group of men honor Mr. Washington for his attitude of conciliation toward the white South; they accept the "Atlanta Compromise" in its broadest interpretation; they recognize, with him, many signs of promise, many men of high purpose and fair judgment, in this section; they know that no easy task has been laid upon a region already tottering under heavy burdens. But, nevertheless, they insist that the way to truth and right lies in straightforward honesty, not in indiscriminate flattery; in praising those of the South who do well and criticisms uncompromisingly those who do ill; in taking advantage of the opportunities at hand and urging their fellows to do the same, but at the same time in remembering that only a firm adherence to their higher ideals and aspirations will ever keep those ideals within the realm of possibility. They do not expect that the free right to vote, to enjoy civic rights, and to be educated, will come in a moment; they do not expect to see the bias and prejudices of years disappear at the blast of a trumpet; but they are absolutely certain that the way for a people to gain their reasonable rights is not by voluntarily throwing them away and insisting that they do not want them; that the way for a people to gain respect is not by continually belittling and ridiculing themselves; that, on the contrary, Negroes must insist continually, in season and out of season, that voting is necessary to modern manhood, that color discrimination is barbarism, and that black boys need education as well as white boys.

In failing thus to state plainly and unequivocally the legitimate demands of their people, even at the cost of opposing an honored leader, the thinking classes of American Negroes would shirk a heavy responsibility,—a responsibility to themselves, a responsibility to the struggling masses, a responsibility to the darker races of men whose future depends so largely on this American experiment, but especially a responsibility to this nation,—this common Fatherland. It is wrong to encourage a man or a people in evil-doing; it is wrong to aid and abet a national crime simply because it is unpopular not to do so. The growing spirit of kindliness and reconciliation between the North and South after the frightful differences of a generation ago ought to be a source of deep congratulation to all, and especially to those whose mistreatment caused the war; but if that reconciliation is to be marked by the industrial slavery and civic death of those same black men, with permanent legislation into a position of inferiority, then those black men, if they are really men, are called upon by every consideration of patriotism and loyalty to oppose such a course by all civilized methods, even though such opposition involves disagreement with Mr. Booker T.

Washington. We have no right to sit silently by while the inevitable seeds are sown for a harvest of disaster to our children, black and white.

* * *

The black men of America have a duty to perform, a duty stern and delicate,—a forward movement to oppose a part of the work of their greatest leader. So far as Mr. Washington preaches Thrift, Patience, and Industrial Training for the masses, we must hold up his hands and strive with him, rejoicing in his honors and glorying in the strength of this Joshua called of God and of man to lead the headless host. But so far as Mr. Washington apologizes for injustice, North or South, does not rightly value the privilege and duty of voting, belittles the emasculating effects of caste distinctions, and opposes the higher training and ambition of our brighter minds,—so far as he, the South, or the Nation, does this,—we must unceasingly and firmly oppose them. By every civilized and peaceful method we must strive for the rights which the world accords to men, clinging unwaveringly to those great words which the sons of the Fathers would fain forget: "We hold these truths to be self-evident: That all men are created equal; that they are endowed by their Creator with certain unalienable rights; that among these are life, liberty, and the pursuit of happiness."

# "The Talented Tenth" (1903)*

The problem of training the Negro is to-day immensely complicated by fact that the whole question of the efficiency and appropriateness of our present systems of education, for any kind of child, is a matter of active debate, in which final settlement seems still afar off. Consequently it often happens that persons arguing for or against certain systems of education for Negroes, have these controversies in mind and miss the real question at issue. The main question, so far as the Southern Negro is concerned, is: What under the present circumstance, must a system of education do in order to raise the Negro as quickly as possible in the scale of civilization? The answer to this question seems to me clear: It must strengthen the Negro's character, increase his knowledge and teach him to earn a living. Now it goes without saying, that it is hard to do all these things simultaneously or suddenly, and that at the same time it will not do to give all the attention to one and neglect the others; we could give black boys trades, but that alone will not civilize a race of ex-slaves; we might simply increase their knowledge of the world, but this would not necessarily make them wish to use this knowledge honestly; we might seek to strengthen character and purpose, but to what end if this people have nothing to eat or to wear? A system of education is not one thing, nor does it have a single definite object, nor is it a mere matter of schools. Education is that whole system of human training within and without the school house walls, which molds and develops men. If then we start out to train an ignorant and unskilled people with a heritage of bad habits, our system of training must set before itself two great aims—the one dealing with knowledge and character, the other part seeking to give the child the technical knowledge necessary for him to earn a living under the present circumstances. These

*From W. E. B. Du Bois, "The Talented Tenth," in the *Negro Problem*... (New York 1903), pp. 56–75.

objects are accomplished in part by the opening of the common schools on the one, and of the industrial schools on the other. But only in part, for there must also be trained those who are to teach these schools—men and women of knowledge and culture and technical skill who understand modern civilization, and have the training and aptitude to impart it to the children under them. There must be teachers, and teachers of teachers, and to attempt to establish any sort of a system of common and industrial school training, without *first* (and I say *first* advisedly) without *first* providing for the higher training of the very best teachers, is simply throwing your money to the winds. School houses do not teach themselves—piles of brick and mortar and machinery do not send out *men*. It is the trained, living human soul, cultivated and strengthened by long study and thought, that breathes the real breath of life into boys and girls and makes them human, whether they be black or white, Greek, Russian or American. Nothing, in these latter days, has so dampened the faith of thinking Negroes in recent educational movements, as the fact that such movements have been accompanied by ridicule and denouncement and decrying of those very institutions of higher training which made the Negro public school possible, and make Negro industrial schools thinkable. It was Fisk, Atlanta, Howard and Straight, those colleges born of the faith and sacrifice of the abolitionists, that placed in the black schools of the South the 30,000 teachers and more, which some, who depreciate the work of these higher schools, are using to teach their own new experiments. If Hampton, Tuskegee and the hundred other industry schools prove in the future to be as successful as they deserve to be, then their success in training black artisans for the South, will be due primarily to the white colleges of the North and the black colleges of the South, which trained the teachers who to-day conduct these institutions. There was a time when the American people believed pretty devoutly that a log of wood with a boy at one end and Mark Hopkins at the other, represented the highest ideal of human training. But in these eager days it would seem that we have changed all that and think it necessary to add a couple of sawmills and a hammer to this outfit, and, at a pinch, to dispense with the services of Mark Hopkins.

I would not deny, or for a moment seem to deny, the paramount necessity of teaching the Negro to work, and to work steadily and skillfully; or seem to depreciate in the slightest degree the important part industrial schools must play in the accomplishment of these ends, but I *do* say, and insist upon it, that it is industrialism drunk with its vision of success, to imagine that its own work can be accomplished without providing for the training of broadly cultured men and women to teach its own teachers, and to teach the teachers of the public schools.

\* \* \*

It is coming to be seen, however, in the education of the Negro, as clearly as it has been in the education of the youths the world over, that it is the *boy* and not the material product, that is the true object of education. Consequently the object of the industrial school came to be the thorough training of boys regardless of the cost of the training, so long as it was thoroughly well done.

Thus, again, in the manning of trade schools we are thrown back upon the higher training as its source and chief support. What is the chief need for the building up of the Negro public school in the South? The Negro race in the South needs teachers to-day above all else. This is the concurrent testimony of all who know the situation. For the supply of this great demand two things are needed—institutions of higher education and money for school houses and salaries. It is usually assumed that a hundred or more institutions for Negro training are to-day turning out so many teachers and college-bred men that the race is threatened with an over-supply. This is sheer nonsense. There are to-day less than 3,000 living Negro college graduates in the United States, and less than 1,000 Negroes in college. Moreover, in the 164 schools for Negroes, 95 per cent of their students are doing elementary and secondary work, work which should be done in the public schools. Over half the remaining 2,157 students are taking high school studies. The mass of so-called "normal" schools for the Negro, are simply doing elementary common school work, or, at most, high school work, with a little instruction in methods. The Negro colleges and the post-graduate courses at other institutions are the only agencies for the broader and more careful training of teachers. The work of these institutions is hampered for lack of funds. It is getting increasingly difficult to get funds for training teachers in the best modern methods, and yet all over the South, from State Superintendents, county officials, city boards and school principals comes the wail, "We need TEACHERS!" and teachers must be trained.

* * *

There was a time when any aged and wornout carpenter could teach in a trade school. But not so to-day. Indeed the demand for college-bred men by a school like Tuskegee, ought to make Mr. Booker T. Washington the firmest friend of higher training. Here he has as helpers the son of a Negro senator, trained in Greek and the humanities, and graduated at Harvard; the son of a Negro congressman and lawyer, trained in Latin and mathematics, and graduated at Oberlin; he has as his wife, a woman who read Virgil and Homer in the same class room with me; he has as college chaplain, a classical graduate of Atlanta University; as teacher of science, a graduate of Fisk; as teacher of history, a graduate of Smith,—indeed some thirty of his chief teachers are college graduates, and instead of studying French grammars in the midst of weeds, or buying pianos for dirty cabins, they are at Mr. Washington's right hand helping him in a noble work. And yet one of the effects of Mr. Washington's propaganda has been to throw doubt upon the expediency of such training for Negroes, as these persons have had.

Men of America, the problem is plain before you. Here is a race transplanted through the criminal foolishness of your fathers. Whether you like it or not the millions are here, and here they will remain. If you do not lift them up, they will pull you down. Education and work are the levers to uplift a people. Work alone will not do it unless inspired by the right ideals and guided by intelligence. Education must not simply teach work—it must teach Life. The Talented Tenth of the Negro race must be made leaders of thought and missionaries of culture among their people. No others can do this work and Negro colleges must train men for it. The Negro race, like all other races, is going to be saved by its exceptional men.

## QUESTIONS

1. What is the relationship of industrial training to the Puritan ethic?

2. Explain Booker T. Washington's claim that industrial education "kills two birds with one stone."

3. Why do you think Washington's Atlanta Compromise was so well received?

4. Describe in your own words what W. E. Du Bois meant by the phrase "the talented tenth."

5. Do you think that the "test" required of Booker T. Washington for admission into Hampton Institute was appropriate? Explain your answer.

6. Explain the newly freed slave's craving for Greek and Latin learning in the aftermath of the Civil War.

7. Describe in your own words Du Bois's criticism of Washington. Explain why Du Bois suggests that it is the duty of the Black men in the United States to oppose the work of their greatest leader—Booker T. Washington.

# CHAPTER

# 12  Plessy and Beyond

It is more than coincidence that a year after Booker T. Washington's famous Atlanta Compromise speech the Supreme Court of the United States legalized the segregation of the races. Focusing on an 1890 Lousiana state law providing for separate railway carriages for the White and colored races, the Court ruled in *Plessy v Ferguson* (1896) that separate but equal facilities are constitutional.

The case centered on Homer Adolph Plessy who was not allowed to sit in the train car designated for "Whites only," even though he was seven-eighths Caucasian and his one-eighth African heritage was not evident in his appearance. Plessy was jailed for refusing to leave the "Whites only" carriage and charged with violating state law. Once the case reached the Supreme Court, the Court reasoned that the separation of the races—even when mandated or sanctioned by law—does not violate the Negroes' rights as guaranteed by the Fourteenth Amendment. Rejecting the argument that prejudice and bigotry can be eliminated only by a forced commingling of the two races, the Court suggested that racial equality will be achieved only through a mutual appreciation of the merits of each race.

In what was to become a very familiar phrase, the *Plessy v Ferguson* decision provided legal sanction for "separate but equal" facilities for coloreds and Whites. For more than fifty years, states throughout the South used this "separate but equal" doctrine to justify dual systems of education for White and colored children and youth. Theoretically, the "colored" schools were equal to those of the Whites, but in reality they received less money, had fewer or inadequate facilities, and paid teachers and staff less than their White counterparts received. They were "separate but equal" in name only.

During the first half of the twentieth century, the NAACP won cases in which there was clear violation of the "separate but equal" doctrine. In the 1930s, NAACP legal strategists turned their attention to education and began focusing on higher and professional education where there was clear violation of the "separated but equal" doctrine. In the South, Negroes were not allowed to attend state-supported institutions offering professional and graduate programs, and there were no public "colored" institutions offering comparable programs. The strategy to attack the obvious violations of the "separate but equal" doctrine bore fruit in 1950; the U.S. Supreme Court ordered the University of Oklahoma to remove all state-imposed restrictions on George McLaurin—a Black educator previously admitted to the doctoral program in education but segregated from other students in the classroom, library, and cafeteria. The Court's decision stated that such restrictions interfered with his opportunity to learn his profession.

On the same day, the Supreme Court ordered the University of Texas Law School to admit Heman M. Sweatt, a Black mail carrier previously enrolled in a makeshift law school hastily established by Texas in an attempt to comply with the "separate but equal" doctrine. The Court ruled that this makeshift law school, consisting of four part-time instructors, three classrooms, and one student, did not offer "substantial equality" to White and Negro students. With the McLaurin and Sweatt decisions, the Supreme Court delivered a clear signal that the "equal" part of the doctrine must be taken seriously.

For more information about the McLaurin and Sweatt decisions, see Diane Ravitch, *The Troubled Crusade: American Education, 1945–1980* (New York: Basic Books, Inc., 1983), pp. 114–124.

# The Separate but Equal Doctrine*

### *Mr. Justice Brown, after Stating the Case, Delivered the Opinion of the Court*

This case turns upon the constitutionality of an act of the General Assembly of the State of Louisiana, passed in 1890, providing for separate railway carriages for the white and colored races....

The information filed in the criminal District Court charged in substance that Plessy, being a passenger between two stations within the State of Louisiana, was assigned by officers of the company to the coach used for the race to which he belonged, but he insisted upon going into a coach used by the race to which he did not belong. Neither in the information nor plea was his particular race or color averred

The petition for the writ of prohibition averred that petitioner was seven eighths Caucasian and one eighth African blood; that the mixture of colored blood was not discernible in him, and that he was entitled to every right, privilege and immunity secured to citizens of the United States of the white race; and that, upon such theory, he took possession of a vacant seat in a coach where passengers of the white race were accommodated, and was ordered by the conductor to vacate said coach and take a seat in another assigned to persons of the colored race, and having refused to comply with such demand he was forcibly ejected with the aid of a police officer, and imprisoned in the parish jail to answer a charge of having violated the above act.

The constitutionality of this act is attacked upon the ground that it conflicts both with the Thirteenth Amendment of the Constitution, abolishing slavery, and the Fourteenth Amendment, which prohibits certain restrictive legislation on the part of the States....

A statute which implies merely a legal distinction between the white and colored races—a distinction which is founded in the color of the two races, and which must always exist so long as white men are distinguished from the other race by color—has no tendency to destroy the legal equality of the two races, or reestablish a state of involuntary servitude. Indeed. we do not understand that the Thirteenth Amendment is strenuously relied upon by the plaintiff in error in this connection....

The object of the [Fourteenth] amendment was undoubtedly to enforce the absolute equality of the two races before the law, but in the nature of things it could not have been

*Plessy v. Ferguson* (1896), 163 U.S. 537.

intended to abolish distinctions based upon color, or to enforce social, as distinguished from political equality, or a commingling of the two race, upon terms unsatisfactory to either. Laws permitting, and even requiring, their separation in places where they are liable to be brought into contact do not necessarily imply the inferiority of either race to the other, and have been generally, if not universally, recognized within the competency of the state legislatures in the exercise of their police power. The most common instance of this is connected with the establishment of separate schools for white and colored children, which has been held to be a valid exercise of the legislative power even by courts of States where the political rights of the colored race have been longest and most earnestly enforced.

\* \* \*

It is claimed by the plaintiff in error that, in any mixed community, the reputation of belonging to the dominant race, in this instance the white race, is *property*, in the same sense that a right of action, or of inheritance, is property. Conceding this to be so, for the purposes of this case, we are unable to see how this statute deprives him of, or in any way affects his right to, such property. If he be a white man and assigned to a colored coach, he may have his action for damages against the company for being deprived of his so called property. Upon the other hand, if he be a colored man and be so assigned, he has been deprived of no property, since he is not lawfully entitled to the reputation of being a white man.

In this connection, it is also suggested by the learned counsel for the plaintiff in error that the same argument that will justify the state legislature in requiring railways to provide separate accommodations for the two races will also authorize them to require separate cars to be provided for people whose hair is of a certain color, or who are aliens, or who belong to certain nationalities, or to enact laws requiring colored people to walk upon one side of the street, and white people upon the other, or requiring white men's houses to be painted white, and colored men's black, or their vehicles or business signs to be of different colors, upon the theory that one side of the street is as good as the other, or that a house or vehicle of one color is as good as one of another color. The reply to all this is that every exercise of the police power must be reasonable, and extend only to such laws as are enacted in good faith for the promotion for the public good, and not for the annoyance or oppression of a particular class....

So far, then, as a conflict with the Fourteenth Amendment is concerned, the case reduces itself to the question whether the statute of Louisiana is a reasonable regulation, and with respect to this there must necessarily be a large discretion on the part of the legislature. In determining the question of reasonableness it is at liberty to act with reference to the established usages, customs and traditions of the people, and with a view to the promotion of their comfort, and the preservation of the public peace and good order. Gauged by this standard, we cannot say that a law which authorizes or even requires the separation of the two races in public conveyances is unreasonable, or more obnoxious to the Fourteenth Amendment than the acts of Congress requiring separate schools for colored children in the District of Columbia, the constitutionality of which does not seem to have been questioned, or the corresponding acts of state legislatures.

We consider the underlying fallacy of the plaintiff's argument to consist in the assumption that the enforced separation of the two races stamps the colored race with a badge of inferiority. If this be so, it is not by reason of anything found in the act, but solely because the colored race chooses to put that construction upon it. The argument necessarily assumes that if, as has been more than once the case, and is not unlikely to be so again, the colored race should become the dominant power in the state legislature, and should enact a law in precisely similar terms, it would thereby relegate the white race to an inferior position. We imagine that the white race, at least, would not acquiesce in this assumption. The argument also assumes that social prejudices may be overcome by legislation, and that equal rights cannot be secured to the negro except by an enforced commingling of the two races. We cannot accept this proposition. If the two races are to meet upon terms of social equality, it must be the result of natural affinities, a mutual appreciation of each other's merits and a voluntary consent of individuals. As was said by the Court of Appeals of New York in *People v. Gallagher,* 93 N.Y. 438, 448, "this end can neither be accomplished nor promoted by laws which conflict with the general sentiment of the community upon whom they are designed to operate. When the government, therefore, has secured to each of its citizens equal rights before the law and equal opportunities for improvement and progress, it has accomplished the end for which it was organized and performed all of the functions respecting social advantages with which it is endowed." Legislation is powerless to eradicate racial instincts or to abolish distinctions based upon physical differences, and the attempt to do so can only result in accentuating the difficulties of the present situation. If the civil and political rights of both races be equal one cannot be inferior to the other civilly or politically. If one race be inferior to the other socially, the Constitution of the United States cannot put them upon the same plane.

*Affirmed.*

### *Mr. Justice Harlan, Dissenting*

The white race deems itself to be the dominant race in this country. And so it is, in prestige, in achievements, in education, in wealth and in power. So, I doubt not, it will continue to be for all time, if it remains true to its great heritage and holds fast to the principles of constitutional liberty. But in view of the Constitution, in the eye of the law, there is in this country no superior, dominant, ruling class of citizens. There is no caste here. Our Constitution is color-blind, and neither knows nor tolerates classes among citizens. In respect of civil rights, all citizens are equal before the law. The humblest is the peer of the most powerful. The law regards man as man, and takes no account of his surroundings or of his color when his civil rights as guaranteed by the supreme law of the land are involved. It is, therefore, to be regretted that this high tribunal, the final expositor of the fundamental law of the land, has reached the conclusion that it is competent for a State to regulate the enjoyment by citizens of their civil rights solely upon the basis of race.

In my opinion, the judgment this day rendered will, in time, prove to be quite as pernicious as the decision made by this tribunal in the *Dred Scott case.* It was adjudged in that case that the descendants of Africans who were imported into this country and sold as slaves were not included nor intended to be included under the word "citizens" in the Constitution, and could not claim any of the rights and privileges which that instrument provided for and secured to citizens of the United States; that at the time of the adoption of the Constitution they were "considered as a subordinate and inferior class of beings, who had been subjugated by the dominant race, and, whether emancipated or not, yet remained subject to their authority, and had no rights or privileges but such as those who held the power and the government might choose to grant them." 19 How. 393, 404. The recent amendments of the Constitution, it was supposed, had eradicated these principles from our institutions. But it seems that we have yet, in some of the States, a dominant race—a superior class of citizens, which assumes to regulate the enjoyment of civil rights, common to all citizens, upon the basis of race. The present decision, it may well be apprehended, will not only stimulate aggressions, more or less brutal and irritating, upon the admitted rights of colored citizens, but will encourage the belief that it is possible, by means of state enactments, to defeat the beneficient purposes which the people of the United States had in view when they adopted the recent amendments of the Constitution, by one of which the blacks of this country were made citizens of the United States and of the States in which they respectively reside, and whose privileges and immunities, as citizens, the States are forbidden to abridge. Sixty millions of whites are in no danger from the presence here of eight millions of blacks. The destinies of the two races, in this country, are indissolubly linked together, and the interests of both require that the common government of all shall not permit the seeds of race hate to be planted under the sanction of law. What can more certainly arouse race hate, what more certainly create and perpetuate a feeling of distrust between these races, than state enactments, which, in fact, proceed on the ground that colored citizens are so inferior and degraded that they cannot be allowed to sit in public coaches occupied by white citizens? That, as all will admit, is the real meaning of such legislation as was enacted in Louisiana....

I am of opinion that the statute of Louisiana is inconsistent with the personal liberty of citizens, white and black, in that State, and hostile to both the spirit and letter of the Constitution of the United States. If laws of like character should be enacted in the several States of the Union, the effect would be in the highest degree mischievous. Slavery, as an institution tolerated by law would, it is true, have disappeared from our country, but there would remain a power in the States, by sinister legislation, to interfere with the full enjoyment of the blessings of freedom; to regulate civil rights, common to all citizens, upon the basis of race; and to place in a condition of legal inferiority a large body of American citizens, now constituting a part of the political community called the People of the United States, for whom, and by whom through representatives, our government is administered. Such a system is inconsistent with the guarantee given by the Constitution to each State of a republican form of government, and may be stricken down by Congressional action, or by the courts in the discharge of their solemn duty to maintain the supreme law of the land, anything in the constitution or laws of any State to the contrary notwithstanding.

For the reasons stated, I am constrained to withhold my assent from the opinion and judgment of the majority.

# Decision on a Separate School of Law for Negroes in Texas (1950)*

### *Certiorari to the Supreme Court of Texas*

### *Mr. Chief Justice Vinson Delivered the Opinion of a Unanimous Court*

This case and *McLaurin* v. *Oklahoma State Regent,*...present differing aspects of this general question: To what extent does the Equal Protection Clause of the Fourteenth Amendment limit the power of a state to distinguish between students of different races in professional

*From *Sweatt* v. *Painter,* 339 U.S. 629.

and graduate education in a state university? Broader issues have been urged for our consideration, but we adhere to the principle of deciding constitutional questions only in the context of the particular case before the Court. We have frequently reiterated that this Court will decide constitutional questions only when necessary to the disposition of the case at hand, and that such decisions will be drawn as narrowly as possible.... Because of this traditional reluctance to extend constitutional interpretations to situations or facts which are not before the Court, much of the excellent research and detailed argument presented in these cases is unnecessary to their disposition.

In the instant case, petitioner filed an application for admission to the University of Texas Law School for the February, 1946 term. His application was rejected solely because he is a Negro. Petitioner thereupon brought this suit for mandamus against the appropriate school officials, respondents here, to compel his admission. At that time, there was no law school in Texas which admitted Negroes.

The State trial court recognized that the action of the State in denying petitioner the opportunity to gain a legal education while granting it to others deprived him of the equal protection of the laws guaranteed by the Fourteenth Amendment. The court did not grant the relief requested, however, but continued the case for six months to allow the State to supply substantially equal facilities. At the expiration of the six months, in December, 1946, the court denied the writ on the showing that the authorized University officials had adopted an order calling for the opening of a law school for Negroes the following February. While petitioner's appeal was pending, such a school was made available, but petitioner refused to register therein. The Texas Court of Civil Appeals set aside the trial court's judgment and ordered the cause "remanded generally to the trial court for further proceedings without prejudice to the rights of any party to this suit."

On remand, a hearing was held on the issue of the equality of the educational facilities at the newly established school as compared with the University of Texas Law School. Finding that the new school offered petitioner "privileges, advantages, and opportunities for the study of law substantially equivalent to those offered by the State to white students at the University of Texas," the trial court denied mandamus. The Court of Civil Appeals affirmed....

The University of Texas Law School, from which petitioner was excluded, was staffed by a faculty of sixteen full-time and three part-time professors, some of whom are nationally recognized authorities in their field. Its student body numbered 850. The library contained over 65,000 volumes. Among the other facilities available to the students were a law review, moot court facilities, scholarship funds, and Order of the Coif affiliation. The school's alumni occupy the most distinguished positions in the private practice of the law and in the public life of the State. It may properly be considered one of the nation's ranking law schools.

The law school for Negroes which was to have opened in February, 1947, would have had no independent faculty or library. The teaching was to be carried on by four members of the University of Texas Law School faculty, who were to maintain their offices at the University of Texas while teaching at both institutions. Few of the 10,000 volumes ordered for the library had arrived; nor was there any full-time librarian. The school lacked accreditation.

Since the trial of this case, respondents report the opening of a law school at the Texas State University for Negroes. It is apparently on the road to full accreditation. It has a faculty of five full-time professors; a student body of 23; a library of some 16,500 volumes serviced by a full-time staff; a practice court and legal aid association; and one alumnus who has become a member of the Texas Bar.

Whether the University of Texas Law School is compared with the original or the new law school for Negroes, we cannot find substantial equality in the educational opportunities offered white and Negro law students by the State. In terms of number of the faculty, variety of courses and opportunity for specialization, size of the student body, scope of the library, availability of law review and similar activities, the University of Texas Law School is superior. What is more important, the University of Texas Law School possesses to a far greater degree those qualities which are incapable of objective measurement but which make for greatness in a law school. Such qualities, to name but a few, include reputation of the faculty, experience of the administration, position and influence of the alumni, standing in the community, traditions and prestige. It is difficult to believe that one who had a free choice between these law schools would consider the question closed.

Moreover, although the law is a highly learned profession, we are well aware that it is an intensely practical one. The law school, the proving ground for legal learning and practice, cannot be effective in isolation from the individuals and institutions with which the law interacts. Few students and no one who has practiced law would choose to study in an academic vacuum, removed from the interplay of ideas and the exchange of views with which the law is concerned. The law school to which Texas is willing to admit petitioner excludes from its student body members of the racial groups which number 85% of the population of the State and include most of the lawyers, witnesses, jurors, judges, and other officials with whom petitioner will inevitably he dealing when he becomes a member of the Texas Bar. With such a substantial and significant segment of society excluded, we cannot conclude that the education offered petitioner is substantially equal to that which he would receive if admitted to the University of Texas Law School.

It may be argued that excluding petitioner from that school is no different from excluding white students from the new law school. This contention overlooks realities. It is unlikely that a member of a group so decisively in the majority, attending a school with rich traditions and prestige which only a history of consistently maintained excellence could command, would claim that the opportunities afforded him for legal education were unequal to those held open to petitioner. That such a claim, if made, would be dishonored by the State, is no answer, "Equal protection of the laws is not achieved through indiscriminate imposition of inequalities." *Shelley* v. *Kraemer,* 334 U.S. 1, 22 (1948).

It is fundamental that these cases concern rights which are personal and present. This Court has stated unanimously that "The State must provide [legal education] for [petitioner] in conformity with the equal protection clause of the Fourteenth Amendment and provide it as soon as it does for applicants of any other group." *Sipuel* v. *Board of Regents,* 332 U.S. 631, 633 (1948). That case "did not present the issue whether a state might not satisfy the equal protection clause of the Fourteenth Amendment establishing a separate law school for Negroes." *Fisher* v. *Hurst,* 333 U.S. 147, 150 (1948). In *Missouri ex rel. Gaines* v. *Canada,* 305 U.S. 337, 351 (1938), the Court, speaking through Chief Justice Hughes, declared that "petitioner's right was a personal one. It was as an individual that he was entitled to the equal protection of the laws, and the State was bound to furnish him within its borders facilities for legal education substantially equal to those which the State there afforded for persons of the white race, whether or not other Negroes sought the same opportunity." These are the only cases in this Court which present the issue of the constitutional validity of race distinctions in state-supported graduate and professional education.

In accordance with these cases, petitioner may claim his full constitutional right: legal education equivalent to that offered by the State to students of other races. Such education is not available to him in a separate law school as offered by the State. We cannot, therefore, agree with respondents that the doctrine of *Plessy* v. *Ferguson,* 163 U.S. 537 (1896) requires affirmance of the judgment below. Nor need we reach petitioner's contention that *Plessy* v. *Ferguson* should be reexamined in the light of contemporary knowledge respecting the purposes of the Fourteenth Amendment and the effects of racial segregation....

We hold that the Equal Protection Clause of the Fourteenth Amendment requires that petitioner be admitted to the University of Texas Law School. The judgment is reversed and the cause is remanded for proceedings not inconsistent with this opinion.

*Reversed.*

## Segregation of a Graduate Student in a State University Ruled Unconstitutional (1950)*

### *Chief Justice Vison Delivered the Opinion of the Court*

...Thus he (McLaurin) was required to sit apart at a designated desk in an anteroom adjoining the classroom; to sit at a designated desk on the mezzanine floor of the library, but not to use the desks in the regular reading room; and to sit at a designated table and to eat at a different time from the other students in the school cafeteria.

To remove these conditions, appellant filed a motion to modify the order and judgment of the District Court. That court held that such treatment did not violate the provisions of the Fourteenth Amendment and denied the motion. This appeal followed.

In the interval between the decision of the court below and the hearing in this Court, the treatment afforded appellant was altered. For some time, the section of the classroom in which appellant sat was surrounded by a rail on which there was a sign stating, "Reserved For Colored", but these have been removed. He is now assigned to a seat in the classroom in a row specified for colored students; he is assigned to a table in the library on the main floor; and he is permitted to eat at the same time in the cafeteria as other students although here again he is assigned to a special table.

It is said that the separations imposed by the State in his case are in form merely nominal. McLaurin uses the same classroom, library and cafeteria as students of other races; there is no indication that the seats to which he is assigned in these rooms have any disadvantage of location. He may wait in line in the cafeteria and there stand and talk with his fellow students, but while he eats he must remain apart.

These restrictions were obviously imposed in order to comply, as nearly as could be, with the statutory requirements of Oklahoma. But they signify that the State, in administering the facilities it affords for professional and graduate study, sets McLaurin apart from the

*From *McLaurin* v. *Oklahoma State Regents.* 339 U.S. 637.

other students. The result is that appellant is handicapped in his pursuit of effective graduate instruction. Such restrictions impair and inhibit his ability to study, to engage in discussions and exchange views with other students, and, in general, to learn his profession.

Our society grows increasingly complex, and our need for trained leaders increases correspondingly. Appellant's case represents, perhaps, the epitome of that need, for he is attempting to obtain an advanced degree in education, to become, by definition, a leader and trainer of others. Those who will come under his guidance and influence must be directly affected by the education he receives. Their own education and development will necessarily suffer to the extent that his training is unequal to that of his classmates. State-imposed restrictions which produce such inequalities cannot be sustained.

It may be argued that appellant will be in no better position when these restrictions are removed, for he may still be set apart by his fellow students. This we think irrelevant. There is a vast differences—a Constitutional difference—between restrictions imposed by the state which prohibit the intellectual commingling of students, and the refusal of individuals to commingle where the state presents no such bar....

The removal of the state restrictions will not necessarily abate individual and group predilections, prejudices and choices. But at the very least, the state will not be depriving appellant of the opportunity to secure acceptance by his fellow students on his own merits.

We conclude that the conditions under which this appellant is required to receive his education deprive him of his personal and present right to the equal protection of the laws. See *Sweatt* v. *Painter,* 339 U.S. We hold that under these circumstances the Fourteenth Amendment precludes differences in treatment by the state based upon race. Appellant, having been admitted to a state-supported graduate school, must receive the same treatment at the hands of the state as students of other races.

## QUESTIONS

1. Summarize in your own words the major arguments of the U.S. Supreme Court in declaring that "separate but equal" facilities are constitutional.

2. Explain the strategy of the NAACP to focus on situations in which there was a clear violation of the "separate but equal" doctrine.

3. Explain why the constitutional questions raised in *Plessy v Ferguson* focus on the Thirteenth and Fourteenth Amendments.

4. Explain in your words Justice Harlan's dissent in the *Plessy v Ferguson* ruling. What is meant by the statement "Our constitution is color-blind"?

5. Did the *Plessy* judgment become, as Justice Harlan predicted, as pernicious as the decision made in the *Dred Scott* case? Explain your answer.

# 13 The Education of the Immigrant

## Common or Special Education

As suggested in Chapter 9, one specific purpose of the common school was to "Americanize" the immigrant. Emerging during the nineteenth century as the dominant form of schooling in the United States, the common school reached virtually every family. Earning its characterization as a nation of immigrants, approximately thirty-five million people immigrated to this country from 1815 to 1915. The largest number came from Germany, but Ireland, Great Britain, Austria-Hungary, Russia, and many other countries also were well represented. As the selection about the Russian girl Mary Antin included here clearly shows, the common school was available to many of these immigrants and played a major role in "Americanizing" them. Thanks in part to the common school, Germans who had retained their language and culture for centuries when transplanted to Russia became "Americanized" in one one generation after settling in Eureka, South Dakota.

Crossing the Atlantic Ocean in pursuit of a better life, these Europeans understood that they would never return. They were psychologically prepared to accept the ways of "the promised land" and to sublimate old world values and customs to those of their new nation. Still, Americanization often produced family tensions as schools encouraged or required immigrant children to abandon their culture and language and to embrace U.S. English and Puritan values. "Look what happens," lamented an immigrant mother, "when we send our children to school. All they learn is to despise us."

Americanization prevailed both in the classroom and schoolyard. Teachers Americanized names (a first-grade Chicano boy named Jesus became Jesse), and ridicule by classmates marked the end of "the Chinese boy's pigtail, the Mexican girl's tortilla, and the Italian child's baroque accent."[1] Common school teachers often served as middle class mothers for immigrant children, giving them baths, teaching them proper manners and appropriate dress, and instilling in them the values of hard work, perseverance, and thrift. By the second or third generation, Americanization won out as immigrants—especially those of European origin—blended into the U.S. mainstream. What they retained of their ethnic heritage was reserved for private family ceremonies.

---

[1]David B. Tyack, ed., *Turning Points in American Educational History* (New York: John Wiley & Sons, 1967) p. 236.

As immigration patterns shifted away from northern and western Europe and toward southern and central Europe as well as from Mexico during the final decades of the nineteenth century, faith in the ability of the common school to Americanize these new immigrants began to wane. Much like school reformers in the aftermath of the Civil War, the idea that certain child races—like the Negroes—required a special education was expanded to include Mexican Americans. Mexican Americans, along with southern and eastern Europeans, were considered docile, illiterate, and lacking in the Anglo-Saxon conceptions of law, order, and government.

With the dawn of a new century, the education of the rapidly increasing Chicano population of the Southwestern United States was of little concern to the dominant Anglo power structure. In many ways, the relationships of the Anglo or white landowning class to the Chicano field worker parallels the Jim Crow South of the time. Just as Negroes, although no longer slaves, were still subservient to the Whites, the Mexican American farm or ranch worker was the peon to the Anglo patron. Racial prejudice prevailed as minority—largely Mexican American—children were not afforded the same quantity or quality of education available to Anglo children.

Much as in the South, a dual system of schooling existed, with the Anglos educated to assume their natural roles as leaders, managers, and owners while Mexican Americans were educated to assume their natural roles as farm and ranch workers. Not only were Mexican Americans schools inferior to those of their Anglo counterparts, but also, because many Mexican American families were compelled to follow the crops to earn a living wage, migrating Chicano children received fragments of education wherever and whenever they could. In the vernacular of the place and time, a patron and peon society emerged as part of a plantation and ranch economy dependent on a large number of docile but hardworking people.

Schools for Mexican American children were like the common school in that their primary purpose was to transform Mexican Americans from half-hearted citizens into lawabiding and useful Americans. Similar to the industrial education that Booker T. Washington and other people had advocated for Negroes, education for Mexican American children was designed to socialize the so-called child races to perform at the lowest levels of society. Just as industrial education represented the solution to the Negro problem, similar kinds of industrial programs characterized Chicano schools in the 1930s. These programs emphasized vocational and manual arts training, the learning of English, and the adoption of such Puritan core values as cleanliness, thrift, and punctuality.

As we discuss in Chapters 14 and 15, the dual castelike systems of education that existed in both the South and Southwest have been eliminated. In addition, the racially motivated industrial education is no longer touted as the answer for educating Black and Chicano children. Still, genuine equal educational opportunity remains an elusive goal. In the Southwest, substantial immigration—both legal and illegal—continues. In some border states, the Mexican American population exceeds 50 percent. Racial tension continues, with some Anglos concerned that these new immigrants are less willing to sublimate their language and culture to the dominant Anglo culture.

There is some truth to this claim in that the host country (the United States) is next door to Mexico. Unlike earlier immigrants, who made a once-in-a-lifetime decision to immigrate to the new world, the new immigrants from Mexico have long traditional and historical ties with inhabitants on both sides of the Rio Grande. Even though we have abandoned the racist idea that we need a special education for such so-called child races as Blacks and Mexican Americans, the question of what it means to be an American remains as elusive as ever. A related and equally problematic question is what kind of education is needed to create and maintain an equilibrium between the common values that all Americans should share and the individual and cultural values that also define us. In a sense, these new immigrants have brought into focus the fallacy of the myth of the U.S. as a cultural melting pot and the schools as its cauldron.

# A Russian Immigrant in the "Promised Land" (1912)*

The knowledge of such things as I am telling leaves marks upon the flesh and spirit. I remember little children in Polotzk with old, old faces and eyes glazed with secrets. I knew how to dodge and cringe and dissemble before I knew the names of the seasons. And I had plenty of time to ponder on these things, because I was so idle. If they had let me go to school, now—But of course they didn't.

There was no free school for girls, and even if your parents were rich enough to send you to a private school, you could not go very far. At the high school, which was under government control, Jewish children were admitted in limited numbers,—only ten to every hundred,—and even if you were among the lucky ones, you had your troubles. The tutor who prepared you talked all the time about the examinations you would have to pass, till you were scared. You heard on all sides that the brightest Jewish children were turned down if the examining officers did not like the turn of their noses. You went up to be examined with the other Jewish children, your heart heavy, about that matter of your nose. There was a special examination for the Jewish candidates, of course; a nine-year-old Jewish child had to answer questions that a thirteen-year-old Gentile was hardly expected to understand. But that did not matter so much. You had been prepared for the thirteen-year-old test. You found the questions quite easy. You wrote your answers triumphantly—and you received a low rating, and there was no appeal.

I used to stand in the doorway of my father's store, munching on an apple that did not taste good any more, and watch the pupils going home from school in twos and threes; the girls in neat brown dresses and black aprons and little stiff hats, the boys in trim uniforms with many buttons. They had ever so many books in the satchels on their backs. They would take them out at home, and read and write, and learn all sorts of interesting things. They looked to me like beings from another world than mine. But those whom I envied had their own troubles, as I often heard. Their school life was one struggle against injustice from instructors, spiteful treatment from fellow students and insults from everybody. Those who, by heroic efforts and transcendent good luck, successfully finished the course, found themselves against a new wall, if they wished to go on. They were turned down at

*From Mary Antin, *The Promised Land* (Boston, 1912) pp. 26–27, 198–200, 203–205.

the universities, which admitted them in the ratio of three Jews to a hundred Gentiles, under the same debarring entrance conditions as at the high school,—especially rigorous examinations, dishonest marking, or arbitrary rulings without disguise. No, the Czar did not want us in the schools....

In America, then, everything was free, as we had heard in Russia. Light was free; the streets were as bright as a synagogue on a holy day. Music was free; we had been serenaded, to our gaping delight, by a brass band of many pieces, soon after our installation on Union Place.

Education was free. That subject my father had written about repeatedly, as comprising his chief hope for us children, the essence of American opportunity, the treasure that no thief could touch, not even misfortune or poverty. It was the one thing that he was able to promise us when he sent for us; surer, safer than bread or shelter. On our second day I was thrilled with the realization of what this freedom of education meant. A little girl from across the alley came and offered to conduct us to school. My father was out, but we five between us had a few words of English by this time. We knew the word school. We understood. This child, who had never seen us till yesterday, who could not pronounce our names, who was not much better dressed than we, was able to offer us the freedom of the schools of Boston! No application made, no questions asked, no examinations, rulings, exclusions; no machinations, no fees. The doors stood open for every one of us. The smallest child could show us the way.

This incident impressed me more than anything I had heard in advance of the freedom of education in America. It was a concrete proof—almost the thing itself. One had to experience it to understand it....

The apex of my civic pride and personal contentment was reached on the bright September morning when I entered the public school. That day I must always remember, even if I live to be so old that I cannot tell my name. To most people their first day at school is a memorable occasion. In my case the importance of the day was a hundred times magnified, on account of the years I had waited, the road I had come, and the conscious ambitions I entertained.

I am wearily aware that I am speaking in extreme figures, in superlatives. I wish I knew of some other way to render the mental life of the immigrant child of reasoning age. I may have been ever so much an exception in acuteness of observation, powers of comparison, and abnormal self-consciousness; none the less were my thoughts and conduct typical of the attitude of the intelligent immigrant child toward American institutions. And what the child thinks and feels is a reflection of the hopes, desires, and purposes of the parents who brought him overseas, no matter how precocious and independent the child may be. Your immigrant inspectors will tell you what poverty the foreigner brings in his baggage, what want in his pockets. Let the overgrown boy of twelve, reverently drawing his letters in the baby class, testify to the noble dreams and high ideals that may be hidden beneath the greasy caftan of the immigrant. Speaking for the Jews, at least, I know I am safe in inviting such an investigation.

Who were my companions on my first day at school? Whose hand was in mine, as I stood, overcome with awe, by the teacher's desk, and whispered my name as my father prompted? Was it Frieda's steady, capable hand? Was it her loyal heart that throbbed, beat for beat with mine, as it had done through all our childish adventures? Frieda's heart did throb that day, but not with my emotions. My heart pulsed with joy and pride and ambition; in her heart longing fought with abnegation. For I was led to the schoolroom, with its sunshine and its singing and the teacher's cheery smile; while she was led to the workshop, with its foul air, care-lined faces, and the foreman's stern command. Our going to school was the fulfilment of my father's best promises to us, and Frieda's share in it was to fashion and fit the calico frocks in which the baby sister and I made our first appearance in a public schoolroom.

I remember to this day the gray pattern of the calico, so affectionately did I regard it as it hung upon the wall—my consecration robe awaiting the beatific day. And Frieda, I am sure, remembers it, too, so longingly did she regard it as the crisp, starchy breadths of it slid between her fingers. But whatever were her longings, she said nothing of them; she bent over the sewing-machine humming an Old-World melody. In every straight, smooth seam, perhaps, she tucked away some lingering impulse of childhood, but she matched the scrolls and flowers with the utmost care. If a sudden shock of rebellion made her straighten up for an instant, the next instant she was bending to adjust a ruffle to the best advantage. And when the momentous day arrived, and the little sister and I stood up to be arrayed, it was Frieda herself who patted and smoothed my stiff new calico, who made me turn round and round, to see that I was perfect, who stooped to pull out a disfiguring basting-thread. If there was anything in her heart besides sisterly love and pride and good-will, as we parted that morning, it was a sense of loss and a woman's acquiescence in her fate; for we had been close friends, and now our ways would lie apart. Longing she felt, but no envy. She did not grudge me what she was denied....

\* \* \*

Father himself conducted us to school. He would not have delegated that mission to the President of the United States. He had awaited the day with impatience equal to mine, and the visions he saw as he hurried us over the sun-flecked pavements transcended all my dreams.... in his primary quest he had failed. There was left him the compensation of intellectual freedom. That he sought to realize in every possible way. He had very little opportunity to prosecute his education, which, in truth, had never been begun. His struggle for a bare living left him no time to take advantage of the public evening school; but he lost nothing of what was to he learned through reading, through attendance at public meetings, through exercising the rights of citizenship. Even here he was hindered by a natural inability to acquire the English language. In time, indeed, he learned to read, to follow a conversation or lecture; but he never learned to write correctly, and his pronunciation remains extremely foreign to this day.

If education, culture, the higher life were shining things to be worshipped from afar, he had still a means left whereby he could draw one step nearer to them. He could send his children to school, to learn all those things that he knew by fame to be desirable. The common school, at least, perhaps high school; for one or two, perhaps even college! His children should be students, should fill his house with books and intellectual company; and thus he would walk by proxy in the Elysian Fields of liberal learning. As for the children themselves, he knew no surer way to their advancement and happiness.

So it was with a heart full of longing and hope that my father led us to school on that first day. He took long strides in his eagerness, the rest of us running and hopping to keep up.

At last the four of us stood around the teacher's desk; and my father, in his impossible English, gave us over in her charge, with some broken word of his hopes for us that his swelling heart could no longer contain. I venture to say that Miss Nixon was struck by something uncommon in the group we made, something outside of Semitic features and the abashed manner of the alien. My little sister was as pretty as a doll, with her clear pink-and-white face, short golden curls, and eyes like blue violets when you caught them looking up. My brother might have been a girl, too, with his cherubic contours of face, rich red color, glossy black hair, and fine eyebrows. Whatever secret fears were in his heart, remembering his former teachers, who had taught with the rod, he stood up straight and uncringing before the American teacher, his cap respectfully doffed. Next to him stood a starved-looking girl with eyes ready to pop out, and short dark curls that would not have made much of a wig for a Jewish bride.

All three children carried themselves rather better than the common run of "green" pupils that were brought to Miss Nixon. But the figure that challenged attention to the group was the tall, straight father, with his earnest face and fine forehead, nervous hands eloquent in gesture, and a voice full of feeling. This foreigner, who brought his children to the school as if it were an act of consecration, who regarded the teacher of the primer class with reverence, who spoke of visions, like a man inspired, in a common schoolroom, was not like other aliens, who brought their children in dull obedience to the law; was not like the native fathers, who brought their unmanageable boys, glad to be relieved of their care. I think Miss Nixon guessed what my father's best English could not convey. I think she divined that by the simple act of delivering our school certificates to her he took possession of America.

# Language*

Assume for the moment that legal immigrants make an economy more efficient. Does that tell us all we need to know in order to understand their impact on our society? A national culture is held together by official rules and informal signals. Through their language, dress, taste, and habits of life, immigrants initially violate the rules and confuse the signals. The United States has prided itself on building a nation out of diverse parts. *E Pluribus Unum* originally referred to the act of political union in which separate colonies became one sovereign state. It now seems more fitting as a token of the cultural adjustments through which immigrant strangers have become Americans. Can the assimilative forces still prevail?

The question arises because most of today's immigrants share one trait: their native language is Spanish.

From 1970 to 1978, the three leading sources of legal immigrants to the U.S. were Mexico, the Philippines, and Cuba. About 42 percent of legal immigration during the seventies was from Latin America. It is thought that about half of all illegal immigrants come from Mexico, and 10 to 15 percent more from elsewhere in Latin America. Including illegal immigrants makes all figures imprecise, but it seems reasonable to conclude that more than half the people who now come to the United States speak Spanish. This is a greater concentration of immigrants in one non-English language group than ever before.

---

*From James Fallows, "The New Immigrants," *Atlantic Monthly,* Nov. 1983, pp. 45–68, 85–89. Reprinted by permission.

Is it a threat? The conventional wisdom about immigrants and their languages is that the Spanish-speakers are asking for treatment different from that which has been accorded to everybody else. In the old days, it is said, immigrants were eager to assimilate as quickly as possible. They were placed, sink or swim, in English-language classrooms, and they swam. But now the Latin Americans seem to be insisting on bilingual classrooms and ballots. "The Hispanics demand that the United States become a bilingual country, with all children entitled to be taught in the language of their heritage, at public expense," Theodore White has written. Down this road lie the linguistic cleavages that have brought grief to other nations.

This is the way many people think, and this is the way I myself thought as I began this project.

The historical parallel closest to today's concentration of Spanish-speaking immigrants is the German immigration of the nineteenth century. From 1830 to 1890, 4.5 million Germans emigrated to the United States, making up one third of the immigrant total. The Germans recognized that command of English would finally ensure for them, and especially for their children, a place in the mainstream of American society. But like the Swedes, Dutch, and French before them, they tried hard to retain the language in which they had been raised.

The midwestern states, where Germans were concentrated, established bilingual schools, in which children could receive instruction in German. In Ohio, German–English public schools were in operation by 1840; in 1837, the Pennsylvania legislature ordered that German-language public schools be established on an equal basis with English-language schools. Minnesota, Maryland, and Indiana also operated public schools in which German was used, either by itself or in addition to English. In *Life with Two Languages,* his study of bilingualism, François Grosjean says, "What is particularly striking about German Americans in the nineteenth century is their constant efforts to maintain their language, culture, and heritage."

"Yet despite everything the Germans could do, their language began to die out. The progression was slow and fraught with pain. For the immigrant, language was the main source of certainty and connection to the past. As the children broke from the Old World culture and tried out their snappy English slang on their parents, the pride the parents felt at such achievements was no doubt mixed with the bittersweet awareness that they were losing control.

At first the children would act as interpreters for their parents; then they would demand the independence appropriate to that role; then they would yearn to escape the coarse ways of immigrant life. And in the end, they would be Americans. It was hard on the families, but it built an assimilated English-language culture.

The pattern of assimilation is familiar from countless novels, as well as from the experience of many people now living. Why, then, is the currently fashionable history of assimilation so different? Why is it assumed, in so many discussions of bilingual education, that in the old days immigrants switched quickly and enthusiastically to English?

One reason is that the experience of Jewish immigrants in the early twentieth century was different from this pattern. German Jews, successful and thoroughly assimilated here in the nineteenth century, oversaw an effort to bring Eastern European Jews into the American mainstream as quickly as possible. In New York City, the Lower East Side's Hebrew Institute, later known as the Educational Alliance, defined its goal as teaching the newcomers "the privileges and duties of American citizenship." Although many Jewish immigrants preserved their Yiddish, Jews generally learned English faster than any other group.

Another reason that nineteenth-century linguistic history is so little remembered lies in the political experience of the early twentieth century. As an endless stream of New Immigrants arrived from Eastern Europe, the United States was awash in theories about the threats the newcomers posed to American economic, sanitary, and racial standards, and the "100 percent Americanism" movement arose. By the late 1880s, school districts in the Midwest had already begun reversing their early encouragement of bilingual education. Competence in English was made a requirement for naturalized citizens in 1906. Pro-English-language leagues sprang up to help initiate the New Immigrants. California's Commission on Immigration and Housing, for example, endorsed a campaign of "Americanization propaganda," in light of "the necessity for all to learn English—the language of America." With the coming of World War I, all German-language activities were suddenly cast in a different light. Eventually, as a result, Americans came to believe that previous immigrants had speedily switched to English, and to view the Hispanics' attachment to Spanish as a troubling aberration.

The term "Hispanic" is in many ways deceiving. It refers to those whose origins can be traced back to Spain *(Hispania)* or Spain's former colonies. It makes a bloc out of Spanish-speaking peoples who otherwise have little in common. The Cuban-Americans, concentrated in Florida, are flush with success. Some of them nurse dreams of political revenge against Castro. They demonstrate little solidarity with such other Hispanics as the Mexican-Americans of Texas, who are much less estranged from their homeland and who have been longtime participants in the culture of the Southwest. The Cuban-Americans tend to be Republicans; most Mexican-Americans and Puerto Ricans are Democrats. The Puerto Ricans, who are U.S. citizens from birth, and who have several generations of contact with American city life behind them, bear little resemblance to the Salvadorans and Guatemalans now pouring northward to get out of the way of war. Economically, the Puerto Ricans of New York City have more in common with American blacks than with most other Hispanic groups. Such contact as Anglo and black residents of Boston and New York have with Hispanic life comes mainly through Puerto Ricans; they may be misled about what to expect from the Mexicans and Central Americans arriving in ever increasing numbers. Along the southern border, Mexican-American children will razz youngsters just in from Mexico. A newcomer; called a "TJ," for Tijuana: it is the equivalent of "hillbilly" or "rube."

Still, "Hispanic" can be a useful word, because it focuses attention on the major question about this group of immigrants: Will their assimilation into an English-speaking culture be any less successful than that of others in the past?

To answer, we must consider what is different now from the circumstances under which the Germans, Poles, and Italians learned English.

The most important difference is that the host country is right next door. The only other non-English-speaking group for which this is true is the French-Canadians. Proximity has predictable consequences. For as long as the Southwest has been part of the United States, there has been a border culture in which, for social and commercial reasons, both languages have been used. There has also been a Mexican-American population accustomed to moving freely across the border, between the cultures, directing its loyalties both ways.

Because it has always been so easy to go home, many Mexicans and Mexican-Americans have displayed the classic sojourner outlook. The more total the break with the mother country, the more pressured immigrants feel to adapt; but for many immigrants from Mexico, whose kin and friends still live across the border and whose dreams center on returning in wealthy splendor to their native villages, the pressure is weak.

Many people have suggested that there is another difference, perhaps more significant than the first. It is a change in the nation's self-confidence. The most familiar critique of bilingual education holds that the nation no longer feels a resolute will to require mastery of the national language. America's most powerful assimilative force, the English language, may therefore be in jeopardy.

It is true that starting in the early 1960s U.S. government policy began to move away from the quick-assimilation approach preferred since the turn of the century. After surveys of Puerto Rican students in New York City and Mexican-Americans in Texas revealed that they were dropping out of school early and generally having a hard time, educational theorists began pushing plans for Spanish-language instruction. The turning point came with *Lau* v. *Nichols,* a case initiated in 1971 by Chinese-speaking students in San Francisco. They sued for "equal protection," on grounds that their unfamiliarity with English denied them an adequate education. In 1974, the Supreme Court ruled in their favor, saying that "those who do not understand English are certain to find their classroom experience wholly incomprehensible and in no way meaningful." The ruling did not say that school systems had to use bilingual programs of the kind that the phrase is now generally understood to mean—that is, classrooms in which both languages are used. The court said that "teaching English to the students…who do not speak the language" would be one acceptable solution. But the federal regulations and state laws that implemented the decision obliged many districts to set up the system of "transitional" bilingual education that has since become the focus of furor.

The rules vary from state to state, but they typically require a school district to set up a bilingual program whenever a certain number of students (often twenty) at one grade level are from one language group and do not speak English well. In principle, bilingual programs will enable them to keep up with the content of, say, their math and history courses while preparing them to enter the English-language classroom.

The bilingual system is accused of supporting a cadre of educational consultants while actually retarding the students' progress into the English-speaking mainstream. In this view, bilingual education could even be laying the foundation for a separate Hispanic culture, by extending the students' Spanish-language world from their homes to their schools.

Before I traveled to some of the schools in which bilingual education was applied, I shared the skeptics' view. What good could come of a system that encouraged, to whatever degree, a language other than the national tongue? But after visiting elementary, junior high, and high schools in Miami, Houston, San Antonio, Austin, several parts of Los Angeles, and San Diego, I found little connection between the political debate over bilingual education and what was going on in these schools.

To begin with, one central fact about bilingual education goes largely unreported. It is a *temporary* program. The time a typical student stays in the program varies from place to place—often two years in Miami, three years in Los Angeles—but when that time has passed, the student will normally leave. Why, then, do bilingual programs run through high school? Those classes are usually for students who are new to the district—usually because their parents are new to the country.

There is another fact about bilingual education, more difficult to prove but impressive to me, a hostile observer. Most of the children I saw were unmistakably learning to speak English.

In the elementary schools, where the children have come straight out of all-Spanish environments, the background babble seems to be entirely in Spanish. The kindergarten and first- to third-grade classrooms I saw were festooned with the usual squares and circles cut from colored construction paper, plus posters featuring Big Bird and charts about the weather and the seasons. Most of the schools seemed to keep a rough balance between English and Spanish in the lettering around the room; the most Spanish environment I saw was in one school in East Los Angeles, where about a third of the signs were in English.

The elementary school teachers were mostly Mexican-American women. They prompted the children with a mixture of English and Spanish during the day. While books in both languages are available in the classrooms, most of the first-grade reading drills I saw were in Spanish. In theory, children will learn the phonetic principle of reading more quickly if they are not trying to learn a new language at the same time. Once comfortable as readers, they will theoretically be able to transfer their ability to English.

In a junior high school in Houston, I saw a number of Mexican and Salvadoran students in their "bilingual" biology and math classes. They were drilled entirely in Spanish on the parts of an amoeba and on the difference between a parallelogram and a rhombus. When students enter bilingual programs at this level, the goal is to keep them current with the standard curriculum while introducing them to English. I found my fears of linguistic separatism rekindled by the sight of fourteen-year-olds lectured to in Spanish. I reminded myself that many of the students I was seeing had six months earlier lived in another country.

The usual next stop for students whose time in bilingual education is up is a class in intensive English, lasting one to three hours a day. These students are divided into two or three proficiency levels, from those who speak no English to those nearly ready to forgo special help. In Houston, a teacher drilled two-dozen high-school-age Cambodians, Indians, Cubans, and Mexicans on the crucial difference between the voiced *th* sound of "this" and the voiceless *th* of "thing." In Miami, a class of high school sophomores included youths from Cuba, El Salvador, and Honduras. They listened as their teacher read a Rockwellesque essay about a student with a crush on his teacher, and then set to work writing an essay of their own, working in words like "garrulous" and "sentimentalize."

One of the students in Miami, a sixteen-year-old from Honduras, said that his twelve-year-old brother had already moved into mainstream classes. Linguists say this is the standard pattern for immigrant children. The oldest children hold on to their first language longest, while their younger sisters and brothers swim quickly into the new language culture.

The more I saw of the classes, the more convinced I became that most of the students were learning English. Therefore, I started to wonder what it is about bilingual education that has made it the focus of such bitter disagreement.

For one thing, most immigrant groups other than Hispanics take a comparatively dim view of bilingual education. Haitians, Vietnamese, and Cambodians are eligible for bilingual education, but in general they are unenthusiastic. In Miami, Haitian boys and girls may learn to read in Creole rather than English. Still, their parents push to keep them moving into English. "A large number of [Haitian] parents come to the PTA meetings, and they don't want interpreters," said the principal of Miami's Edison Park Elementary School last spring. "They want to learn English. They don't want notices coming home in three languages. When they come here, unless there is total noncommunication, they will try to get through to us in their broken English. The students learn the language *very* quickly."

Bilingual education is inflammatory in large part because of what it symbolizes, not because of the nuts and bolts of its daily operation. In reality, bilingual programs move students into English with greater or lesser success; in reality, most Spanish-speaking parents understand that mastery of English will be their children's key to mobility. But in the political arena, bilingual education presents a different face. To the Hispanic ideologue, it is a symbol of cultural pride and political power. And once it has been presented that way, with full rhetorical flourish, it naturally strikes other Americans as a threat to the operating rules that have bound the country together.

Once during the months I spoke with and about immigrants I felt utterly exasperated. It was while listening to two Chicano activist lawyers in Houston who demanded to know why their people should be required to learn English at all. "It is unrealistic to think people can learn it that quickly," one lawyer said about the law that requires naturalized citizens to pass a test in English. *"Especially when they used to own this part of the country,* and when Spanish was the *historic language* of this region."

There is a historic claim for Spanish—but by the same logic there is a stronger claim for, say, Navajo as the historic language of the Southwest. The truth is that for more than a century the territory has been American and its national language has been English.

I felt the same irritation welling up when I talked with many bilingual instructors and policy-makers. Their arguments boiled down to: What's so special about English? They talked about the richness of the bilingual experience, the importance of maintaining the children's abilities in Spanish—even though when I watched the instructors in the classroom I could see that they were teaching principally English.

In my exasperation, I started to think that if such symbols of the dignity of language were so provocative to me, a comfortable member of the least-aggrieved ethnic group, it might be worth reflecting on the comparable sensitivities that lie behind the sentiments of the Spanish-speaking.

Consider the cases of Gloria Ramirez and Armandina Flores, who taught last year in the bilingual program at the Guerra Elementary School, in the Edgewood Independent School District, west of San Antonio.

San Antonio has evaded questions about the balance between rich and poor in its school system by carving the city up into independent school districts. Alamo Heights is the winner under this approach, and Edgewood is the loser. The Edgewood School District is perennially ranked as one of the poorest in the state. The residents are almost all Mexican-Americans or Mexicans. It is a settled community, without much to attract immigrants, but many stop there briefly on their way somewhere else, enough to give Edgewood a sizable illegal-immigrant enrollment.

In the middle of a bleak, sunbaked stretch of fields abutting a commercial vegetable farm, and within earshot of Kelly Air Force Base, sits Edgewood's Guerra School. It is an ordinary-looking but well-kept one-story structure that was built during the Johnson Administration. Nearly all the students are Mexican or Mexican-American.

Gloria Ramirez, who teaches first grade, is a compact, attractive woman of thirty-three, a no-nonsense veteran of the activist movements of the 1960s. Armandina Flores, a twenty-seven-year-old kindergarten teacher, is a beauty with dark eyes and long hair. During classroom hours, they deliver "Now, children" explanations of what is about to happen in both Spanish and English, although when the message really must get across, it comes in Spanish.

Both are remarkable teachers. They have that spark often thought to be missing in the public schools. There is no hint that for them this is just a job, perhaps because it symbolizes something very different from the worlds in which they were raised.

Gloria Ramirez was born in Austin, in 1950. Both of her parents are native Texans, as were two of her grandparents, but her family, like many other Mexican-American families, "spoke only Spanish when I was growing up," she says. None of her grandparents went to school at all. Her parents did not go past the third grade. Her father works as an auto-body mechanic; her mother raised the six children, and recently went to work at Austin State Hospital as a cleaner.

Ramirez began learning English when she started school; but the school, on Austin's east side, was overwhelmingly Mexican-American, part of the same culture she'd always known. The big change came when she was eleven. Her family moved to a working-class Anglo area in South Austin. She and her brother were virtually the only Mexican-Americans at the school. There was no more Spanish on the playground, or even at home. "My parents requested that we speak more English to them from then on," she says. "Both of them could speak it, but neither was comfortable."

"Before then, I didn't realize I had an accent. I didn't know until a teacher at the new school pointed it out in a ridiculing manner. I began learning English out of revenge." For six years, she took speech classes. "I worked hard so I could sound—like this," she says in standard American. She went to the University of Texas, where she studied history and philosophy and became involved in the Mexican-American political movements of the 1970s. She taught bilingual-education classes in Boston briefly before coming home to Texas.

Armandina Flores was born in Ciudad Acuña, Mexico, across the river from Del Rio, Texas. Her mother, who was born in Houston, was an American citizen, but *her* parents had returned to Mexico a few months after her birth, and she had never learned English. Flores's father was a Mexican citizen. When she reached school age, she began commuting across the river to a small Catholic school in Del Rio, where all the other students were Chicano. When she was twelve and about to begin the sixth grade, her family moved to Del Rio and she entered an American public school.

At that time, the sixth grade was divided into tracks, which ran from 6-1 at the bottom to 6-12. Most of the Anglos were at the top; Armandina Flores was initially placed in 6-4. She showed an aptitude for English and was moved up to 6-8. Meanwhile, her older sister, already held back once, was in 6-2. Her parents were proud of Armandina's progress; they began to depend on her English in the family's dealings in the Anglo world. She finished high school in Del Rio, went to Our Lady of the Lake College in San Antonio, and came to Edgewood as an aide in 1978, when she was twenty-two.

Considered one way, these two stories might seem to confirm every charge made by the opponents of bilingual education. Through the trauma of being plucked from her parents' comfortable Spanish-language culture and plunged into the realm of public language, Gloria Ramirez was strengthened, made a cosmopolitan and accomplished person. Her passage recalls the one Richard Rodriguez describes in *Hunger of Memory,* an autobiography that has become the most eloquent text for opponents of bilingual programs.

"Without question, it would have pleased me to hear my teachers address me in Spanish when I entered the classroom," Rodriguez wrote. "I would have felt much less afraid.... But I would have delayed—for how long postponed?—having to learn the language of public society."

Gloria Ramirez concedes that the pain of confused ethnicity and lost loyalties among Mexican-Americans is probably very similar to what every other immigrant group has endured. She even admits that she was drawn to bilingual education for political as well as educational reasons. As for Armandina Flores, hers is a calmer story of successful assimilation, accomplished without the crutch of bilingual education.

Yet both of these women insist, with an edge to their voices, that their students are fortunate not to have the same passage awaiting them.

It was a very wasteful process, they say. They swam; many others sank. "You hear about the people who make it, but not about all the others who dropped out, who never really learned," Ramirez says. According to the Mexican-American Legal Defense and Education Fund, 40 percent of Hispanic students drop out before they finish high school, three times as many as among Anglo students.

"Many people around here don't feel comfortable with themselves in either language," Ramirez says. Flores's older sister never became confident in English; "she feels like a lower person for it." She has just had a baby and is anxious that he succeed in English. Ramirez's older brother learned most of his English in the Marines. He is married to a Mexican immigrant and thinks that it is very important that their children learn English. And that is more likely to happen, the teachers say, if they have a transitional moment in Spanish.

Otherwise, "a child must make choices that concern his survival," Ramirez says. "He can choose to learn certain words, only to survive; but it can kill his desire to learn, period. Eventually he may be able to deal in the language, but he won't be educated." If the natural-immersion approach worked, why, they ask, would generation after generation of Chicanos, American citizens living throughout the Southwest, have lived and died without ever fully moving into the English-language mainstream?

These two teachers, and a dozen others with parallel experience, might be wrong in their interpretation of how bilingual education works. If so, they are making the same error as German, Polish, and Italian immigrants. According to the historians hired by the Select Commission, "Immigrants argued, when given the opportunity, that the security provided them by their cultures eased rather than hindered the transition." Still, there is room for reasonable disagreement about the most effective techniques for bringing children into English. A former teacher named Robert Rossier, for example, argues from his experience teaching immigrants that intensive courses in English are more effective than a bilingual transition. Others line up on the other side.

But is this not a question for factual resolution rather than for battles about linguistic and ethnic pride? Perhaps one approach will succeed for certain students in certain situations and the other will be best for others. The choice between bilingual programs and intensive-English courses, then, should be a choice between methods, not ideologies. The wars over bilingual education have had a bitter, symbolic quality. Each side has invested the issue with a meaning the other can barely comprehend. To most Mexican-American parents and children, bilingual education is merely a way of learning English; to Hispanic activists, it is a symbol that they are at last taking their place in the sun. But to many other Americans, it sounds like a threat not to assimilate.

"It is easy for Americans to take for granted, or fail to appreciate, the strength of American culture," says Henry Cisneros, the mayor of San Antonio. Cisneros is the first Mexican-American mayor of the country's most heavily Hispanic major city, a tall, grave man of thirty-six who is as clear a demonstration of the possibilities of ethnic assimilation as John Kennedy was. Cisneros gives speeches in Spanish and in English. Over the door that leads to his chambers, gilt letters spell out "Office of the Mayor" and, underneath, *"Oficina del Alcalde."* "I'm talking about TV programs, McDonald's, automobiles, the Dallas Cowboys. It is very pervasive. Mexican-Americans *like* the American way of life."

"These may sound like just the accouterments," Cisneros says. "I could also have mentioned due process of law; relations with the police; the way supermarkets work; the sense of participation, especially now that more and more Mexican-Americans are in positions of leadership. All of the things that shape the American way of life are indomitable."

In matters of civic culture, many Mexican-Americans, especially in Texas, act as custodians of the values the nation is said to esteem. They emphasize family, church, and patriotism of the most literal sort, expressed through military service. In the shrinelike position of honor in the sitting room, the same place where black families may have portraits of John F. Kennedy or Martin Luther King, a Mexican-American household in Texas will display a picture of the son or nephew in the Marines. Every time I talked with a Mexican-American about assimilation and separatism, I heard about the Mexican-American heroes and martyrs who have served in the nation's wars.

All the evidence suggests that Hispanics are moving down the path toward assimilation. According to a survey conducted in 1982 by Rodolfo de la Garza and Robert Brischetto for the Southwest Voter Registration Education Project, 11 percent of Chicanos (including a large number of illegal immigrants) were unable to speak English. The younger the people, the more likely they were to speak English. Ninety-four percent of those between the ages of eighteen and twenty-five could speak English, versus 78 percent of those aged sixty-six to eighty-seven. Not surprisingly, the English-speakers were better educated, had better jobs, and were less likely to have two foreign-born parents than the Spanish-speakers.

The details of daily life in Hispanic centers confirm these findings. The first impression of East Los Angeles or Little Havana is of ubiquitous Spanish, on the billboards and in the air. The second glance reveals former Chicano activists, now in their late thirties, bemused that their children have not really learned Spanish, or second-generation Cubans who have lost interest in liberating the motherland or in being Cubans at all.

Ricardo Romo says that when he taught Chicano studies at UCLA, his graduate students would go into the San Antonio *barrio* but could not find their way around, so much had they lost touch with the Spanish language. At a birthday party for a Chicano intellectual in Texas, amid piñatas and plates laden with *fajitas,* a birthday cake from a bakery was unveiled. It said "Happy Birthday" in Spanish—misspelled. There was pathos in that moment, but it was pathos that countless Italians, Poles, and Jews might understand.

With Mexico next door to the United States, the Mexican-American culture will always be different from that of other ethnic groups. Spanish will be a living language in the United States longer than any other alternative to English. But the movement toward English is inescapable.

In only one respect does the Hispanic impulse seem to me to lead in a dangerous direction. Hispanics are more acutely aware than most Anglos that, as a practical reality, English is the national language of commerce, government, and mobility. But some have suggested that, in principle, it should not be this way.

They invoke the long heritage of Mexican-Americans in the Southwest. As "Californios" or "Tejanos," the ancestors of some of these families lived on and owned the territory before the Anglo settlers. Others came across at the turn of the century, at a time of Mexican upheaval; still others came during the forties and fifties, as workers. They have paid taxes, fought in wars, been an inseparable part of the region's culture. Yet they were also subject to a form of discrimination more casual than the segregation of the Old South, but having one of the same effects. Because of poverty or prejudice or gerrymandered school districts, many Mexican-Americans were, in effect, denied education. One result is that many now in their fifties and sixties do not speak English well. Still, they are citizens, with the right of citizens to vote. How are they to exercise their right if to do so requires learning English? Do they not deserve a ballot printed in a language they can understand?

In the early seventies, the issue came before the courts, and several decisions held that if voters otherwise eligible could not understand English, they must have voting materials prepared in a more convenient language. In 1975, the Voting Rights Act amendments said that there must be bilingual ballots if more than 5 percent of the voters in a district were members of a "language minority group." The only "language minority groups" eligible under this ruling were American Indians, Alaskan natives, Asian-Americans (most significantly, Chinese and Filipinos), and Spanish-speakers. A related case extracted from the Sixth Circuit Court of Appeals the judgment that "the national language of the United States is English."

So it is that ballots in parts of the country are printed in Spanish, or Chinese, or Tagalog, along with English. This is true even though anyone applying for naturalization must still pass an English-proficiency test, which consists of questions such as "What are the three branches of government?' and "How long are the terms of a U.S. Senator and member of Congress?" The apparent inconsistency reflects the linguistic reality that many native-born citizens have not learned the national language.

By most accounts, the bilingual ballot is purely a symbol. The native-born citizens who can't read English often can't read Spanish, either. As a symbol, it points in the wrong direction, away from a single national language in which the public business will be done. Its only justification is the older generation, which was excluded from schools. In principle, then, it should be phased out in several years.

But there are those who feel that even the present arrangement is too onerous. Rose Matsui Ochi, an assistant to the mayor of Los Angeles, who served on the Select Commission, dissented from the commission's recommendation to keep the English-language requirement for citizenship. She wrote in her minority opinion, "Abolishing the requirement recognizes the inability of certain individuals to learn English." Cruz Reynoso, the first Mexican-American appointee to the California Supreme Court, was also on the Select

Commission, and he too dissented. "America is a *political* union—not a cultural, linguistic, religious or racial union," he wrote. "Of course, we as individuals would urge all to learn English, for that is the language used by most Americans, as well as the language of the marketplace. But we should no more demand English-language skills for citizenship than we should demand uniformity of religion. That a person wants to become a citizen and will make a good citizen is more than enough."

Some Chicano activists make the same point in less temperate terms. Twice I found myself in shouting matches with Mexican-Americans who asked me who I thought I was to tell them—after all the homeboys who had died in combat, after all the insults they'd endured on the playground for speaking Spanish—what language they "should" speak.

That these arguments were conducted in English suggests the theoretical nature of the debate. Still, in questions like this, symbolism can be crucial. "I have sympathy for the position that the integrating mechanism of a society is language," Henry Cisneros says. "The U.S. has been able to impose fewer such integrating mechanisms on its people than other countries, but it needs some tie to hold these diverse people, Irish, Jews, Czechs, together as a nation. Therefore, I favor people learning English and being able to conduct business in the official language of the country."

"The *unum* demands only certain things of the *pluribus,*" Lawrence Fuchs says. "It demands very little. It demands that we believe in the political ideals of the republic, which allows people to preserve their ethnic identity. Most immigrants come from repressive regimes; we say, we're asking you to believe that government should *not* oppress you. Then it only asks one other thing: that in the wider marketplace and in the civic culture, you use the official language. No other society asks so little.

"English is not just an instrument of mobility. It is a sign that you really are committed. If you've been here five years, which you must to be a citizen, and if you are reasonably young, you should be able to learn English in that time. The rest of us are entitled to that."

Most of the young people I met—the rank and file, not the intellectuals who espouse a bilingual society—seemed fully willing to give what in Fuchs's view the nation asks. I remember in particular one husky Puerto Rican athlete at Miami Senior High School who planned to join the Navy after he got his diploma. I talked to him in a bilingual classroom, heard his story, and asked his name. He told me, and I wrote *"Ramon."* He came around behind me and looked at my pad. "No, no!" he told me. "You should have put R-A-Y-M-O-N-D."

# A U.S. Bureau of Education Official on Education and the Chinese Migration (1875)*

## II.—Results to Be Arrived At

This incoming element, then, which must either greatly hamper or greatly help our national prosperity, which, perhaps we should say, must either overwhelm and smother, or immeasurably enlarge and enrich our political and social life, is to be controlled, not

*From H. N. Day, "The Chinese Migration," as quoted in U S. Bureau of Education, *Report of the Commissioner of Education for the Year 1870* (Washington, D.C., 1871). pp. 428–430.

checked; and we cannot too carefully and steadily keep before us the definite end to which all the particulars of this control should be directed. It is, in a proper sense perhaps of that expression, but a high peculiar sense, to be utilized. It is to be utilized after the laws of its own nature—after the principles of rational freedom in the most exact reciprocity of duty and privilege. It is to be assimilated to our own life and incorporated into it. The thorough Americanization of this new element is the comprehensive result which all political and individual endeavors in regard to them should seek. It is to be assimilated to the highest, completest form of our civilization, as intelligent, free, Christian.

It will prove a terrible pest and bane if it be allowed to have a place in our social system only as a foreign element, as fungous or parasitic. China has never known caste; America knows it no more. The institutions of both countries alike repel and abominate it. Only the greed or the tyranny of individuals, or of communities among us, can, and then only in spite of our fundamental laws and in audacious resistance to them, make a servile class of these immigrants; and the true way to prevent this result is not to stop back the stream, but arrest the iniquity that would poison it. Full and exact equality of social duty and privilege is the fundamental principle of all true and wise policy in the treatment of immigrants to our shores. The indispensable condition of our highest national well-being is the organic membership of all the races, all the kindreds, all the families, all the individuals dwelling among us, so that each shall minister and be ministered to, nourish and be nourished by, all the rest—one common pulsation beating through every element in our system.

Nor need any alarm be taken from outcries against the horrors of "amalgamation" and "miscegenation." These are mere bug-bears, invented by political cunning to frighten silly men, who do not understand that the freedom of our life and institutions assures, in the main, that social connections and alliances will be between parties best suited to each other, and therefore that public morality and decency will not be shocked by unseemly unions. At all events, history shows that whatever evil of this kind may arise, it is sporadic and exceptional, and can only be aggravated by governmental interference.

Chinese civilization has much that is in common to what is peculiar to American as distinguished from European civilization. Its principles of social equality, as before alluded to, its submission to law and authority rather than to hereditary and personal rule, its love of home and family, its requirement of universal education, its enforcement of political responsibility, are true American principles; and fresh importations will but help to overthrow and exterminate what of hostility to the free working of these principles the feudal and out-of-door life of European society has introduced among us. The characteristic vices of Chinese life are rather moral and religious than political, as their superstition, their idolatry, their gambling propensities, their love of opium, which last vice, it should be remarked, is but of recent introduction and of limited extent, forced, in a sense, upon them by foreign cupidity and power against their established laws. These vices are not to be kept out by a futile attempt to stop the providentially-ordered intercourse between nations, but to be cured by suitable moral means. Most certainly it would be very unwise to oppose their spread by closing the channels of intercommunication between members of our own political body. Fusion, rather than fencing and walling into separate fields, is the true result which wisdom prescribes.

This thorough incorporation into our common national life involves some particulars of policy which it may not be amiss to specify.

*The Adoption of the American Language*

The citizens of this country should speak the same language incorruptly. Diversity of dialects may possibly consist with a certain national unity and integrity; it is certainly ever a hinderance to it. The thoughts and sentiments of a people to be in accord and sympathy, to be healthful and nourishing in the fullest extent, must flow in and out, to and from the different parts, through the channel of a single dialect. A pure, uncorrupt English should be held forth as the indispensable attainment of every American citizen. Any corruption of our noble speech by foreign dialectic intermixtures, any *patois,* should be everywhere and by every means discountenanced and opposed. It is gratifying to learn that the Chinese immigrant shows no proclivity in himself to that miserable jargon called *Pigeon-English.* In North Adams he has nothing of it, knows nothing of it, desires nothing of it.

On the other hand, and positively, no more efficient means of assimilating foreigners to our mariners, our institutions, our national life, than the learning, the reading, the speaking our language habitually; than the habitual admission of all thoughts and sentiments, and the habitual utterance of them through the common speech of American life.

*Adoption of American Dress and Habits*

In common with the foreign dialect, the foreign dress and all the personal habits which are foreign to our manners should be replaced by such as are properly American. Every conspicuous badge of alienism should be avoided. It is one of the favorable prognostics of the experiment at North Adams that the American dress is adopted, so far as taste and comfort dictate. The fact indicates how far the treatment which the stranger receives at our hands may keep him from that isolation which is betrayed by the foreign dress and speech; how far that isolation, where it exists, is attributable to the social atmosphere into which he is brought.

*Adoption of American Homes*

A thorough American domestication is to be sought. The family life, as has been stated, is the predominant characteristic of the Chinese. The love and reverence paid among them to parents and to ancestors, the religious sentiments that they are trained to cherish toward the home of the family should be provided with the opportunities of gratification. They should be guided and helped to homes in America, where all the sacred relics of the departed may be securely and permanently enshrined, where the strong family feeling may be indulged and cherished. The low, narrow superstition that defies this worthy domestic disposition is to be eliminated by lifting and enlarging the filial sentiment from the earthly to the heavenly Father, so that the piety which rightly and naturally begins, and is fostered toward the natural parent, shall develop into a love and reverence for the eternal and supreme. There will be difficulty in this at the start. Work on railroads and in mines, and first employment in factories and in private households, must, of course, hinder separate establishment in dwellings. But certainly the settling down in families in the midst of native Americans, so that all the neighborhood intercourse of common life shall be in a fully American atmosphere, must have an influence in Americanizing that cannot be too highly estimated.

Most earnestly to be deprecated is the isolation of foreigners, and especially of Chinamen into separate villages, towns, or wards. The testimony is that the Chinaman is not more clannish than other men; but it is purely natural that common origin, common estrangement in regard to the land of their adoption, common dialect, should breed common sympathies, and should draw together. Thorough and complete Americanization is, however, hindered by all such isolation.

As the man is fashioned in the training of the child, and as the spirit of the nation is shaped in the family, it is of the first importance that not only the family life be maintained and protected, but also in order to the completest fusion that this family life be impregnated by the true American spirit, and be shaped after a pure American and Christian pattern. The family spirit which so characterizes the Chinaman should not be eradicated and supplanted, but only elevated and expanded.

### Adoption of American Manners

In like manner a full initiation into the peculiar social usages and manners of American life, so far, at least, as worthy, is to be desired, as also a free introduction into that vast diversity of our arts and occupations, as likewise into our religious usages and habits. Into this whole social life, this new element may bring in something that will liberalize, expand, enrich, as well as purify and elevate our manners, but it should be carefully grafted into the fundamental principles and spirit of our social order and economy, and not root itself and grow up a distinct and isolated growth.

### Admission to Citizenship

Finally, on the broadest, surest grounds of a true and wise policy, the Chinaman should be brought to a free participation in our political life. Intelligence and morality, indeed, should be the conditions of political rights and privileges; but such conditions only as are accorded to others should be imposed on him. His wonted training and spirit, as already observed, do not predispose him to seek political privileges, rather to shun them. He, therefore, needs no unusual checks. He is to be nationalized in his feelings and views, his characteristic family spirit being expanded into the proper love of country as the characteristic filial spirit rises and swells into reverence for the Divine Father of all. This is the only safe result for him, as for the country. The sordid calculations of political partisanship will doubtless often prompt to strong opposition to the naturalization of the Chinaman, perhaps sometimes seek to effect it too hastily, and with too much disregard of settled limitations and safeguards. The dangers of the too free admission of foreigners to citizenship will be as much exaggerated in the one case as underrated in the other. The one safe, desirable course is, under suitable limitations and conditions of intelligence, morality, time of residence, and the like, to bring in all that dwell among us into the full exercise of all political rights, and the corresponding participation in all political burdens and responsibilities.

### III.—Method of Attainment

To the question, now, how such thorough assimilation of this foreign element to American life after its highest type is best to be accomplished, all the facts in the case point to the answer: *By education under a right popular sentiment.*

This right popular sentiment in regard to the whole Chinese question is indispensable even to much success in any educational effort, for this must itself spring from an enlightened, philanthropic feeling, and be guided and sustained by this feeling, while all educational endeavors may be effectually prostrated by a strong popular sentiment arrayed in hostility, and bent on oppression or extermination. It is most important, therefore, that the public mind be carefully and accurately informed in respect to all the facts and principles involved in this question. It should be lifted above the low, mean selfishness which vitalizes the caste spirit in every form, whether industrial or political. It should be familiarized with the lofty, worthy views that are inspired at once by that superintending providence which has brought the swelling tide of population onward till it has reached our waiting continent, that it may spread over its wastes a reclaiming, regenerating life; and also by that noble spirit of philanthropy which from the first has extended a hand of welcome to all the oppressed and crushed from other lands.

## Q U E S T I O N S

1. Describe in your own words what freedom of education meant to Mary Antin, a Russian immigrant in the nineteenth century.

2. Explain how Mexican Americans in the Southwestern United States experienced a life situation similar to that of the Blacks in the southern part of the nation.

3. Compare the new immigrants from Mexico and Central and South America to the immigrants largely from Europe during the nineteenth century.

4. To Mary Antin's parents, was their dream of their children walking with Americans as Americans worth the cost? Explain your answer.

5. How important is it that all immigrants begin to speak English as soon as possible?

6. Should English speakers in the United States be obligated to learn another language? Why or why not?

# 14 The *Brown* Decisions

By the midtwentieth century, the NAACP's strategy of stressing the "equal" half of the separate but equal doctrine was having an effect. For example, in 1945 South Carolina spent three times as much for the education of each White child as it did for each Black child. Although still unacceptable, this expenditure represented considerable improvement from 1930, when the state spent eight times as much to educate a White child as it did to educate a Black child. With their successes in stressing that treatment, if separate, must be equal, the NAACP had established the foundation for challenging the constitutionality of the separate but equal doctrine.

In the early 1950s, court cases in Kansas, South Carolina, Virginia, and Delaware had been filed seeking admission of Black children to all-White schools. Once these cases reached the U.S. Supreme Court, Thurgood Marshall and other NAACP attorneys argued that the constitutional rights of their clients—the Black students—were being denied because segregated public schools were not equal and could not be made equal. Using the *Brown v the Board of Education of Topeka, Kansas,* case to rule on all four cases, the Supreme Court agreed that their decision must go beyond a comparison of the tangible differences between schools for Whites and "colored" (equipment, buildings, teacher salaries, etc.) to a consideration of the effect of segregation itself on public education. Recognizing the importance of educational opportunity for anyone wishing to succeed, the Supreme Court concluded that such an opportunity in which the state had undertaken to provide it became a right that must be available to all children on equal terms.

Convinced by the arguments presented by the NAACP, the Court concluded that segregation of White and Black children has a detrimental effect on the minority child. Segregation, especially when sanctioned by law, tends to stigmatize minority children as being inferior, thus affecting their desire to learn. In a landmark decision, this May 1954 ruling declared that separate educational facilities are inherently unequal. The doctrine of "separate but equal" has no place in public education.

A year later, in the *Brown II* ruling, the Supreme Court charged local school authorities in the South with the responsibility for eliminating segregated educational facilities. Instructing state and local governments to move "with all deliberate speed" in solving this problem, the ruling indicated that the federal courts would determine if local plans and actions constituted good faith in complying with the principles established in *Brown v Board of Education of Topeka, Kansas.* For many Black people the long-awaited integrated society would soon be a reality, and equality of educational opportunity would be theirs. If Blacks were euphoric, many Southerners were outraged. But as schools opened their doors each fall with little or no changes in the makeup of their student body, neither the jubilation of the Blacks nor the anger of the Whites was justified. As we discuss in the next Chapter the idea that Blacks and other so-called child races required a special education remained very much alive.

# Brown v. Board of Education (1954)*

### *Mr. Chief Justice Warren Delivered the Opinion of the Court*

These cases come to us from the States of Kansas, South Carolina, Virginia, and Delaware. They are premised on different facts and different local conditions, but a common legal question justifies their consideration together in this consolidated opinion.[1]

In each of the cases, minors of the Negro race, through their legal representatives, seek the aid of the courts in obtaining admission to the public schools of their community, on a nonsegregated basis. In each instance, they had been denied admission to schools attended by white children under laws requiring or permitting segregation according to race. This segregation was alleged to deprive the plaintiffs of the equal protection of the laws under the Fourteenth Amendment. In each of the cases other than the Delaware case, a three-judge federal district court denied relief to the plaintiffs on the so-called "separate but equal" doctrine announced by this Court in *Plessy* v. *Ferguson,* 163 U.S. 537. Under

---

*From *Brown et al* v. *Board of Education of Topeka et al.,* 347 U.S. 483 (1954).

[1]In the Kansas case, *Brown* v. *Board of Education,* the plaintiffs are Negro children of elementary school age residing in Topeka. They brought this action in the United States District Court for the District of Kansas to enjoin enforcement of Kansas statute which permits, but does not require, cities of more than 15,000 population to maintain separate school facilities for Negro and white students. Kan. Gen. Stat. § 72-1724 (1949). Pursuant to that authority, the Topeka Board of Education elected to establish segregated elementary schools. Other public schools in the community, however, are operated on a nonsegregated basis. The three-judge District Court, convened under 28 U.S.C. § 2281 and 2284, found that segregation in public education has a detrimental effect upon Negro children, but denied relief on the ground that the Negro and white schools were substantially equal with respect to buildings, transportation, curricula, and educational qualifications of teachers. 98 F. Supp. 797. The case is here on direct appeal under 28 U.S.C. § 1253.

In the South Carolina case, *Briggs* v. *Elliott,* the plaintiffs are Negro children of both elementary and high school age residing in Clarendon County. They brought this action in the United States District Court for the Eastern District of South Carolina to enjoin enforcement of previsions in the state constitution and statutory code which require the segregation of Negroes and whites in public schools. S.C. Const., Art. XI, § 7; S.C. Code § 5377 5377 (1942). The three-judge District Court, convened under 28 U.S.C. § 2281 and 2284, denied the requested relief. The court found that the Negro schools were inferior to the white schools and ordered the defendants to begin immediately to equalize the facilities. But the court sustained the validity of the contested provisions and denied the plaintiffs admission to the white schools during the equalization program. 98 F. Supp. 529. This Court vacated the District Court's judgement and remanded the case for the purpose of obtaining the court's views on a report filed by the defendants concerning the progress made in the equalization program. 342 U.S. 350. On remand, the District Court found that substantial equality had been achieved except for buildings and that the defendants were proceeding to rectify this inquality as well. 103 F. Supp. 920. The case is again here on direct appeal under 28 U.S.C. § 1253.

*Footnote continues*

that doctrine, equality of treatment is accorded when the races are provided substantially equal facilities, even though these facilities be separate. In the Delaware case, the Supreme Court of Delaware adhered to that doctrine, but ordered that the plaintiffs be admitted to the white schools because of their superiority to the Negro schools.

The plaintiffs contend that segregated public schools are not "equal" and cannot be made "equal," and that hence they are deprived of the equal protection of the laws. Because of the obvious importance of the question presented, the Court took jurisdiction. Argument was heard in the 1952 Term and reargument was heard this Term on certain questions propounded by the Court.

Reargument was largely devoted to the circumstances surrounding the adoption of the Fourteenth Amendment in 1868. It covered exhaustively consideration of the Amendment in Congress, ratification by the states, then-existing practices in racial segregation, and the views of proponents and opponents of the Amendment. This discussion and our own investigation convince us that, although these sources cast some light, it is not enough to resolve the problem with which we are faced. At best, they are inconclusive. The most avid proponents of the post-War Amendments undoubtedly intended them to remove all legal distinctions among "all persons born or naturalized in the United States." Their opponents, just as certainly, were antagonistic to both the letter and the spirit of the Amendments and wished them to have the most limited effect. What others in Congress and the state legislatures had in mind cannot be determined with any degree of certainty.

An additional reason for the inconclusive nature of the Amendment's history, with respect to segregated schools, is the status of public education at that time. In the South, the movement toward free common schools, supported by general taxation, had not yet taken hold. Education of white children was largely in the hands of private groups. Education of

---

[1](Continued) In the Virginia case, *Davis* v. *County School Board,* the plaintiffs are Negro children of high school age residing in Prince Edward County. They brought this action in the United States District Court for the Eastern District of Virginia to enjoin enforcement of provisions in the state constitution and statutory code which require the segregation of Negroes and whites in public schools. Va. Const., § 140; Va. Code § 22–221 (1950). The three-judge District Court, convened under 28 U.S.C. § 2281 and 2284, denied the requested relief. The court found the Negro school inferior in physical plant, curricula, and transportation and to "proceed with all reasonable diligence and dispatch to remove" the inequality in physical plant. But, as in the South Carolina case, the court sustained the validity of the contested provisions and denied the plaintiffs admission to the white schools during the equalization program. 103 F. Supp. 337. The case is here on direct appeal under 28 U.S.C. § 1253.

In the Delaware case, *Gebhart* v. *Belton,* the plaintiffs are Negro children of both elementary and high school age residing in New Castle County. They brought this action in the Delaware Court of Chancery to enjoin enforcement of provisions in the state constitution and statutory code which require the segregation of Negroes and whites in public schools. Del. Const., Art. X, § 2; Del. Rev. Code § 2631 (1935). The Chancellor gave judgment for the plaintiffs and ordered their immediate admission to schools previously attended only by white children, on the ground that the Negro schools were inferior with respect to teacher training, pupil-teacher ratio, extracurricular activities, physical plant, and time and distance involved in travel. 87 A 2d 862. The Chancellor also found that segregation itself results in an inferior education for Negro children (see note 10, *infra*), but did not rest his decision on that ground. *Id.,* at 865. The Chancellor's decree was affirmed by the Supreme Court of Delaware, which intimated, however, that the defendants might be able to obtain a modification of the decree after equalization of the Negro and white schools had been accomplished. 91 A. 2d 137, 152. The defendants, contending only that the Delaware courts had erred in ordering the immediate admission of the Negro plaintiffs to the white school, applied to this Court for certiorari. The writ was granted, 344 U.S. 891. The plaintiffs, who were successful below, did not submit a cross-petition.

Negroes was almost nonexistent, and practically all of the race were illiterate. In fact, any education of Negroes was forbidden by law in some states. Today, in contrast, many Negroes have achieved outstanding success in the arts and sciences as well as in the business and professional world. It is true that public school education at the time of the Amendment had advanced further in the North, but the effect of the Amendment on Northern States was generally ignored in the congressional debates. Even in the North, the conditions of public education did not approximate those existing today. The curriculum was usually rudimentary; ungraded schools were common in rural areas; the school term was but three months a year in many states; and compulsory school attendance was virtually unknown. As a consequence, it is not surprising that there should be so little in the history of the Fourteenth Amendment relating to its intended effect on public education.

In the first cases in this Court construing the Fourteenth Amendment, decided shortly after its adoption, the Court interpreted it as proscribing all state-imposed discriminations against the Negro race. The doctrine of "separate but equal" did not make its appearance in this Court until 1896 in the case of *Plessy* v. *Ferguson, supra,* involving not education but transportation. American courts have since labored with the doctrine for over half a century. In this Court, there have been six cases involving the "separate but equal" doctrine in the field of public education. In *Cumming* v. *County Board of Education,* 175 U.S. 528, and *Gong Lum* v. *Rice,* 275 U.S. 78, the validity of the doctrine itself was not challenged. In more recent cases, all on the graduate school level, inequality was found in that specific benefits enjoyed by white students were denied to Negro students of the same educational qualifications. *Missouri ex rel. Gaines* v. *Canada,* 305 U.S. 337; *Sipuel* v. *Oklahoma,* 332 U.S. 631; *Sweatt* v. *Painter,* 339 U.S. 629: *McLaurin* v. *Oklahoma State Regents,* 339 U.S. 637. In none of these cases was it necessary to re-examine the doctrine to grant relief to the Negro plaintiff. And in *Sweatt* v. *Painter, supra,* the Court expressly reserved decision on the question whether *Plessy* v. *Ferguson* should be held inapplicable to public education.

In the instant cases, that question is directly presented. Here, unlike *Sweatt* v. *Painter,* there are findings below that the Negro and white schools involved have been equalized, or are being equalized, with respect to buildings, curricula, qualifications and salaries of teachers, and other "tangible" factors. Our decision, therefore, cannot turn on merely a comparison of these tangible factors in the Negro and white schools involved in each of the cases. We must look instead to the effect of segregation itself on public education.

In approaching this problem, we cannot turn the clock back to 1868 when the Amendment was adopted, or even to 1896 *Plessy* v. *Ferguson* was written. We must consider public education in the light of its full development and its present place in American life throughout the Nation. Only in this way can it be determined if segregation in public schools deprives these plaintiffs of the equal protection of the laws.

Today, education is perhaps the most important function of state and local governments. Compulsory school attendance laws and the great expenditures for education both demonstrate our recognition of the importance of education to our democratic society. It is required in the performance of our most basic public responsibilities, even service in the armed forces. It is the very foundation of good citizenship. Today it is a principal instrument in awakening the child to cultural values, in preparing him for later professional training, and in helping him to adjust normally to his environment. In these days, it is doubtful that any child may reasonably be expected to succeed in life if he is denied the opportunity of an education. Such an opportunity, where the state has undertaken to provide it, is a right which must be made available to all on equal terms.

We come then to the question presented: Does segregation of children in public schools solely on the basis of race, even though the physical facilities and other "tangible" factors may be equal, deprive the children of the minority group of equal educational opportunities? We believe that it does.

In *Sweatt* v. *Painter,supra,* in finding that a segregated law school for Negroes could not provide them equal educational opportunities, this Court relied in large part on "those qualities which are incapable of objective measurement but which make for greatness in a law school." In *McLaurin* v. *Oklahoma State Regents, supra,* the Court, in requiring that a Negro admitted to a white graduate school be treated like all other students, again resorted to intangible considerations: "…his ability to study, to engage in discussions and exchange views with other students, and, in general, to learn his profession." Such considerations apply with added force to children in grade and high schools. To separate them from others of similar age and qualifications solely because of their race generates a feeling of inferiority as to their status in the community that may affect their hearts and minds in a way unlikely ever to be undone. The effect of this separation on their educational opportunities was well stated by a finding in the Kansas case by a court which nevertheless felt compelled to rule against the Negro plaintiffs:

> Segregation of white and colored children in public schools has a detrimental effect upon the colored children. The impact is greater when it has the sanction of the law; for the policy of separating the races is usually interpreted as denoting the inferiority of the negro group A sense of inferiority affects the motivation of a child to learn. Segregation with the sanction of law, therefore, has a tendency to [retard] the educational and mental development of negro children and to deprive them of some of the benefits they would receive in a racial[ly] integrated school system.

Whatever may have been the extent of psychological knowledge at the time of *Plessy* v. *Ferguson,* this finding is amply supported by modern authority.[2] Any language in *Plessy* v. *Ferguson* contrary to this finding is rejected.

We conclude that in the field of public education the doctrine of "separate but equal" has no place. Separate educational facilities are inherently unequal. Therefore, we hold that the plaintiffs and others similarly situated for whom the actions have been brought are, by reason of the segregation complained of, deprived of the equal protection of the laws guaranteed by the Fourteenth Amendment. This disposition makes unnecessary any discussion whether such segregation also violates the Due Process Clause of the Fourteenth Amendment.

Because these are class actions, because of the wide applicability of this decision, and because of the great variety of local conditions, the formulation of decrees in these

---

[2]K. B. Clark, Effect of Prejudice and Discrimination on Personality Development (Midcentury White House Conference on Children and Youth, 1950); Witmer and Kotinsky, Personality in the Making (1952), c. VI; Deutscher and Chein, The Psychological Effects of Enforced Segregation: A Survey of Social Science Opinion, 26 J. Psychol. 259 (1948): Chein, What are the Psychological Effects of Segregation Under Conditions of Equal Facilities?, 3 Int. J. Opinion and Attitude Res. 229 (1949); Brameld, Educational Costs, in Discrimination and National Welfare (MacIver, ed., 1949), 44–48; Frazier, The Negro in the United States (1949), 674–681. And see generally Myrdal, An American Dilemma (1944).

cases presents problems of considerable complexity. On reargument, the consideration of appropriate relief was necessarily subordinated to the primary question—the constitutionality of segregation in public education. We have now announced that such segregation is a denial of the equal protection of the laws. In order that we may have the full assistance of the parties in formulating decrees, the cases will be restored to the docket, and the parties are requested to present further argument on Questions 4 and 5 previously propounded by the Court for the reargument this Term. The Attorney General of the United States is again invited to participate. The Attorneys General of the states requiring or permitting segregation in public education will also be permitted to appear as *amici curiae* upon request to do so by September 15, 1954, and submission of briefs by October 1, 1954.

*It is so ordered.*

## "With All Deliberate Speed" (1955)*

### *Mr. Chief Justice Warren Delivered the Opinion of the Court*

These cases were decided on May 17, 1954. The opinions of that date, declaring the fundamental principle that racial discrimination in public education is unconstitutional, are incorporated herein by reference. All provisions of federal, state, or local law requiring or permitting such discrimination must yield to this principle. There remains for consideration the manner in which relief is to be accorded.

Because these cases arose under different local conditions and their disposition will involve a variety of local problems, we requested further argument on the question of relief. In view of the nationwide importance of the decision, we invited the Attorney General of the United States and the Attorneys General of all states requiring or permitting racial discrimination in public education to present their views on that question. The parties, the United States, and the States of Florida, North Carolina, Arkansas, Oklahoma, Maryland, and Texas filed briefs and participated in the oral argument.

These presentations were informative and helpful to the Court in its consideration of the complexities arising from the transition to a system of public education freed of racial discrimination. The presentations also demonstrated that substantial steps to eliminate racial discrimination in public schools have already been taken, not only in some of the communities in which these cases arose, but in some of the states appearing as *amici curiae,* and in other states as well. Substantial progress has been made in the District of Columbia and in the communities in Kansas and Delaware involved in this litigation. The defendants in the cases coming to us from South Carolina and Virginia are awaiting the decision of this Court concerning relief.

Full implementation of these constitutional principles may require solution of varied local school problems. School authorities have the primary responsibility for elucidating, assessing, and solving these problems; courts will have to consider whether the action of school authorities constitutes good faith implementation of the governing constitutional principles. Because of their proximity to local conditions and the possible need for further

*From *Brown* v. *Board of Education.* 349 U.S. 294.

hearings, the courts which originally heard these cases can best perform this judicial appraisal. Accordingly, we believe it appropriate to remand the cases to those courts.

In fashioning and effectuating the decrees, the courts will be guided by equitable principles. Traditionally, equity has been characterized by a practical flexibility in shaping its remedies and by a facility for adjusting and reconciling public and private needs. These cases call for the exercise of these traditional attributes of equity power. At stake is the personal interest of the plaintiffs in admission to public schools as soon as practicable on a nondiscriminatory basis. To effectuate this interest may call for elimination of a variety of obstacles in making the transition to school systems operated in accordance with the constitutional principles set forth in our May 17, 1954, decision. Courts of equity may properly take into account the public interest in the elimination of such obstacles in a systematic and effective manner. But it should go without saying that the vitality of these constitutional principles cannot be allowed to yield simply because of disagreement with them.

While giving weight to these public and private considerations, the courts will require that the defendants make a prompt and reasonable start toward full compliance with our May 17, 1954, ruling. Once such a start has been made, the courts may find that additional time is necessary to carry out the ruling in an effective manner. The burden rests upon the defendants to establish that such time is necessary in the public interest and is consistent with good faith compliance at the earliest practicable date. To that end, the courts may consider problems related to administration, arising from the physical condition of the school plant, the school transportation system, personnel, revision of school districts and attendance areas into compact units to achieve a system of determining admission to the public schools on a nonracial basis, and revision of local laws and regulations which may be necessary in solving the foregoing problems. They will also consider the adequacy of any plans the defendants may propose to meet these problems and to effectuate a transition to a racially nondiscriminatory school system. During this period of transition, the courts will retain jurisdiction of these cases.

The judgments below, except that in the Delaware case, are accordingly reversed and the cases are remanded to the District Courts to take such proceedings and enter such orders and decrees consistent with this opinion as are necessary and proper to admit to public schools on a racially nondiscriminatory basis with all deliberate speed the parties to these cases. The judgement in the Delaware case—ordering the immediate admission of the plaintiffs to schools previously attended only by white children—is affirmed on the basis of the principles stated in our May 17, 1954, opinion, but the case is remanded to the Supreme Court of Delaware for such further proceedings as that Court may deem necessary in light of this opinion.

*It is so ordered.*


# QUESTIONS

1. Explain the arguments by Thurgood Marshall and other NAACP attorneys suggesting that segregated public schools were not equal and could not be made equal.

2. What other states besides Kansas had cases filed seeking admission of Black children to all-White schools?

3. What role did the *Plessy v Ferguson* decision play in the federal district court decision to deny access of the Black children to all-White schools?

4. Summarize the explanation provided in the 1954 *Brown* decision regarding the Fourteenth Amendment's lack of effect on public education.

5. Explain in your own words the impact that "intangible considerations"—raised in both the *McLaurin* and *Sweatt* cases—had in the 1954 *Brown* decision.

6. Describe in your own words the "psychological" knowledge that the U.S. Supreme Court found so compelling in ruling that the doctrine of "separate but equal" has no place in public education.

7. After declaring "separate but equal" unconstitutional, why did the Supreme Court wait a year to issue directives for implementing the decision?

8. What role, if any, did the legacy of local control of education contribute to the decision in the 1955 *Brown* ruling to allow federal district courts to assume responsibility for implementing the 1954 decision? Explain your answer.

9. Would it have been better for the Supreme Court to demand the immediate end of segregated public schools rather than encouraging school districts—under the supervision of federal district courts—to "move with all deliberate speed" toward unitary systems?

# CHAPTER

# 15 Affirmative Action

## The Next Step

Even though the *Brown* v. *the Board of Education of Topeka, Kansas,* decisions made racially segregated schools illegal, desegregation proceeded at a snail's pace. A decade after the first *Brown* ruling, only 2 percent of black students were attending school with White children. In the South where *de jure* segregation was common, local school districts established "freedom of choice" plans, ostensibly allowing any child in the district to attend the school of his or her choice. In reality, dual systems for Whites and "Colored" remained largely intact as the economic and social forces essentially denied Black children the opportunity to attend schools with White children. By the mid-1960s, federal courts began to lose patience with White southern intransigence. The courts' impatience, when combined with federal legislation such as the Civil Rights Act of 1964 and the Elementary and Secondary Education Act of 1965, resulted in substantial integration of the public schools during the next decade.

Title VI of the 1964 Civil Rights Act forbids discrimination in any federally funded program, but since little federal aid was going to U.S. schools, the law had little impact on the schools. This changed the next year, with the passage of the Elementary and Secondary Education Act. By making substantial federal dollars available to needy school districts, the ESEA loaded the weapon established by Title VI of the 1964 Civil Rights Act. To be eligible for these federal funds, school districts had to demonstrate that "no person...shall, on the grounds of race, color, or national origin, be excluded from participation in, be denied the benefits of, or be subjected to discrimination under any program or activity receiving Federal financial assistance."

The Supreme Court joined Congress in taking affirmative action to eliminate racially segregated schools in a 1968 case known as *Green* v *County School Board of New Kent, Virginia.* In its ruling, the Supreme Court held that school authorities were "clearly charged with the affirmative duty to take whatever steps might be necessary to convert to a unitary system in which racial discrimination would be eliminated root and branch." In short, this ruling placed the burden on school districts to come up with realistic plans for eliminating dual systems immediately. The growing impatience with school districts' circumvention of the *Brown* decision for more than a decade led inevitably to busing as a means of achieving an integrated school system.

Building on the decision in the *Green* case that "the burden on a school board today is to come forward with a plan that promises realistically to work now...," the Supreme Court ordered busing as the means for achieving a unitary school in the *Swann v Charlotte-*

*Mecklenburg Board of Education case.* Charlotte-Mecklenburg, a combined city-county school system in North Carolina enrolling more than 84,000 students in 1968–1969, had submitted to the federal district court a "freedom of choice" plan that purportedly abolished the dual system of schooling for Negro and White students. In reality, during the 1968–1969 school year, 14,000 of the 29,000 Black students in the district attended schools that were 99 percent Black. Because this plan did not comply with the spirit of the *Brown* decisions, the Supreme Court ordered Charlotte-Mecklenburg to eliminate the dual system immediately and establish a unitary system without delay.

The Court held that school authorities have an obligation to prepare students for a pluralistic world. Hence, the ratio of Black and White students in each school should reflect the proportion in the district as a whole. If the district failed or refused to achieve such a racial balance, a federal district court would step in and impose a remedy ensuring a unitary school district. The district's inability to develop an acceptable plan resulted in a Court-ordered busing plan designed to ensure a racially integrated school system.

Virtually everyone agreed that absent any previous history of racial discrimination, school children should be allowed to attend the school nearest their home. In Charlotte and other school districts across the land, the social goal of eliminating racial discrimination took precedence over the individual preference for the neighborhood school. Busing, as a means of achieving racially integrated schools, continued well into the 1980s to be a controversial issue. In response to public opinion polls suggesting that the majority of Americans opposed it, court ordered busing became a political issue at the local, state, and national levels. In some cases, court-ordered busing contributed to "White flight" as middle- and upper-class families abandoned city public schools for suburban public and private schools. Even the Black community questioned the desirability of busing because Black children were generally bused more often and further than were White children.

Busing, more than any recent phenomenon, brings into the focus the age-old conflict between individual wants and societal demands. In the United States, where school reform has replaced revolutions as the mechanism for social change, busing compels us to revisit the question of how much can or should schools contribute to correcting old wrongs and/or to promoting the common good.

# The Civil Rights Act of 1964*

## *Title IV—Public Education*

Under this title the U.S. Office of Education is authorized to:

**a.** conduct a national survey to determine the availability of equal educational opportunity;

**b.** provide technical assistance, upon request, to help States, political subdivisions or school districts carry out school desegregation plans;

---

*From U.S. Commission on Civil Rights, Civil Rights Digest, *Special Bulletin* (August, 1964), Appendix.

   **c.** arrange training institutes to prepare teachers and other school personnel to deal with desegregation problems;

   **d.** make grants enabling school boards to employ specialists for in-service training programs.

In addition, the Attorney General is authorized to file civil suits seeking to compel desegregation of public schools, including public colleges.

Before filing such a suit the Attorney General must have received a signed complaint from a pupil or parent and must have determined that the complainant, according to standards set forth in the Act, is unable to bring the action. The Attorney General is also required to notify the school board and give it a reasonable period of time to correct the alleged condition before filing suit.

* * *

### *Title VI—Federally Assisted Programs*

Under this title every Federal agency which provides financial assistance through grants, loans or contracts is required to eliminate discrimination on the grounds of race, color or national origin in these programs.

For example, this title would require the following:

   **a.** hospitals constructed with Federal funds would have to serve all patients without regard to race, color or national origin;

   **b.** elementary and secondary schools constructed, maintained and operated with Federal funds would have to admit children without regard to race, color or national origin;

   **c.** State employment services financed by Federal funds would have to refer qualified job applicants for employment without discrimination;

   **d.** schools for the deaf and the blind operated with Federal funds would have to serve the deaf and blind of any color;

   **e.** colleges and universities receiving funds for their general operation or for the construction of special facilities, such as research centers, would have to admit students without discrimination;

   **f.** construction contractors receiving funds under Federal public work programs would have to hire employees without discrimination.

Action by a Federal agency to carry out the requirements of this title may include the terminating of programs where discrimination is taking place or refusal to grant assistance to such a program.

Each agency is required to publish rules or regulations to carry out the purposes of the title. These rules and regulations are subject to the approval of the President.

Compliance actions are subject to the following conditions:

   **a.** notice must be given of alleged failure to comply and an opportunity for a hearing must be provided;

   **b.** in the event assistance is to be cut off, a written report must be submitted to Congress 30 days before the cut-off date;

   **c.** compliance action may be appealed to the courts.

Social security and veteran's benefits, and other Federal benefits distributed directly to individuals are not affected by this law.

Federal assistance in the form of insurance or guaranty—for example, FHA insured loans—are not covered by this title (however, the President's Executive Order prohibiting discrimination in Federally aided housing remains in effect).

# President Lyndon Johnson's Call upon Congress to Pass Elementary and Secondary Education Act (1965)*

*To the Congress of the United States:*

In 1787, the Continental Congress declared in the Northwest Ordinance:
"Schools and the means of education shall forever be encouraged."
America is strong and prosperous and free because for 178 years we have honored that commitment.

In the United States today—

One-quarter of all Americans are in the Nation's classrooms.

High school attendance has grown eighteenfold since the turn of the century—six times as fast as the population.

College enrollment has advanced eightfold. Americans today support a fourth of the world's institutions of higher learning and a third of its professors and college students.

In the life of the individual, education is always an unfinished task.
And in the life of this Nation, the advancement of education is a continuing challenge.
There is a darker side to education in America:

One student out of every three now in the fifth grade will drop out before finishing high school—if the present rate continues.

Almost a million young people will continue to quit school each year—if our schools fail to stimulate their desire to learn.

Over 100,000 of our brightest high school graduates each year will not go to college—and many others will leave college—if the opportunity for higher education is not expanded.

The cost of this neglect runs high—both for the youth and the Nation:

Unemployment of young people with an eighth grade education or less is four times the national average.

Jobs filled by high school graduates rose by 40 percent in the last 10 years. Jobs for those with less schooling decreased by nearly 10 percent.

We can measure the cost in even starker terms. We now spend about $450 a year per child in our public schools. But we spend $1,800 a year to keep a delinquent youth in a detention home, $2,500 a year for a family on relief, $3,500 a year for a criminal in State prison.

*From House Document No. 45, 89th Cong., 1st Sess. (1965), pp. 1–3.

The growing numbers of young people reaching school age demand that we move swiftly even to stand still.

> Attendance in elementary and secondary schools will increase by 4 million in the next 5 years; 400,000 new classrooms will be needed to meet this growth. But almost one-half million of the Nation's existing classrooms are already more the 30 years old.
>
> The post-World War II boom in babies has now reached college age. And by 1970, our colleges must be prepared to add 50 percent more enrollment to their presently over-crowded facilities.

In the past, Congress has supported an increasing commitment to education in America. Last year, I signed historic measures passed by the 88th Congress to provide—

> Facilities badly needed by universities, colleges, and community colleges;
> Major new resources for vocational training;
> More loans and fellowships for students enrolled in higher education; and
> Enlarged and improved training for physicians, dentists, and nurses.

I propose that the 89th Congress join me in extending the commitment still further. I propose that we declare a national goal of

### *Full Educational Opportunity*

Every child must be encouraged to get as much education as he has the ability to take.

We want this not only for his sake—but for the Nation's sake.

Nothing matters more to the future of the country: not our military preparedness, for armed might is worthless if we lack the brainpower to build a world of peace; not our productive economy, for we cannot sustain growth without trained manpower, not our democratic system of government, for freedom is fragile if citizens are ignorant.

We must demand that our schools increase not only the quantity but the quality of America's education. For we recognize that nuclear age problems cannot be solved with horse-and-buggy learning. The three R's of our school system must be supported by the three T's—teachers who are superior, techniques of instruction that are modern, and thinking about education which places it first in all our plans and hopes.

Specifically, four major tasks confront us—

> to bring better education to millions of disadvantaged youth who need it most;
> to put the best educational equipment and ideas and innovations within reach of all students;
> to advance the technology of teaching and the training of teachers; and
> to provide incentives for those who wish to learn at every stage along the road to learning.

Our program must match the magnitude of these tasks. The budget on education which I request for fiscal year 1966 will contain a total of $4.1 billion. This includes $1.1 billion to finance programs established by the 88th Congress. I will submit a request for $1.5 billion in new obligational authority to finance the programs described in this message. This expenditure is a small price to pay for developing our Nation's most priceless resource.

In all that we do, we mean to strengthen our State and community education systems. Federal assistance does not mean Federal control—as past programs have proven. The late Senator Robert Taft declared:

> Education is primarily a State function—in the field of education, as in the fields of health, relief. and medical care, the Federal Government has a secondary obligation to see that there is a basic floor under those essential services for all adults and children in the United States.

In this spirit, I urge that we now push ahead with the No. 1 business of the American people—the education of our youth in preschools, elementary and secondary schools, and in the colleges and universities.

# Eliminate Racial Discrimination Root and Branch*

### *Mr. Justice Brennan Delivered the Opinion of a Unanimous Court (1968)*

Petitioners brought this action in March 1965 seeking injunctive relief against respondent's continued maintenance of an alleged racially segregated school system. New Kent County is a rural county in Eastern Virginia. About one-half of its population of some 4,500 are Negroes. There is no residential segregation in the county; persons of both races reside throughout. The school system has only two schools, the New Kent school on the east side of the county and the George W. Watkins school on the west side. In a memorandum filed May 17, 1966, the District Court found that the "school system serves approximately 1,300 pupils, of which 740 are Negro and 550 are White. The School Board operates one white combined elementary and high school [New Kent], and one Negro combined elementary and high school [George W. Watkins]. There are no attendance zones. Each school serves the entire county." The record indicates that 21 school buses—11 serving the Watkins school and 10 serving the New Kent school—travel overlapping routes throughout the county to transport pupils to and from the two schools.

The segregated system was initially established and maintained under the compulsion of Virginia constitutional and statutory provisions mandating racial segregation in public education.... The respondent School Board continued the segregated operation of the system after the *Brown* decisions, presumably on the authority of several statutes enacted by Virginia in resistance to those decisions. Some of these statutes were held to be unconstitutional on their face or as applied. One statute, the Pupil Placement Act (1964), not repealed until 1966, divested local boards of authority to assign children to particular schools and placed that authority in a State Pupil Placement Board. Under that Act children were each year automatically reassigned to the school previously attended unless upon their application the State Board assigned them to another school; students seeking enrollment for the first time were also assigned at the discretion of the State Board. To September 1964, no Negro pupil had applied for admission to the New Kent school under this statute and no white pupil had applied for admission to the Watkins school.

*From *Green v. School Board of New Kent County*, 391 U.S. 430.

The School Board initially sought dismissal of this suit on the ground that petitioners had failed to apply to the State Board for assignment to New Kent school. However, on August 2, 1965, five months after the suit was brought, respondent School Board, in order to remain eligible for federal financial aid, adopted a "freedom-of-choice" plan for desegregating the schools. Under that plan, each pupil except those entering the first and eighth grades, may annually choose between the New Kent and Watkins schools and pupils not making a choice are assigned to the school previously attended; first and eighth grade pupils must affirmatively choose a school....

The pattern of separate "white" and "Negro" schools in the New Kent County school system established under compulsion of state laws is precisely the pattern of segregation to which *Brown I* and *Brown II* were particularly addressed, and which *Brown I* declared unconstitutionally denied Negro school children equal protection of the laws. Racial identification of the system's schools was complete, extending not just to the composition of student bodies at the two schools but to every facet of school operations—facility, staff, transportation, extracurricular activities and facilities. In short, the State, acting through the local school board and school officials, organized and operated a dual system, part "white" and part "Negro."

It was such dual systems that 14 years ago *Brown I* held unconstitutional and a year later *Brown II* held must be abolished; school boards operating such school systems were *required* by *Brown II* "to effectuate a transition to a racially nondiscriminatory school system...." It is of course true that for the time immediately after *Brown II* the concern was with making an initial break in a long-established pattern of excluding Negro children from schools attended by white children. The principal focus was on obtaining for those Negro children courageous enough to break with tradition a place in the "white" schools.... Under *Brown II* that immediate goal was only the first step, however. The transition to a unitary, nonracial system of public education was and is the ultimate end to be brought about; it was because of the "complexities arising from the transition to a system of public education freed of racial discrimination" that we provided for "all deliberate speed" in the implementation of the principles of *Brown I.*

\* \* \*

It is against this background that 13 years after *Brown II* commanded the abolition of dual systems we must measure the effectiveness of respondent School Board's "freedom-of-choice" plan to achieve that end. The School Board contends that it has fully discharged its obligation by adopting a plan by which every student, regardless of race, may "freely" choose the school he will attend. The Board attempts to cast the issue in its broadest form by arguing that its "freedom-of-choice" plan may be faulted only by reading the Fourteenth Amendment as universally requiring "compulsory integration," a reading it insists the wording of the Amendment will not support. But the argument ignores the thrust of *Brown II*. In the light of the command of that case, what is involved here is the question whether the Board has achieved the "racially nondiscriminatory school system" *Brown II* held must be effectuated in order to remedy the established unconstitutional deficiencies of its segregated system. In the context of the state-imposed segregated pattern of long standing, the fact that in 1965 the Board opened the doors of the former "white" school to Negro children and of the "Negro" school to white children merely begins, not ends, our inquiry whether the Board has taken steps adequate to abolish its dual, segregated system. *Brown II* was a call for the dismantling of well-entrenched dual systems tempered by an awareness that complex and multifaceted problems would arise which would require time and flexibility for a successful resolution. School boards such as the respondent then operating state-compelled dual systems were nevertheless clearly charged with the affirmative duty to take whatever steps might be necessary to convert to a unitary system in which racial discrimination would be eliminated root and branch.... The constitutional rights of Negro school children articulated in *Brown I* permit no less than this; and it was to this end that *Brown II* commanded school boards to bend their efforts.

In determining whether respondent School Board met that command by adopting its "freedom-of-choice" plan, it is relevant that this first step did not come until some 11 years after *Brown I* was decided and 10 years after *Brown II* directed the making of a "prompt and reasonable start." This deliberate perpetuation of the unconstitutional dual system can only have compounded the harm of such a system. Such delays are no longer tolerable, for "the governing constitutional principles no longer hear the imprint of newly enunciated doctrine." Moreover, a plan that at this late date fails to provide meaningful assurance of prompt and effective disestablishment of a dual system is also intolerable. "The time for mere 'deliberate speed' has run out;"..."the context in which we must interpret and apply this language [of *Brown II*] to plans for desegregation has been significantly altered." The burden on a school board today is to come forward with a plan that promises realistically to work, and promises realistically to work *now*.

The obligation of the district courts, as it always has been, is to assess the effectiveness of a proposed plan in achieving desegregation. There is no universal answer to complex problems of desegregation; there is obviously no one plan that will do the job in every case. The matter must be assessed in light of the circumstances present and the options available in each instance. It is incumbent upon the school board to establish that its proposed plan promises meaningful and immediate progress toward disestablishing state-imposed segregation. It is incumbent upon the district court to weigh that claim in light of the facts at hand and in light of any alternatives which may be shown as feasible and more promising in their effectiveness. Where the court finds the board to be acting in good faith and the proposed plan to have real prospects for dismantling the state-imposed dual system "at the earliest practicable date," then the plan may be said to provide effective relief. Of course, the availability to the board of other more promising courses of action may indicate a lack of good faith; and at the least it places a heavy burden upon the board to explain its preference for an apparently less effective method. Moreover, whatever plan is adopted will require evaluation in practice, and the court should retain jurisdiction until it is clear that state-imposed segregation has been completely removed....

We do not hold that "freedom of choice" can have no place in such a plan. We do not hold that a "freedom-of-choice" plan might of itself be unconstitutional, although that argument has been urged upon us. Rather, all we decide today is that in desegregating a dual system a plan utilizing "freedom of choice" is not an end in itself....

Although the general experience under "freedom of choice" to date has been such as to indicate its ineffectiveness as a tool of desegregation, there may well be instances in which it can serve as an effective device. Where it offers real promise of aiding a desegregation program to effectuate conversion of a state-imposed dual system to a unitary, nonracial system there might be no objection to allowing such a device to prove itself in operation. On the other hand, if there are reasonably available other ways, such for illustration as zoning, promising speedier and more effective conversion to a unitary, nonracial school system, "freedom of choice" must be held unacceptable.

The New Kent School Board's "freedom-of-choice" plan cannot be accepted as a sufficient step to "effectuate a transition" to a unitary system. In three years of operation not a single white child has chosen to attend Watkins school and although 115 Negro children enrolled in New Kent school in 1967 (up from 35 in 1965 and 111 in 1966) 85% of the Negro children in the system still attend the all-Negro Watkins school. In other words, the school system remains a dual system. Rather than further the dismantling of the dual system, the plan has operated simply to burden children and their parents with a responsibility which *Brown II* placed squarely on the School Board. The Board must be required to formulate a new plan and, in light of other courses which appear open to the Board, such as zoning, fashion steps which promise realistically to convert to a system without a "white" school and a "Negro" school, but just schools.

…The case is remanded to the District Court for further proceedings consistent with this opinion.

# Court-Ordered Busing*

### *Syllabus*

The Charlotte-Mecklenburg school system, which includes the city of Charlotte, North Carolina, had more than 84,000 students in 107 schools in the 1968–1969 school year. Approximately 29% (24,000) of the pupils were Negro, about 14,000 of whom attended 21 schools that were at least 99% Negro. This resulted from a desegregation plan approved by the District Court in 1965, at the commencement of this litigation. In 1968, petitioner Swann moved for further relief based on *Green v. County School Board,* 391 U.S. 430, which required school boards to come forward with a plan that promises realistically to work…now…until it is clear that state-imposed segregation has been completely removed.

The District Court ordered the school board in April 1969 to provide a plan for faculty and student desegregation. Finding the board's submission unsatisfactory, the District Court appointed an expert to submit a desegregation plan. In February 1970, the expert and the board presented plans, and the court adopted the board's plan, as modified, for the junior and senior high schools, and the expert's proposed plan for the elementary schools. The Court of Appeals affirmed the District Court's order as to faculty desegregation and the secondary school plans, [p*2] but vacated the order respecting elementary schools, fearing that the provisions for pairing and grouping of elementary schools would unreasonably burden the pupils and the board. The case was remanded to the District Court for reconsideration and submission of further plans. This Court granted certiorari and directed reinstatement of the District Court's order pending further proceedings in that court. On remand the District Court received two new plans, and ordered the board to adopt a plan,

*Swann v. Charlotte-Mecklenburg Board of Education, 402 U.S. 1 (1971)(USSC+).

or the expert's plan would remain in effect. After the board "acquiesced" in the expert's plan, the District Court directed that it remain in effect.

### *Held:*

**1.** Today's objective is to eliminate from the public schools all vestiges of state-imposed segregation that was held violative of equal protection guarantees by *Brown v. Board of Education,* 347 U.S. 483, in 1954. P. 15.

**2.** In default by the school authorities of their affirmative obligation to proffer acceptable remedies, the district courts have broad power to fashion remedies that will assure unitary school systems. P. 16.

**3.** Title IV of the Civil Rights Act of 1964 does not restrict or withdraw from the federal courts their historic equitable remedial powers. The proviso in 42 U.S.C. § 2000c-6 was designed simply to foreclose any interpretation of the Act as expanding the existing powers of the federal courts to enforce the Equal Protection Clause. Pp. 16–18.

**4.** Policy and practice with regard to faculty, staff, transportation, extracurricular activities, and facilities are among the most important indicia of a segregated system, and the first remedial responsibility of school authorities is to eliminate invidious racial distinctions in those respects. Normal administrative practice should then produce schools of like quality, facilities, and staffs. Pp. 18–19.

**5.** The Constitution does not prohibit district courts from using their equity power to order assignment of teachers to achieve a particular degree of faculty desegregation. *United States v. Montgomery County Board of Education,* 395 U.S. 225, was properly followed by the lower courts in this case. Pp. 19–20.

**6.** In devising remedies to eliminate legally imposed segregation, local authorities and district courts must see to it that future school construction and abandonment are not used and do not serve to perpetuate or reestablish a dual system. Pp. 20–21. [p*3]

**7.** Four problem areas exist on the issue of student assignment:

   **1.** *Racial quotas.* The constitutional command to desegregate schools does not mean that every school in the community must always reflect the racial composition of the system as a whole; here the District Court's very limited use of the racial ratio—not as an inflexible requirement, but as a starting point in shaping a remedy—was within its equitable discretion. Pp. 22–25.

   **2.** *One-race schools.* While the existence of a small number of one-race, or virtually one-race, schools does not, in itself, denote a system that still practices segregation by law, the court should scrutinize such schools and require the school authorities to satisfy the court that the racial composition does not result from present or past discriminatory action on their part. Pp. 25–26.

   An optional majority-to-minority transfer provision has long been recognized as a useful part of a desegregation plan, and to be effective such arrangement must provide the transferring student free transportation and available space in the school to which he desires to move. Pp. 26–27.

**3.** *Attendance zones.* The remedial altering of attendance zones is not, as an interim corrective measure, beyond the remedial powers of a district court. A student assignment plan is not acceptable merely because it appears to be neutral, for such a plan may fail to counteract the continuing effects of past school segregation. The pairing and grouping of noncontiguous zones is a permissible tool; judicial steps going beyond contiguous zones should be examined in light of the objectives to be sought. No rigid rules can be laid down to govern conditions in different localities. Pp. 27–29. [p*4]

**4.** *Transportation.* The District Court's conclusion that assignment of children to the school nearest their home serving their grade would not effectively dismantle the dual school system is supported by the record, and the remedial technique of requiring bus transportation as a tool of school desegregation was within that court's power to provide equitable relief. An objection to transportation of students may have validity when the time or distance of travel is so great as to risk either the health of the children or significantly impinge on the educational process; limits on travel time will vary with many factors, but probably with none more than the age of the students. Pp. 29–31. [p*4]

**8.** Neither school authorities nor district courts are constitutionally required to make year-by-year adjustments of the racial composition of student bodies once a unitary system has been achieved. Pp. 31–32.

431 F.2d 138, affirmed as to those parts in which it affirmed the District Court's judgment. The District Court's order of August 7, 1970, is also affirmed.

## QUESTIONS

**1.** Distinguish between *de jure* and *de facto* segregation..

**2.** How were "freedom of choice" plans a part of the southern intransigence in complying with the Brown rulings?

**3.** Explain the relationship between Title VI of the 1964 Civil Rights Act and the 1965 Elementary and Secondary Education Act.

**4.** Do you agree that court-ordered busing of children was necessary in order to end the racial segregation of U.S. public schools?

**5.** Explain why the U.S. Supreme Court ruled in the *Green v School Board of New Kent County* case that "the time for mere deliberate speed" had run out.

**6.** Was busing to eliminate a dual system of schooling the best solution for the Charlotte-Mecklenburg School System? Explain your answers.

# 16 Enter Bakke

Voices asserting that affirmative action programs violated the constitutional rights of nonminorities surfaced in the mid-1970s. Allan Bakke's suit against the University of California is the best known and most significant of such cases. Bakke, a White male, was denied admission to the UC-Davis Medical School in 1973 and again in 1974. In both years, minority applicants with test scores lower than Bakke's gained admission. Filing suit in the Superior Court of California, Bakke alleged that UC-Davis's special admission program for minority candidates resulted in his not being accepted to the medical school.

The UC-Davis Medical School reserved 16 of its 100 annual slots for applicants from minority groups (Blacks, Latinos, Asians, American Indians). Applicants from these groups were rated for admission by a separate committee and were not ranked against candidates in the general admission process. Bakke alleged that the special admissions program denying him admission on the basis of his race was in violation of the equal protection clause of the Fourteenth Amendment.

The intent of the Davis special admissions program was to expand access to higher professional education to heretofore excluded groups. Members of minority groups competed with nonminorities for eighty-four seats, but only among themselves for the sixteen special seats. Bakke, a nonminority, claimed discrimination solely on the basis of race.

In its ruling on this case, the U.S. Supreme Court expressed sympathy for the University's desire for a heterogenuous student body but questioned the means used to achieve this. Pointing to Harvard's process of considering race, along with other factors, in selecting candidates for admission, Justice Powell emphasized the need to consider each applicant as an individual regardless of race. While noting that UC-Davis Medical School's preferential program was seriously flawed for disregarding individual rights as guaranteed by the Fourteenth Amendment, Justice Powell suggested that it was possible to consider race as one of several criteria in admitting candidates. The UC-Davis preferential admission program was declared unconstitutional, and Bakke was admitted to the medical school. At the same time, the Supreme Court affirmed the validity of race-conscious admission programs so long as candidates are treated as individuals rather than as members of a group.

Even though support for affirmative-action programs and procedures has eroded in recent years, the Bakke ruling in support of carefully crafted race-conscious admission programs remains in force except in the fifth federal court district. In Texas, Oklahoma, and Lousiana, race-conscious admission programs have been ruled unconstitutional in the more recent *Hopwood* case. Because the Supreme Court has refused to review the ruling of the federal court for the fifth district, the *Hopwood* decision affects only the states within that district.

# The Case of Reverse Discrimination*

## *Syllabus*

The Medical School of the University of California at Davis (hereinafter Davis) had two admissions programs for the entering class of 100 students—the regular admissions program and the special admissions program. Under the regular procedure, candidates whose overall undergraduate grade point averages fell below 2.5 on a scale of 4.0 were summarily rejected. About one out of six applicants was then given an interview, following which he was rated on a scale of 1 to 100 by each of the committee members (five in 1973 and six in 1974), his rating being based on the interviewers' summaries, his overall grade point average, his science courses grade point average, his Medical College Admissions Test (MCAT) scores, letters of recommendation, extracurricular activities, and other biographical data, all of which resulted in a total "benchmark score." The full admissions committee then made offers of admission on the basis of their review of the applicant's file and his score, considering and acting upon applications as they were received. The committee chairman was responsible for placing names on the waiting list and had discretion to include persons with "special skills." A separate committee, a majority of whom were members of minority groups, operated the special admissions program. The 1973 and 1974 application forms, respectively, asked candidates whether they wished to be considered as "economically and/or educationally disadvantaged" applicants and members of a "minority group" (blacks, Chicanos, Asians, American Indians). If an applicant of a minority group was found to be "disadvantaged," he would be rated in a manner similar to the one employed by the general admissions committee. Special candidates, however, did not have to meet the 2.5 grade point cutoff and were not ranked against candidates in the general admissions process. About one-fifth of the special applicants were invited for interviews in 1973 and 1974, following which they were given benchmark scores, and the top choices were then given to the general admissions committee, which could reject special candidates for failure to meet course requirements or other specific deficiencies. The special committee continued to recommend candidates until 16 special admission selections had been made. During a four-year period, 63 minority [p*2661 students were admitted to Davis under the special program and 44 under the general program. No disadvantaged whites were admitted under the special program, though many applied. Respondent, a white male, applied to Davis in 1973 and 1974, in both years being considered only under the general admissions program. Though he had a 468 out of 500 score in 1973, he was rejected, since no general applicants with scores less than 470 were being accepted after respondent's application, which was filed late in the year, had been processed and

*Regents of the Univ. of Cal.* v. *Bakke,* 438 U.S. 265 (1978) (USSC+)

completed. At that time, four special admission slots were still unfilled. In 1974 respondent applied early, and though he had a total score of 549 out of 600, he was again rejected. In neither year was his name placed on the discretionary waiting fist. In both years, special applicants were admitted with significantly lower scores than respondent's. After his second rejection, respondent filed this action in state court for mandatory, injunctive, and declaratory relief to compel his admission to Davis, alleging that the special admissions program operated to exclude him on the basis of his race in violation of the Equal Protection Clause of the Fourteenth Amendment, a provision of the California Constitution, and 167 § 601 of Title VI of the Civil Rights Act of 1964, which provides, *inter alia,* that no person shall on the ground of race or color be excluded from participating in any program receiving federal financial assistance. Petitioner cross-claimed for a declaration that its special admissions program was lawful. The trial court found that the special program operated as a racial quota, because minority applicants in that program were rated only against one another, and 16 places in the class of 100 were reserved for them. Declaring that petitioner could not take race into account in making admissions decisions, the program was held to violate the Federal and State Constitutions and Title VI. Respondent's admission was not ordered, however, for lack of proof that he would have been admitted but for the special program. The California Supreme Court, applying a strict scrutiny standard, concluded that the special admissions program was not the least intrusive means of achieving the goals of the admittedly compelling state interests of integrating the medical profession and increasing the number of doctors willing to serve minority patients. Without passing on the state constitutional or federal statutory grounds, the court held that petitioner's special admissions program violated the Equal Protection Clause. Since petitioner could not satisfy its burden of demonstrating that respondent, absent the special program, would not have been admitted, the court ordered his admission to Davis.

*Held:* The judgment below is affirmed insofar as it orders respondent's admission to Davis and invalidates petitioner's special admissions program, [p*267] but is reversed insofar as it prohibits petitioner from taking race into account as a factor in its future admissions decisions.

18 Cal.3d 34, 553 P.2d 1152, affirmed in part and reversed in part.

MR. JUSTICE POWELL concluded:

**1.** Title VI proscribes only those racial classifications that would violate the Equal Protection Clause if employed by a State or its agencies. Pp. 281–287.

**2.** Racial and ethnic classifications of any sort are inherently suspect and call for the most exacting judicial scrutiny. While the goal of achieving a diverse student body is sufficiently compelling to justify consideration of race in admissions decisions under some circumstances, petitioner's special admissions program, which forecloses consideration to persons like respondent, is unnecessary to the achievement of this compelling goal, and therefore invalid under the Equal Protection Clause. Pp. 287–320.

**3.** Since petitioner could not satisfy its burden of proving that respondent would not have been admitted even if there had been no special admissions program, he must be admitted. P. 320.

MR. JUSTICE BRENNAN, MR. JUSTICE WHITE, MR. JUSTICE MARSHALL, and MR. JUSTICE BLACKMUN concluded:

**1.** Title VI proscribes only those racial classifications that would violate the Equal Protection Clause if employed by a State or its agencies. Pp. 328–355.

**2.** Racial classifications call for strict judicial scrutiny. Nonetheless, the purpose of overcoming substantial chronic minority underrepresentation in the medical profession is sufficiently important to justify petitioner's remedial use of race. Thus, the judgment below must be reversed in that it prohibits race from being used as a factor in university admissions. Pp. 355–379.

MR. JUSTICE STEVENS, joined by THE CHIEF JUSTICE, MR. JUSTICE STEWART, and MR. JUSTICE REHNQUIST, being of the view that whether race can ever be a factor in an admissions policy is not an issue here; that Title VI applies; and that respondent was excluded from Davis in violation of Title VI, concurs in the Court's judgment insofar as it affirms the judgment of the court below ordering respondent admitted to Davis. Pp. 408–421.

### *Opinions*

POWELL, J., announced the Court's judgment and filed an opinion expressing his views of the case, in Parts I, III-A, and V-C of which WHITE, J., joined; and in Parts I and V-C of which BRENNAN, MARSHALL, and BLACKMUN, JJ., joined. BRENNAN, WHITE, MARSHALL, and BLACKMUN, [p*268] JJ., filed an opinion concurring in the judgment in part and dissenting in part, *post,* p. 324. WHITE, J., *post,* p. 379. MARSHALL, J., *post,* p. 387, and BLACKMUN, J., *post,* p. 402, filed separate opinions. STEVENS, J., filed an opinion concurring in the judgment in part and dissenting in part, in which BURGER, C.J., and STEWART and REHNQUIST, JJ., joined, *post,* p. 408. [p*269]

### *POWELL, J., Judgment of the Court*

MR. JUSTICE POWELL announced the judgment of the Court.

This case presents a challenge to the special admissions program of the petitioner, the Medical School of the University of California at Davis, which is designed to assure the admission [p*270] of a specified number of students from certain minority groups. The Superior Court of California sustained respondent's challenge, holding that petitioner's program violated the California Constitution, Title VI of the Civil Rights Act of 1964, 42 U.S.C. § 2000d *et seq.,* and the Equal Protection Clause of the Fourteenth Amendment. The court enjoined petitioner from considering respondent's race or the race of any other applicant in making admissions decisions. It refused, however, to order respondent's admission to the Medical School, holding that he had not carried his burden of proving that he would have been admitted but for the constitutional and statutory violations. The Supreme Court of California affirmed those portions of the trial court's judgment declaring the special admissions program unlawful and enjoining petitioner from considering the race of any applicant.[*] [p*271] It modified that portion of the judgment denying respondent's requested injunction and directed the trial court to order his admission.

For the reasons stated in the following opinion, I believe that so much of the judgment of the California court as holds petitioner's special admissions program unlawful and directs that respondent be admitted to the Medical School must be affirmed. For the reasons expressed in a separate opinion, my Brothers THE CHIEF JUSTICE, MR. JUSTICE STEWART, MR. JUSTICE REHNQUIST, and MR. JUSTICE STEVENS concur in this judgment. [p*272]

I also conclude, for the reasons stated in the following opinion, that the portion of the court's judgment enjoining petitioner from according any consideration to race in its admissions process must be reversed. For reasons expressed in separate opinions, my Brothers MR. JUSTICE BRENNAN, MR. JUSTICE WHITE, MR. JUSTICE MARSHALL, and MR. JUSTICE BLACKMUN concur in this judgment.

## Affirmative Action Denied

IN THE UNITED STATES COURT OF APPEALS

FOR THE FIFTH CIRCUIT

———————

No. 94-50569

———————

CHERYL J. HOPWOOD, et al.,

Plaintiffs-Appellees,

VERSUS

STATE OF TEXAS, et al.,

Defendants-Appellees,

VERSUS

THURGOOD MARSHALL LEGAL SOCIETY

and

BLACK PRE-LAW ASSOCIATION,

Movants-Appellants.

_____

Appeals from the United States District Court

for the Western District of Texas

_____

March 18, 1996

Before SMITH, WIENER, and DeMOSS, Circuit Judges.

JERRY E. SMITH, Circuit Judge:

With the best of intentions, in order to increase the enrollment of certain favored classes of minority students, the University of Texas School of Law ("the law school") discriminates in favor of those applicants by giving substantial racial preferences in its admissions program. The beneficiaries of this system are blacks and Mexican Americans, to the detriment of whites and non-preferred minorities. The question we decide today in No. 94-50664 is whether the Fourteenth Amendment permits the school to discriminate in this way.

We hold that it does not. The law school has presented no compelling justification, under the Fourteenth Amendment or Supreme Court precedent, that allows it to continue to elevate some races over others, even for the wholesome purpose of correcting perceived racial imbalance in the student body. "Racial preferences appear to 'even the score' ... only if one embraces the proposition that our society is appropriately viewed as divided into races, making it right that an injustice rendered in the past to a black man should be compensated for by discriminating against a white." City of Richmond v. J.A. Croson Co., 488 U.S. 469, 528 (1989) (Scalia, J., concurring in the judgment).

As a result of its diligent efforts in this case, the district court concluded that the law school may continue to impose racial preferences. See _Hopwood_ v. _Texas,_ 861 F. Supp. 551 (W.D. Tex. 1994). In No. 94-50664, we reverse and remand, concluding that the law school may not use race as a factor in law school admissions. Further, we instruct the court to reconsider the issue of damages in accordance with the legal standards we now explain. In No. 94-50569, regarding the denial of intervention by two black student groups, we dismiss the appeal for want of jurisdiction.

\* \* \*

In summary, we hold that the University of Texas School of Law may not use race as a factor in deciding which applicants to admit in order to achieve a diverse student body, to combat the perceived effects of a hostile environment at the law school, to alleviate the law school's poor reputation in the minority community, or to eliminate any present effects of past discrimination by actors other than the law school. Because the law school has proffered these justifications for its use of race in admissions, the plaintiffs have satisfied their burden of showing that they were scrutinized under an unconstitutional admissions system. The plaintiffs are entitled to reapply under an admissions system that invokes none of these serious constitutional infirmities. We also direct the district court to reconsider the question of damages, and we conclude that the proposed intervenors properly were denied intervention.

In No. 94-50569, the appeal is DISMISSED for want of jurisdiction. In No. 94-50664, the judgment is REVERSED and REMANDED for further proceedings in accordance with this opinion.

WIENER, Circuit Judge, specially concurring.

"We judge best when we judge least, particularly in controversial matters of high public interest."(63) In this and every other appeal, we should decide only the case before us, and should do so on the narrowest possible basis. Mindful of this credo, I concur in part and, with respect, specially concur in part.

The sole substantive issue in this appeal is whether the admissions process employed by the law school for 1992 meets muster under the Equal Protection Clause of the Fourteenth Amendment. The law school offers alternative justifications for its race-based admissions process, each of which, it insists, is a compelling interest: (1) remedying the present effects of past discrimination (present effects) and (2) providing the educational benefits that can be obtained only when the student body is diverse (diversity). (64) As to present effects, I concur in the panel opinion's analysis: Irrespective of whether the law school or the University of Texas system as a whole is deemed the relevant governmental unit to be tested, (65) neither has established the existence of present effects of past discrimination sufficient to justify the use of a racial classification. (66) As to diversity, however, I respectfully disagree with the panel opinion's conclusion that diversity can never be a compelling governmental interest in a public graduate school. Rather than attempt to decide that issue, I would take a considerably narrower path—and, I believe, a more appropriate one—to reach an equally narrow result: I would assume arguendo that diversity can be a compelling interest but conclude that the admissions process here under scrutiny was not narrowly tailored to achieve diversity.

# QUESTIONS

1. Explain Alan Bakke's assertion that the special admission program of the UC-Davis Medical School violated his rights under the Fourteenth Amendment.

2. Given the decision of the U.S. Fifth Circuit Court of Appeals, is it still legal to consider race as an admission criterion in the United States? Explain your answer.

3. Is it possible to consider race as a factor in selecting candidates for admission and also to treat each applicant as an individual regardless of race? Explain your answer.

# SUGGESTIONS FOR FURTHER READING

James D. Anderson, *The Education of Blacks in the South, 1860–1935.* (Chapel Hill: University of North Carolina Press, 1988).

Robert L. Church and Michael W. Sedlak, *Education in the United States: An Interpretive History.* (New York: The Free Press, 1976).

Ruben Donato, *The Other Struggle for Equal Schools: Mexican Americans during the Civil Rights Era.* (Albany: State University of New York Press, 1997).

Louis R. Harlan, *Booker T. Washington: The Wizard of Tuskegee, 1901–1915.* (New York; Oxford University Press).

Henry J. Perkinson, *The Imperfect Panacea: American Faith in Education.* (New York: Random House, 1968).

Henry J. Perkinson, *Two Hundred Years of American Educational Thought.* (New York: David McKay Company, Inc., 1976).

Diane Ravitch, *The Troubled Crusade: American Education, 1945–1980.* (New York: Basic Books, Inc., Publishers, 1983).

David B. Tyack, ed., *Turning Points in American Educational History.* (New York: John Wiley and Sons, 1967).

# PART FOUR

# Contemporary Issues
## Equity, Inclusion, and Abuse

# 17 Financial Equity

## Local Control Revisited

It is obvious that equity in funding for U.S. public schools has not been achieved. Because a major portion of the money for U.S. public schools comes from local property taxes, great inequities exist in the number of dollars available to schools. Schools in high property-wealth districts—those home to industries, high-end businesses, and expensive private residences—are able to generate much more school revenue than are districts dependent on a tax base of primarily working-class families. Is this fair? Is it constitutional? Do such inequities violate the equal protection clause of the Fourteenth Amendment? The questions were first raised in the *Rodriquez* case in San Antonio, Texas.

The case known as *SAISD v Rodriquez* originated in the Edgewood Independent School District in San Antonio, Texas. Of the forty-nine discrete and insular school districts operating in Bexar County, Texas, in 1947, none had greater financial problems than Edgewood. Located in the southwestern part of the city of San Antonio, the students attending Edgewood schools were largely children of Mexican American immigrants. The already crowded conditions were compounded after World War II as Edgewood became a haven for Mexican Americans seeking employment at the adjacent military bases. Unlike other neighborhoods in San Antonio—Olmos Park, Terrrell Hills, and Alamo Heights, for example—Edgewood had no restrictive covenants limiting or prohibiting Mexican Americans from purchasing homes.

Edgewood's school population increased from 1,586 in 1939 to more than 6,600 students in 1949. With little or no additional revenue, the district had to place 2,400 pupils and 70 classrooms on half-day sessions beginning in 1949. A congressional committee investigating the need for federal subsidies to school districts serving large numbers of children from military families characterized the Edgewood situation as the worst of any school district in the country.

The attention that the Edgewood situation received contributed to the passage by the Texas Legislature of the Gilmer-Aikin educational funding bill in 1949. The bill established the Foundation School Program providing state funding to ensure a minimal education for each child in the state. Local districts could enrich the program with additional revenues raised through property taxes. The Gilmer-Aikin legislation had a positive impact, but it did not result in equalization of funding for education in Bexar County, San Antonio, or in Texas. Property-poor districts like Edgewood had to rely almost entirely on state revenue, whereas property-rich districts like Alamo Heights could and did generate revenues to raise the per-pupil expenditures considerably above the minimal level.

Further complicating Edgewood's plight, school districts within Bexar County began consolidating in 1947. By 1951, the number of districts had been reduced from forty-nine to fourteen. Consolidation of districts with similar tax bases made sense as a strategy for eliminating duplication and reducing costs. In the urban center of the county, the San Antonio ISD (Independent School District) annexed several smaller common school districts but refused Edgewood's request to become a part of the city's school system. For similar reasons, the Alamo Heights School District turned down SAISD's invitation to become part of the city system. In short, rather than the wealth of the city as a whole contributing to the education of Edgewood's children, their tax base consisted primarily of substandard private dwellings often with dirt floors and without plumbing and electricity.

This system of school finance resulted in two-and-one-quarter times more public funds expended for the education of a student in Alamo Heights as in Edgewood. The obvious discrepancies in the educational opportunities for students attending schools five miles apart led Demetrio Rodriquez, a member of the Edgewood Concerned Parents Association, to complain of mismanagement by the Edgewood school board and administration. Upon investigating this complaint, Arthur Gochman, the Association's attorney, discovered that Edgewood's problem was not mismanagement but inadequate and inequitable funding. Gochman and Rodriquez decided to sue the state of Texas, contending that the state's method of school finance violated the equal protection clause of the Fourteenth Amendment. Although initially named as defendants in this case, the San Antonio Independent School District (SAISD) and other school districts in the county supported Edgewood's claim that the state system of school funding adversely affected the poorer districts.

On December 23, 1971, a federal district court ruled in favor of Rodriquez. This court ordered the state of Texas to abandon its current method of educational finance and to reallocate funds so that "the educational opportunities afforded the children attending Edgewood ISD and other children of the state of Texas, are not a function of wealth other than the wealth of the state as a whole." The district court stayed its ruling for two years to give the legislature sufficient time to devise a school finance plan in compliance with the constitutional mandate. Rather than initiate reform, the state of Texas appealed the decision to the U.S. Supreme Court. On March 21, 1973, in a 5-to-4 decision, the Supreme Court reversed the district court's decision and sustained the constitutionality of the Texas system of school finance. Since the initial filing of the case and initial ruling in 1971, four liberal Supreme Court justices had been replaced by President Nixon appointees who were more willing to defer to the policies of the state legislatures and less willing to extend the equal protection clause. By one vote, the Texas system of public school finance and San Antonio's dramatic inequities had withstood constitutional scrutiny.

In spite of the reluctance of the Supreme Court to address the inequities in school funding that exist in virtually every state, the issue will not go away. Throughout the 1970s and 1980s, the legislatures of Texas and other states passed legislation designed to ensure greater equity in school funding. With the focus now at the state level, the question is, Does the state system of public school finance comply with the constitutional mandates of that state? The Texas Supreme Court has answered that question in the negative, declaring on October 2, 1989, that the state's system for financing public school was unconstitutional because of "glaring disparities" between what rich and poor school districts spend on education. In a 9-to-0 decision, the court found that the funding inequity violated a provision of the Texas Constitution requiring the state legislature to support and maintain "an efficient system" for the "general diffusion of knowledge." According to Associate Justice Oscar Mauzy, children who live in poor districts and children who live in rich districts must be afforded a substantially equal opportunity to have access to public funds.

Even though progress toward greater equity in school funding has been achieved in Texas and other states, the fundamental problem remains. As illustrated in Chapter 6, historically, local control of public education has been the bedrock of U.S. society. Financial responsibility has usually been associated with this control with the local community levying property taxes to support public education. Even though the percentage of local funding of the local, state, and federal pie allocated in support of public education has decreased in recent history and continues to vary from state to state and from district to district, local funding remains a significant component of the funding for public education. As long as public education is significantly tied to local property taxes, inequities in school finance will continue. Because local control of public education remains a high priority for this nation, equity in funding to ensure equal educational opportunity is likely to remain an elusive, and perhaps conflicting, dream.

# One Scholar/One Dollar*

## *Syllabus*

The financing of public elementary and secondary schools in Texas is a product of state and local participation. Almost half of the revenues are derived from a largely state-funded program designed to provide a basic minimum educational offering in every school. Each district supplements state aid through an *ad valorem* tax on property within its jurisdiction. Appellees brought this class action on behalf of school children said to be members of poor families who reside in school districts having a low property tax base, making the claim that the Texas system's reliance on local property taxation favors the more affluent and violates equal protection requirements because of substantial inter-district disparities in per-pupil expenditures resulting primarily from differences in the value of assessable property among the districts. The District Court, finding that wealth is a "suspect" classification and that education is a "fundamental" right, concluded that the system could be upheld only upon a showing, which appellants failed to make, that there was a compelling state interest for the system. The court also concluded that appellants failed even to [p*2] demonstrate a reasonable or rational basis for the State's system.

*Held:*

**1.** This is not a proper case in which to examine a State's laws under standards of strict judicial scrutiny, since that test is reserved for cases involving laws that operate to the

---

*San Antonio Independent School District v. Rodriquez, 411 U.S. 1 (1973)(USSC+)

disadvantage of suspect classes or interfere with the exercise of fundamental rights and liberties explicitly or implicitly protected by the Constitution. Pp. 18–44.

    **a.** The Texas system does not disadvantage any suspect class. It has not been shown to discriminate against any definable class of "poor" people or to occasion discriminations depending on the relative wealth of the families in any district. And, insofar as the financing system disadvantages those who, disregarding their individual income characteristics, reside in comparatively poor school districts, the resulting class cannot be said to be suspect. Pp. 18–28.

    **b.** Nor does the Texas school financing system impermissibly interfere with the exercise of a "fundamental" right or liberty. Though education is one of the most important services performed by the State, it is not within the limited category of rights recognized by this Court as guaranteed by the Constitution. Even if some identifiable quantum of education is arguably entitled to constitutional protection to make meaningful the exercise of other constitutional rights, here there is no showing that the Texas system fails to provide the basic minimal skills necessary for that purpose. Pp. 29–39.

    **c.** Moreover, this is an inappropriate case in which to invoke strict scrutiny, since it involves the most delicate and difficult questions of local taxation, fiscal planning, educational policy, and federalism, considerations counseling a more restrained form of review. Pp. 40–44.

    **2.** The Texas system does not violate the Equal Protection Clause of the Fourteenth Amendment. Though concededly imperfect, the system bears a rational relationship to a legitimate state purpose. While assuring a basic education for every child in the State, it permits and encourages participation in and significant control of each district's schools at the local level. Pp. 44–53.

    337 F.Supp. 280, reversed.

    POWELL, J., delivered the opinion of the Court, in which BURGER, C. J., and STEWART, BLACKMUN, and REHNQLTIST, JJ., joined. [p*3] STEWART, J., filed a concurring opinion, *post*, p. 59. BRENNAN, J., filed a dissenting opinion, *post*, p. 62. WHITE, J., filed a dissenting opinion, in which DOUGLAS and BRENNAN, JJ., joined, *post*, p. 63, MARSHALL, J., filed a dissenting opinion, in which DOUGLAS, J., joined, *post*, p. 70. [p*4]

### *Opinions*

#### *POWELL, J., Opinion of the Court*

MR. JUSTICE POWELL delivered the opinion of the Court.

    This suit attacking the Texas system of financing public education was initiated by Mexican-American parents whose children attend the elementary and secondary [p*5] schools in the Edgewood Independent School District, an urban school district in San Antonio, Texas. They brought a class action on behalf of school children throughout the State who are members of minority groups or who are poor and reside in school districts having a low property tax base. Named as defendants were the State Board of Education, the Commissioner of Education, the State Attorney General, and the Bexar County (San Antonio) Board of Trustees.

The complaint [p*6] was filed in the summer of 1968, and a three-judge court was impaneled in January, 1969. In December, 1971, the panel rendered its judgment in a per curiam opinion holding the Texas school finance system unconstitutional under the Equal Protection Clause of the Fourteenth Amendment. The State appealed, and we noted probable jurisdiction to consider the far-reaching constitutional questions presented. 406 U.S. 966 (1972). For the reasons stated in this opinion, we reverse the decision of the District Court.

\* \* \*

Until recent times, Texas was a predominantly rural State, and its population and property wealth were spread [p* 8] relatively evenly across the State. Sizable differences in the value of assessable property between local school districts became increasingly evident as the State became more industrialized and as rural-to-urban population shifts became more pronounced. The location of commercial and industrial property began to play a significant role in determining the amount of tax resources available to each school district. These growing disparities in population and taxable property between districts were responsible in part for increasingly notable differences in levels of local expenditure for education. In due time, it became apparent to those concerned with financing public education that contributions from the Available School Fund were not sufficient to ameliorate these disparities. Prior to 1939, the Available School Fund contributed money to every school district at a rate of $17.50 per school-age child. Although the amount was increased several times in the early 1940's, [p*9] the Fund was providing only $46 per student by 1945.

Recognizing the need for increased state funding to help offset disparities in local spending and to meet Texas' changing educational requirements, the state legislature, in the late 1940's, undertook a thorough evaluation of public education with an eye toward major reform. In 1947, an 18-member committee, composed of educators and legislators, was appointed to explore alternative systems in other States and to propose a funding scheme that would guarantee a minimum or basic educational offering to each child and that would help overcome inter-district disparities in taxable resources. The Committee's efforts led to the passage of the Gilmer-Aikin bills, named for the Committee's co-chairman, establishing the Texas Miniumum Foundation School Program. Today, this Program accounts for approximately half of the total educational expenditures in Texas.

The Program calls for state and local contributions to a fund earmarked specifically for teacher salaries, operating expenses, and transportation costs. The State, supplying funds from its general revenues, finances approximately 80% of the Program, and the school districts are responsible—as a unit—for providing the remaining 20%. The districts' share, known as the Local Fund Assignment, is apportioned among the school districts [p* 10] under a formula designed to reflect each district's relative taxpaying ability. The Assignment is first divided among Texas' 254 counties pursuant to a complicated economic index that takes into account the relative value of each county's contribution to the State's total income from manufacturing, mining, and agricultural activities. It also considers each county's relative share of all payrolls paid within the State and, to a lesser extent, considers each county's share of all property in the State. Each county's assignment is then divided among its school districts on the basis of each district's share of assessable property within the county. The district, in turn, finances its share of the Assignment out of revenues from local property taxation.

## QUESTIONS

1. Should the amount of funds available for the education of children be roughly the same for all students in the county, state, nation? Is this desirable? Is it feasible?

2. Why were the financial problems in the Edgewood Independent School District (EISD) in San Antonio deemed to be among the worst in the nation in the post–World War II period?

3. Why did it make sense for the San Antonio Independent School District (SAISD) to seek consolidation with the Alamo Heights Independent School District and to reject EISD's request to become part of the SAISD?

4. Why did SAISD and Alamo Heights ISD join forces with Edgewood ISD in questioning the fairness and legality of the state of Texas's system of school finance?

5. Explain why the state is ultimately responsible for the manner in which schools are financed in the United States. What influence, if any, does the Tenth Amendment have on this issue?

# CHAPTER

# 18 Mainstreaming and Inclusion
## Out of Sight/Out of Mind

$W$hile a doctoral candidate and later a visiting assistant professor at George Peabody College for Teachers in Nashville, I often explored the city on my bicycle. Allow me to share my discoveries during one such glorious spring weekend in Nashville.

I started out around ten in the morning and rode from my residence near the Peabody campus to Hillsboro Village. I meandered down side streets, gazing at the beautiful, well-maintained older homes. As I made my way over to West End, I thought how good it was to be alive on such a beautiful day. I rode by Nashville's version of the Parthenon in Centennial Park and pedaled south out of the city to Radnor Lake. I returned to campus via Franklin Road and Curtiswood Lane by the governor's mansion and by expansive homes of country music stars.

The next day, I took a bicycle ride, once again, heading downtown. I followed Church Street to the center of the city, turning down Printer's Alley and passing the municipal auditorium, heading west, away from downtown. After crossing the railroad tracks, I turned left on Jefferson Street and headed south toward Fisk University. Eventually, I came to the campus of Tennessee State University, a historically Black institution. What I saw there was in sharp contrast to my ride of the previous day. Poverty was evident in this part of Nashville, yet I was less than a mile away from the affluent area of the city. My weekend cycling made it obvious that poverty amidst plenty is prevalent in our society. More significantly, my second ride made obvious how easy it is to ignore real social problems by avoiding contact with them—keeping them out of sight and thus out of mind.

Many people often avoid confrontations with poverty and racism. As long as we do not have to see it, we tend not to think about it.

As we discuss in Chapters 11, 12, 13, 14, 15, 16, and 18, education and race continue to be major issues in the United States. Other groups—notably those with mental and physical disabilities—also have similar educational history. These people are different; they trouble us in deep, irrational ways. We prefer them to be somewhere else, not cruelly treated, but away from us; out of sight and thus out of mind. We have often segregated them in separate institutions and, as a result, have often dehumanized them.

In recent years—as part of the movement asserting that all children have the right to an education—children with disabilities are no longer being ignored. The basis for asserting that all children, including those with disabilities, have a right to education originates in the *Brown v the Board of Education of Topeka, Kansas,* case. Although originally directed toward schools segregated by race, the rationale that "In these days, it is doubtful that any child may reasonably be expected to succeed in life if he is denied the opportunity of an education. Such an opportunity, where the state has undertaken to provide it, is a right, which must be made available to all on equal terms" has more recently been applied to children and youth with disabilities.

Although the arguments presented in the *Brown* case challenged public school segregation on the basis of race, the basic principle of equal opportunity for an education was carried forward in the arguments presented on behalf of children with disabilities in two seminal court cases: *PARC v the State of Pennsylvania* and *Mills v Board of Education of Washington, DC.* The plaintiffs in the *PARC* case were fourteen school-age children with mental disabilities. The court ruled in favor of the plaintiffs, asserting that all children are educable and that "a mentally retarded person can benefit at any point in his life and development from a program of education."

In the *Mills* decision, the Court went a step further. Here, the Court declared that no child could be excluded from a regular school assignment unless adequate alternative education services appropriate to the child's needs are provided. The Court ruled "that the District of Columbia shall provide to each child of school age a free and suitable publicly supported education, regardless of the degree of the child's mental, physical, or emotional disability or impairment." Remember, the U.S. Constitution does not expressly provide for the right to an education, but when states explicitly take on this role, the Courts have ruled that such an education must be made available to all on an equal basis.

In 1975, the U.S. Congress passed the Education for All Handicapped Children Act (PL 94-142). Even though Congress reaffirmed that education is the states' responsibility, PL 94-142 asserts that any state seeking or receiving federal funds to support its system of education must ensure for all handicapped children the right to an education. One chief aim of PL 94-142 is to bridge the gulf between special and common education. With the enactment of this legislation, it became much more difficult to shunt children with disabilities aside, out of sight/out of mind, in special-education classrooms. Whenever possible, children with disabilities are to be "mainstreamed" into the regular classroom.

The Individual with Disabilities Act (IDEA), enacted by Congress in 1990, is both an extension of PL 94-142 and a departure from it. Even though it was a significant break with a dual system characterized by a self-contained special education classroom, PL 94-142 sustained elements of the traditional ideas that viewed children with disabilities as different from other children. Even though PL 94-142 endorsed mainstreaming children with disabilities into regular classrooms, the added language of "to the extent possible" enabled people unwilling or unable to conceive of "special needs" children as essentially the same as any other child to excuse and/or maintain the status quo. Language such as "the least restrictive environment" resulted in the continuing isolation and treatment of some special needs children in segregated classrooms or facilities.

Contrast this to IDEA's championing of the common humanity of all children. Undeniably, some children need additional help or assistance, but such special assistance or support should be available in an inclusive or regular classroom. PL 94-142 took a significant step in the right direction, but IDEA established the inclusive classroom—an educational environment that enables all children to learn—as the ideal.

U.S. society's tendency to emphasize differences between special needs and so-called normal children creates a false dichotomy. All children—indeed all people—need assistance to learn certain skills at certain times. A good educator identifies a student's need and provides the appropriate intervention or strategy best suited to addressing that particular need. To borrow imagery sometimes associated with the field of literacy, there must be a "goodness of fit" between the teaching strategy used and a child's readiness to learn. For children to learn, there needs to be a "goodness of fit" that addresses each child's needs by matching the content being taught to the appropriate methods used in teaching it. Even though differences and/or needs vary by degrees and require different levels of intervention, the characteristics of a good educational experience are basically the same for all students. A good education means ensuring such a "goodness of fit" for all children regardless of their disabilities or special needs. At the most fundamental level, this is the goal of IDEA.

If we treat children with disabilities in a different manner, we rob them and us of the similarity and commonality that defines us all. We can no longer allow schools to segregate children from one another. Schools must foster a healthy respect for differences among individuals; but regardless of skin color, gender, ethnic origin, or disability, students must not be shunted aside—out of sight and out of mind. At the most fundamental level, mainstreaming and inclusion are moral issues. They are, in effect, efforts to assure that all human beings have the right to develop to their full potential. By retrieving children being dehumanized in out of sight/out of mind institutions and mainstreaming them into the inclusive classroom, schools can foster an appreciation for both the unique and common attributes of each human being.

# The Inclusion Revolution*

Six-year-old Joseph Ford seemed an unlikely revolutionary. This exceptionally bright, cute little boy sought only to enter the first grade of the public "magnet school" attended by his older sisters. But Joe lived in Chicago where school officials had very different plans for him.

They were adamant that Joe should attend a segregated school for children who, like him, had physical disabilities. Children with such severe physical disabilities as Joe simply did not go to the city's outstanding magnet schools.

School officials extolled the benefits of all the physical therapy Joe would receive in the segregated school and insisted that he could not be educated in a magnet school. Joe's mom reasoned through the problem somewhat differently. She knew no amount of physical therapy would "cure" his cerebral palsy and that he would eventually have to earn his living using his superior intellect.

After a year-long struggle involving federal regulatory agencies and the highest officials in the school system, Joe won entry into the magnet school.

Even after he was allowed to enroll, the work was not over for Joe and his family. They had to overcome such barriers as school employees with negative attitudes, staff who

*From Joy Rogers, "The Inclusion Revolution," *Phi Delta Kappa Research Bulletin,* No. 11 (May 1993), pp. 343–350. Reprinted with permission from Phi Delta Kappa International.

often lacked skill at modifying instruction for him, and odd traditions (such as segregated school buses) within the school district. Joe's experience has been paralleled by hundreds of children in hundreds of communities throughout the country as parents have increasingly demanded and won integrated schooling for their children with disabilities. Parents whose children have severe learning and behavior problems have fought to assure that their children will have classmates who behave appropriately as role models. Pioneering kids like Joe have opened the schoolhouse doors in each of their communities for others to follow.

What's happened to Joe? He continues to thrive and is now a successful third grader. He is a bright, loving young man with strikingly mature values and an excellent chance to seize the future his parents have always believed he can attain. Not every child in a school which claims to be using inclusion has been as fortunate.

### *So Many Words*

Many different terms have been used to describe inclusion of students with disabilities in "regular" classes. None of these terms actually appears in federal law, but all have been used to express varying beliefs about what the law means—or should mean.

*Mainstreaming:*   This term has generally been used to refer to the selective placement of special education students in one or more "regular" education classes. Mainstreaming proponents generally assume that a student must "earn" his or her opportunity to be mainstreamed through the ability to "keep up" with the work assigned by the teacher to the other students in the class. This concept is closely linked to traditional forms of special education service delivery.

*Inclusion:*   This term is used to refer to the commitment to educate each child, to the maximum extent appropriate, in the school and classroom he or she would otherwise attend. It involves bringing the support services to the child (rather than moving the child to the services) and requires only that the child will benefit from being in the class (rather than having to keep up with the other students). Proponents of inclusion generally favor newer forms of education service delivery such as the ones under the heading, "What Does Inclusion Look Like?"

*Full Inclusion:*   This term is primarily used to refer to the belief that instructional practices and technological supports are presently available to accommodate all students in the schools and classrooms they would otherwise attend if not disabled. Proponents of full inclusion tend to encourage that special education services generally be delivered in the form of training and technical assistance to "regular" classroom teachers.

*Regular Education Initiative:*   This phrase was coined by a former federal education official, Madeline Will, and has generally been used to discuss either the merger of the governance of special and "regular" education or the merger of the funding streams of each. It is not generally used to discuss forms of service delivery.

### *Why Try Inclusion?*

Two different lines of reasoning have converged in the inclusion movement. The first line of reasoning is the civil rights argument that segregated education is inherently unequal and, therefore, a violation of the rights of the children who are segregated. The second line of reasoning is that empirical analysis of the outcomes from established special education programs indicate that they just haven't worked. In spite of the steady expansion of a costly special education bureaucracy, the children served in special education programs have not shown the expected benefits in development of academic, social, or vocational skills.

In some schools, special and "regular" education personnel co-exist side by side, but do not work together. Teachers have separate classrooms, are paid from separate budgets, and work with different curricular materials. Scarce resources are hoarded rather than shared. In an inclusive school, resources are more efficiently used and reach the maximum number of children.

### The "Down Side" of Inclusion

In one school claiming to be using inclusion, an observer noted 44 second graders watching a filmstrip as a science lesson with only one teacher in the room. The 44 children included a group of special education students, a group of limited English proficient students, and a "regular" class. Two other teachers assigned to the group were out of the classroom. Few educators would attempt to defend this kind of instruction as inclusion—nor could it easily be defended as science instruction either! Inclusion cannot be viewed as a way of eliminating special education costs. It is simply a way of reconceptualizing special education service delivery: the traditional model requires bringing the child to the special education services and the inclusion model requires bringing the special education services to the child.

Similar problems have arisen where school administrators have tried to assign several children with severe disabilities to the same classroom. Although mild disabilities are relatively common (affecting about one child in ten), severe disabilities are far less common (affecting only about one child in a hundred). Thus, if four or five children with severe disabilities are placed with the same class of about 25 children, it is statistically extremely unlikely that the classroom is actually the room to which all of those children would possibly have been assigned if they had not been disabled. This is not inclusion. Such arrangements tend not to be beneficial to any of the children in the class—and create extremely frustrating work environments for the teachers who are assigned to such classes. It is easy to see why teachers in such situations might feel ineffective or exploited! Inclusion works when all staff members in the school accept their fair share of responsibility for all the children who live within the school's attendance area.

### How Does Inclusion Affect Classmates?

Some misguided efforts at inclusion have simply moved children with disabilities into general education classrooms and left them for their classmates to teach. Although tutoring others can often be a good way to learn for both the included child and the tutor, if peer tutoring becomes the predominant mode of instruction, then neither child is receiving appropriate services.

The presence of an included classmate should provide opportunities for growth for the entire class.

- Classmates can develop a sense of responsibility and the enhanced self-esteem which results from such responsibility
- Classmates' understanding of the range of human experience can be enhanced

- Classmates can benefit from their disabled classmates as role models in coping with disabilities. As a result of advancements in medical science, most of those presently nondisabled children will survive to become persons with disabilities themselves one day.
- Classmates are enriched by the opportunity to have had friends with disabilities who successfully managed their affairs and enjoyed full lives.

Effective teachers do not permit a classroom environment in which any child is the victim of ridicule. They arrange learning environment in which every child has opportunities to lead and to experience successes, and they value diversity because it helps them prepare their students to be capable citizens in a democracy.

### What Are "Supplementary Aids and Services?"

Classroom teachers have sometimes been disappointed to discover that every included child does not come with his/her own full-time aide. The determination about what supplementary aids and services are needed is unique for each child and is specified in the child's Individualized Educational Program (IEP). Very few children have individual aides either in special education classes or when included in general classes. Indeed, managing paraprofessionals adds another time-consuming duty for which some teachers are poorly prepared. An incident in one school illustrates how aides can actually interfere with inclusion. In that school the child's individual aide befriended the classroom aide. The result was that instead of being with his classmates at lunch time, that child was seated alone with the two adult aides who enjoyed each others' company at lunch. Aides are very important in some situations, but the addition of adults in a classroom is not a panacea.

The most common supplementary aids and services are actually consultation and training for the teacher. For example, a teacher receiving a blind student for the first time may need initial guidance in how to arrange the classroom and may need continuing suggestions on how to adapt his or her lesson plans to help the blind student understand the concept to be taught.

Electronic aids and services are becoming increasingly common. Some students will use computers, speech synthesizers, FM amplification systems, etc. Other very important aids and services may be much less technologically sophisticated. Simple accommodations such as large print books, preferential seating, behavior management programs, or a modified desk are sufficient for many students with severe disabilities to be successfully included.

In schools where inclusion works well, it is important for the classroom teacher to have regular access to support staff who can help the teacher find equipment or procedures which permit all the children in the class to benefit from the instruction.

Some children need life-sustaining equipment previously unfamiliar in educational settings. Some children need suctioning, clean intermittent catheterization, or frequent positioning changes. Some children need daily medication, access to an epinephrine "pen," or blood sugar monitoring. Necessary supports may include both the equipment and the trained personnel needed to do these tasks. If children are carriers of communicable diseases for which immunization is available, necessary supports for their teachers can include immunization against those diseases.

People who have not seen children with disabilities successfully included in public school classes sometimes create barriers to inclusion because they may fear what they do not understand.

In some communities, teachers have feared that they will be asked to do new or difficult tasks without sufficient training and support. Administrators may fear loss of state or federal reimbursement unless special education students are placed in special education classrooms. Parents of nondisabled students may fear that their children will not get a fair share of the teacher's attention. Parents of the students with disabilities may fear that their children will lose special services which have been helpful.

However, a rapidly growing "track record" of inclusion indicates that, when done with care, inclusion does not create unreasonable demands on teachers or deprive classmates of learning opportunities. Indeed, inclusive classrooms offer some unique benefits for all who participate.

### What Does Inclusion Look Like?

Effective inclusion is characterized by its virtual invisibility. One cannot go to look at the special education classrooms in an inclusive school because there are none. Children with disabilities are not clustered into groups of persons with similar disabilities, but are dispersed in whatever classrooms they would otherwise attend. There are not lots of little rooms labeled "LD Resource," "Emotionally Disturbed," "Speech," or "Trainable." In an inclusive school, special education teachers do not have their own classrooms, but are assigned to other roles such as team teaching in classrooms that serve both disabled and nondisabled students together.

The schools that most readily adopt the concept of inclusion are generally those that already embrace instructional practices which are designed to provide challenging learning environments to children with very diverse learning characteristics. Such practices include heterogeneous grouping, peer tutoring, multi-age classes, middle school structures, "no-cut" athletic policies, cooperative learning, and development of school media centers which stimulate students' electronic access to extensive databases for their own research.

Each of these innovations has been demonstrated in numerous studies to enhance teachers' capacities to meet the individual needs of students.

### What If the Included Student Can't Keep Up with the Class?

Each included student has an Individualized Education Program (IEP) which specifies what he or she needs to learn and, sometimes, that may not mean that the student will be learning the same things as the other students. The teacher's job is to arrange instruction that benefits all the students—even though the various students may derive different benefits. For example, most of the students in the class may be learning the total number of degrees in the angles of a triangle while the included student may be learning to recognize a triangle. Good teachers maximize the opportunities for all students to learn even though they may be learning at different levels. In general, good teachers help their included students to accomplish just as many as possible of the goals of the classroom and to function just as close as possible to the way that their peers function. Good administrators do not evaluate teachers with included students on the basis of the average academic achievement scores of their classes, but rather on the progress made by all the students.

### *An Inclusion Checklist For Your School*

_____  1. Do we genuinely start from the premise that each child belongs in the classroom he or she would otherwise attend if not disabled (or do we cluster children with disabilities into special groups, classrooms, or schools)?

_____  2. Do we individualize the instructional program for all the children whether or not they are disabled and provide the resources that each child needs to explore individual interests in the school environment (or do we tend to provide the same sorts of services for most children who share the same diagnostic label)?

_____  3. Are we fully committed to maintenance of a caring community that fosters mutual respect and support among staff, parents, and students in which we honestly believe that nondisabled children can benefit from friendships with disabled children and disabled children can benefit from friendships with nondisabled children (or do our practices tacitly tolerate children teasing or isolating some as outcasts)?

_____  4. Have our general educators and special educators integrated their efforts and their resources so that they work together as integral parts of a unified team (or are they isolated in separate rooms or departments with separate supervisors and budgets)?

_____  5. Does our administration create a work climate in which staff are supported as they provide assistance to each other (or are teachers afraid of being presumed to be incompetent if they seek peer collaboration in working with students)?

_____  6. Do we actively encourage the full participation of children with disabilities in the life of our school including co-curricular and extracurricular activities (or do they participate only in the academic portion of the school day)?

_____  7. Are we prepared to alter support systems for students as their needs change through the school year so that they can achieve, experience successes, and feel that they genuinely belong in their school and classes (or do we sometimes provide such limited services to them that the children are set up to fail)?

_____  8. Do we make parents of children with disabilities fully a part of our school community so they also can experience a sense of belonging (or do we give them a separate PTA and different newsletters)?

_____  9. Do we give children with disabilities just as much of the full school curriculum as they can master and modify it as necessary so that they can share elements of these experiences with their classmates (or do we have a separate curriculum for children with disabilities)?

_____ **10.** Have we included children with disabilities supportively as in many as possible of the same testing and evaluation experiences as their nondisabled classmates (or do we exclude them from these opportunities while assuming that they cannot benefit from the experiences)?

This checklist may help school personnel in evaluating whether their practices are consistent with the best intentions of the inclusion movement. Rate your school with a + for each item where the main statement best describes your school and a 0 for each item where the parenthetical statement better describes your school. Each item marked 0 could serve as the basis for discussion among the staff. Is this an area in which the staff sees need for further development? Viewed in this context, an inclusive school would not be characterized by a particular set of practices as much as the commitment of its staff to continually develop its capacity to accommodate the full range of individual differences among learners.

### What Skills Do Teachers Need in Inclusive Classrooms?

Most experienced teachers are quick to note that the students who come to them are increasingly needful of special attention. Whether or not the students are classified as special education students, the complexity of social problems which impact on children in the nineties means that far more children need extra help. In addition to schoolwork, children may need help finding adequate food, being safe from abuse, and developing motivation to learn.

The diversity of children in today's schools is often already very great. The inclusion of a child with a disability into this mix is most likely to add one child who has more needs than the others, but not needs that are more severe than needs already represented in the class. The best teachers in inclusive classrooms are simply the best teachers. The best teachers teach each individual student rather than try to gear instruction to the average of a group. The best teachers have a high degree of "with-itness," that is, they are highly aware of the dynamics of their classrooms. The best teachers are versatile. They are comfortable using many different teaching techniques and can readily shift among them as needed. The best teachers enjoy and value all their students—attitudes which are visible to others as they teach.

Inclusion has become such a value laden word that it is currently very difficult to state opposition to inclusion. However the pressure to appear to be inclusive may create many problematic practices that either do not have inclusive effects or, in some cases, do not fit within the existing knowledge base of educational practice. Thus, extensive debate on the question of whether "inclusion" is a good idea has produced much heat, but little light. More useful outcomes are likely to result when the staff of a school works together to determine how it can meet the needs of those specific children who live in its attendance area. The preceding check-list...may help school personnel in evaluating whether their practices are consistent with the best intentions of the inclusion movement.

## Does Federal Law Require Inclusion?

The Individuals with Disabilities Education Act requires that "Each public agency shall insure: (a) Each handicapped child's educational placement: (1) is determined at least annually: (2) is based on his or her individualized education program: and (3) is as close as possible to the child's home: (b) The various alternative placements included under Reg. 300.551 are available to the extent necessary to implement the individualized education program for each handicapped child; (c) Unless a handicapped child's individualized education program requires some other arrangement, the child is educated in the school which he or she would attend if not handicapped; and (d) In selecting the least restrictive environment, consideration is given to any potential harmful effect on the child or on the quality of services which he or she needs." (34 CFR 300.552)

Section 504 of the Rehabilitation Act of 1973 requires that "A recipient [of federal funds] to which this subpart applies shall educate, or shall provide for the education of, each qualified handicapped person in its jurisdiction with persons who are not handicapped to the maximum extent appropriate to the needs of the handicapped person. A recipient shall place a handicapped person in the regular educational environment operated by the recipient unless it is demonstrated by the recipient that the education of the person in the regular environment with the use of supplementary aids and services cannot be achieved satisfactorily. Whenever a recipient places a person in a setting other than the regular educational environment pursuant to this paragraph, it shall take into account the proximity of the alternate setting to the person's home." (34 CFR 104.34)

In plain language, these regulations appear to require that schools make a significant effort to find an inclusive solution for a child. How far must schools go? In recent years, the federal courts have been interpreting these rules to require that children with very severe disabilities must be included in the classroom they would otherwise attend if not disabled even when they cannot do the academic work of the class if there is a potential social benefit, if the class would stimulate the child's linguistic development, or if the other students could provide appropriate role models for the student. In one recent case of interest, a court ordered a school district to place a child with an IQ of 44 in a regular second-grade classroom while rejecting the school district's complaints about expenses as exaggerated (Board of Education, Sacramento City Unified School District v. Holland, 786 F.Supp.874 (ED Cal. 1992)). In another case a federal court rejected a school district's argument that a child would be so disruptive as to significantly impair the education of the other children (Oberti v. Board of Education of the Borough of Clementon School District. 789 F.Supp. 132.2 (D.N.J. 1992)). Educators need to be aware of such developments in the federal courts because court findings in one case tend to set precedent for future courts considering similar matters. These developments suggest that parents are increasingly able to go to the courts to force reluctant school districts to include their children in "regular" classes in situations where the child may not be able to "keep up" with the standard work of the class.

## Q U E S T I O N S

1. Explain how the phrase "out of sight/out of mind" refers to both people of color and people with disabilities.

2. Do you think it makes sense to apply the rationale of the *Brown* decision to special needs children and youth? Explain your answer.

3. Discuss how IDEA is both an extension of and a departure from PL 94-142—The Education for All Handicapped Children Act.

4. From the IDEA perspective, describe the ideal learning environment for any and all children.

5. Describe in your own words the two basic arguments for trying inclusion.

6. Describe an effective teacher in an inclusive classroom.

# CHAPTER

# 19 Testing
## A History of Abuse

The relationship between testing and education is complex. We can trace our nation's fascination with standardized testing back to the late nineteenth century. As the hierarchical and bureaucratic structure of schooling characterized in Chapter 8 as the "one best system" emerged in the latter half of the nineteenth century, the need to measure and compare things and people began to gain favor in U.S. schools. In an effort to create an efficient, meritorious system that sorted students into academic tracks based on ability and aptitude, a science of testing or measurement was needed. Thanks to efforts of the U.S. followers of French scientist Alfred Binet, the foundation for such a science was established during the early twentieth century.

Alfred Binet's interest in the measurement of intelligence led him to construct a set of tasks to assess directly various aspects of reasoning. While working for the French ministry of education, Binet developed techniques for identifying those children whose lack of success in normal classrooms suggested the need for special education. Binet brought together a series of short tasks related to everyday problems, supposedly involving such basic reasoning processes as ordering, comprehension, invention, and correction. Through trial and error, Binet identified an age level for each task. The level assigned corresponded to the youngest age that a child should be able to complete the task successfully. For example, a normal three-year-old boy should be able to point to his nose, eyes, and mouth. A normal ten-year-old child should be able to construct a sentence using such words as *Paris, fortune,* and *gutter.* Using such tasks, the examiner would lead an individual subject through a series of tasks graded in order of difficulty. A child began the Binet scale with the task identified for the youngest age and proceeded in sequence until the child could no longer complete the tasks. The age associated with the last task performed successfully became the child's mental age.

Binet published three versions of the scale before his death in 1911. His goal was to remove the superficial effects of clearly acquired knowledge in his testing, but he never claimed that his scale measured anything as complex or malleable as intelligence. Realizing that his number or intelligent quotient was but a rough empirical guide constructed for a limited purpose, Binet understood that intelligence could be augmented by good education. Similar to lenses correcting a deficiency in sight, Binet believed that his scale could identify mildly retarded and learning-disabled children in need of special help.

Binet's scale was destined for different purposes once it reached the United States. U.S. psychologists, most notably H. H. Goddard, Lewis Terman, and R. M. Yerkes, changed Binet's intentions and invented what scientist Stephen Jay Gould refers to as the hereditarian theory of IQ. Goddard, director of research at the Vineland Training School for Feebleminded Girls and Boys in New Jersey, translated Binet's work into English and advocated using Binet's scale to identify human capabilities and limitations. Unlike Binet, Goddard believed that intelligence was hereditary and that the test scores were measures of a single, innate entity. Agreeing with Binet that the test worked best in identifying low-grade defectives or morons, Goddard championed using the scale to identify and institutionalize all people with a mental age between eight and twelve.

Lewis Terman expanded and popularized Binet's scale in the United States. Binet's last version of the scale consisted of fifty-four tasks graded from prenursery to the mid-teenage years. Terman increased the number of tasks to ninety and extended the scale to the level of superior adults. A professor at Stanford University, Terman's new Stanford-Binet Scale became the standard by which all subsequent IQ tests would be measured. Terman standardized the scale so that so-called average children would score 100 at each age. More significantly, he became a powerful advocate for using the scale to sort children into vocational or professional tracks based on their performance on the Stanford-Binet IQ test. Terman believed that if all people were tested and sorted into roles appropriate for their intelligence, a more just and efficient society could result. Like Goddard, Terman believed that an individual's intellectual capacity was both immutable and inherited. More important, he believed that by using the Stanford-Binet Scale he could—in less than an hour—ascertain an individual's intellectual potential.

Goddard and Terman were joined by a Harvard psychologist R. M. Yerkes in expanding the use of the hereditarian theory of IQ. Motivated, in part, by a desire to advance the relatively new discipline of psychology, Yerkes convinced the U.S. Army to administer IQ tests to all recruits during World War I. Yerkes presided over the testing of 1.75 million recruits during the Great War. With the development of the Army Alpha and Beta tests (written and pictorial tests that supposedly correlate highly with the Stanford-Binet test), the era of mass testing had begun. Although originally intended to sort recruits into suitable military placements and to identify officer-training candidates, the Army never used the tests for these purposes.

Instead, the data were used in support of a powerful racist ideology suggesting that northern Europeans and their descendants were superior to the darker-skinned peoples of southern and eastern Europe. Based on these data, the average mental age of the White American male was just above that of a moron at 13. To people embracing the hereditary theory of IQ, this shockingly low score suggested that the pure Yankee stock had already been diluted through indiscriminate breeding of the poor and feebleminded. To some people, the data supported ethnic or racist stereotypes, with the Russian, Italian, and Polish recruit showing a mental age clustering around 11 and the Black recruit at the bottom of the scale, with a mental age of 10.41.

The low scores on these tests are understandable for a variety of reasons. When one realizes that the average U.S. recruit had not attended high school, a mental age of 13 is not surprising. When one realizes that most recruits from countries scoring low on these tests were recent immigrants with limited English language skills, their low average score takes on a different meaning. When one factors in the pervasive impact of centuries of slavery and racism, the poor showing by Blacks and other so-called child races is understandable.

The reality is that these tests measured education and familiarity with mainstream U.S. culture, not innate intelligence.

Despite these flaws, the impact of these tests has been significant. This was the beginning of the mass testing movement, and the data from the Army Alpha and Beta exams offered scientific support to the popular prejudices of the time. The so-called scientific data contributed to the passage of an immigration bill in 1924 that basically denied immigration of people from countries whose genetic stock was considered inferior.

Although no longer referred to as the Scholastic Aptitude Test, the development of the SAT further illustrates our nation's almost unbridled faith in the efficacy of testing. During the 1930s, James Bryant Conant sought to transform Harvard College from a regional institution into a national institution for selecting and educating the country's natural aristocracy. As the first modern scientist to become president of Harvard University, Conant sought to identify the country's best and brightest young men and admit them to Harvard as undergraduates.

To fulfill this vision, Conant turned to Henry Chauncey, a devotee of the new field of mental testing. Chauncey, along with Wilbur Bender, discovered the Scholastic Aptitude Test (SAT) developed by Princeton University's Carl Brigham. Convinced that the SAT was a pure test of intelligence, Conant and Chauncey replaced the essay tests used for college admission with the SAT. During World War II, Chauncey perfected the techniques of large-scale testing by administering the SAT to 300,000 people nationwide on a single day. Together with Conant, Chauncey established the Educational Testing Service after the war and persuaded colleges and universities across the country to use the SAT as the major admission criterion.

Although an achievement or, as it is now called, an assessment test, the SAT purportedly identified candidates with the aptitude for college-level work. In a society enamored with technology and numbers, the SAT quickly developed a luster all its own. Because applicants paid to take the exam, colleges and universities eagerly used it to provide them with an easy, cheap, and defensible way of justifying admission decisions.

What began as Conant's noble albeit flawed vision of ensuring access to higher education based solely on merit has evolved into a convenient mechanism for determining an individual's access to higher education on the basis—at best—of reasonable achievement or—at worst—of privileged knowledge and information. Whatever the case, Conant's dream of using the SAT to identify students capable of becoming our natural aristocracy has not been realized.

Assessment is a natural and important component of an effective educational program, but the history of testing is significantly a history of abuse. Both the changes of Binet's intent and the inflated expectations for the Scholastic Aptitude Test suggest that we pause before automatically and unthinkingly embracing testing as the panacea for our current or any educational malaise. Even though tests—including standardized tests—can be a useful tool in enhancing learning, this history alerts us to the potential for abuse. In a society in which local control of education has been a paramount virtue, reliance on standardized achievement tests that are not aligned with the local, state, or national standards is unfair. In today's world, where kids can be held back, required to attend summer school, or denied a diploma for failing to achieve a required score on a standardized test, congruence between the curriculum (what is taught) and what is tested is essential. Before educators lose pay and/or their jobs for their students' failure to score high enough on standardized exams, external factors affecting learning, such as the students' family background, poverty, and readiness to learn, must be considered. In short, given this history of abuse, a dose of healthy skepticism is appropriate concerning claims that testing is the answer to our educational dilemmas.

For more information concerning the abuse of testing, see Stephen Jay Gould, *The Mismeasure of Man* (New York: W.W. Norton & Company, 1981), pp. 146–233; and Nicholas Lemann, "Behind the SAT," *Newsweek* (September 6, 1999), pp. 52–57.

# The Psychological Method of Measuring Intelligence (1905)*

In order to recognize the inferior states of intelligence we believe that three different methods should be employed. We have arrived at this synthetic view only after many years of research, but we are now certain that each of these methods renders some service. These methods are:

1. *The medical method,* which aims to appreciate the anatomical, physiological, and pathological signs of inferior intelligence.
2. *The pedagogical method,* which aims to judge of the intelligence according to the sum of acquired knowledge.
3. *The psychological method,* which makes direct observations and measurements of the degree of intelligence.

From what has gone before it is easy to see the value of each of these methods. The medical method is indirect because it conjectures the mental from the physical. The pedagogical method is more direct, but the psychological is the most direct of all because it aims to measure the state of the intelligence as it is at the present moment. It does this by experiments which oblige the subject to make an effort which shows his capability in the way of comprehension, judgment, reasoning, and invention.

### I. The Psychological Method

The fundamental idea of this method is the establishment of what we shall call a measuring scale of intelligence. This scale is composed of a series of tests of increasing difficulty, starting from the lowest intellectual level that can be observed, and ending with that of average normal intelligence. Each group in the series corresponds to a different mental level.

This scale properly speaking does not permit the measure of the intelligence, because intellectual qualities are not superposable, and therefore cannot be measured as linear surfaces are measured, but are on the contrary, a classification, a hierarchy among

*From Alfred Binet and Theodore Simon, *The Development of Intelligence in Children.* Elizabeth S. Kite, trans. (Baltimore 1916) pp. 40–44.

diverse intelligences; and for the necessities of practice this classification is equivalent to a measure. We shall therefore be able to know, after studying two individuals, if one rises above the other and to how many degrees, if one rises above the average level of other individuals considered as normal, or if he remains below. Understanding the normal progress of intellectual development among normals, we shall be able to determine how many years such an individual is advanced or retarded. In a word we shall be able to determine to what degrees of the scale idiocy, imbecility, and moronity correspond.

The scale that we shall describe is not a theoretical work; it is the result of long investigations, first it the Salpêtrière, and afterwards in the primary schools of Paris, with both normal and subnormal children. These short psychological questions have been given the name of tests. The use of tests is today very common, and there are even contemporary authors who have made a specialty of organizing new tests according to theoretical views, but who have made no effort to patiently try them out in the schools. Theirs is an amusing occupation, comparable to a person's making a colonizing expedition into Algeria, advancing always only upon the map, without taking off his dressing gown. We place but slight confidence in the tests invented by these authors and we have borrowed nothing from them. All the tests which we propose have been repeatedly tried, and have been retained from among many, which after trial have been discarded. We can certify that those which are here presented have proved themselves valuable.

We have aimed to make all our tests simple, rapid, convenient, precise, heterogeneous, holding the subject in continued contact with the experimenter, and bearing principally upon the faculty of judgment. Rapidity is necessary for this sort of examination. It is impossible to prolong it beyond twenty minutes without fatiguing the subject. During this maximum of twenty minutes, it must be turned and turned about in every sense, and at least ten tests must be executed, so that not more than about two minutes can be given to each. In spite of their interest, we were obliged to proscribe long exercises. For example, it would be very instructive to know how a subject learns by heart a series of sentences. We have often tested the advantage of leaving a person by himself with a lesson of prose or verse after having said to him, "Try to learn as much as you can of this in five minutes." Five minutes is too long for our test, because during that time the subject escapes us; it may be that he becomes distracted or thinks of other things; the test loses its clinical character and becomes too scholastic. We have therefore reluctantly been obliged to renounce testing the rapidity and extent of the memory by this method. Several other equivalent examples of elimination could be cited. In order to cover rapidly a wide field of observation, it goes without saying that the tests should be heterogeneous.

Another consideration. Our purpose is to evaluate a level of intelligence. It is understood that we here separate natural intelligence and instruction. It is the intelligence alone that we seek to measure, by disregarding insofar as possible, the degree of instruction which the subject possesses. He should, indeed, be considered by the examiner as a complete ignoramus knowing neither how to read nor write. This necessity forces us to forego a great many exercises having a verbal, literary or scholastic character. These belong to a pedagogical examination. We believe that we have succeeded in completely disregarding the acquired information of the subject. We give him nothing to read, nothing to write, and submit him to no test in which he might succeed by means of rote learning. In fact we do not even notice his inability to read if a case occurs. It is simply the level of his natural intelligence that is taken into account.

But here we must come to an understanding of what meaning to give to that word so vague and so comprehensive, "the intelligence." Nearly all the phenomena with which psychology concerns itself are phenomena of intelligence; sensation, perception, are intellectual manifestations as much as reasoning. Should we therefore bring into our examination the measure of sensation after the manner of the psycho-physicists? Should we put to the test all of his psychological processes? A slight reflection has shown us that this would indeed be wasted time.

It seems to us that in intelligence there is a fundamental faculty, the alteration or the lack of which, is of the utmost importance for practical life. This faculty is judgment, otherwise called good sense, practical sense, initiative, the faculty of adapting one's self to circumstances. To judge well, to comprehend well, to reason well, these are the essential activities of intelligence. A person may be a moron or an imbecile if he is lacking in judgment, but with good judgment he can never be either. Indeed the rest of the intellectual faculties seem of little importance in comparison with judgment. What does it matter, for example, whether the organs of sense function normally? Of what import that certain ones are hyperesthetic, or that others are anesthetic or are weakened? Laura Bridgman, Helen Keller and their fellow-unfortunates were blind as well as deaf, but this did not prevent them from being very intelligent. Certainly this is demonstrative proof that the total or even partial integrity of the senses does not form a mental factor equal to judgment. We may measure the acuteness of the sensibility of subjects; nothing could be easier. But we should do this, not so much to find out the state of their sensibility as to learn the exactitude of their judgment.

The same remark holds good for the study of the memory. At first glance, memory being a psychological phenomenon of capital importance, one would be tempted to give it a very conspicuous part in an examination of intelligence. But memory is distinct from and independent of judgment. One may have good sense and lack memory. The reverse is also common. Just at the present time we are observing a backward girl who is developing before our astonished eyes a memory very much greater than our own. We have measured that memory and we are not deceived regarding it. Nevertheless that girl presents a most beautifully classic type of imbecility.

As a result of all this investigation, in the scale which we present we accord the first place to judgment; that which is of importance to us is not certain errors which the subject commits, but absurd errors, which prove that he lacks judgment. We have even made special provision to encourage people to make absurd replies. In spite of the accuracy of this directing idea, it will be easily understood that it has been impossible to permit of its regulating exclusively our examinations. For example, one can not make tests of judgment on children of less than two years when one begins to watch their first gleams of intelligence. Much is gained when one can discern in them traces of coordination, the first delineation of attention and memory. We shall therefore bring out in our lists some tests of memory; but so far as we are able, we shall give these tests such a turn as to invite the subject to make absurd replies, and thus under cover of a test of memory, we shall have an appreciation of their judgment.

# Lewis Terman on the Theory and Practice
# of Intelligence Testing (1916)*

Another important use of intelligence tests is in the study of the factors which influence mental development. It is desirable that we should be able to guard the child against influences which affect mental development unfavorably; but as long as these influences have not been sifted, weighed, and measured, we have nothing but conjecture on which to base our efforts in this direction.

When we search the literature of child hygiene for reliable evidence as to the injurious effects upon mental ability of malnutrition, decayed teeth, obstructed breathing, reduced sleep, bad ventilation, insufficient exercise, etc., we are met by endless assertion painfully unsupported by demonstrated fact. We have, indeed, very little exact knowledge regarding the mental effects of any of the facts just mentioned. When standardized mental tests have come into more general use, such influences will be easy to detect wherever they are really present.

Again, the most important question of heredity is that regarding the inheritance of intelligence, but this is a problem which cannot be attacked at all without some accurate means of identifying the thing which is the object of study. Without the use of scales for measuring intelligence we can give no better answer as to the essential difference between a genius and a fool than is to be found in legend and fiction.

Applying this to school children, it means that without such tests we cannot know to what extent a child's mental performances are determined by environment and to what extent by heredity. Is the place of the so-called lower classes in the social and industrial scale the result of their inferior native endowment, or is their apparent inferiority merely a result of their inferior home and school training? Is genius more common among children of the educated classes than among the children of the ignorant and poor? Are the inferior races really inferior, or are they merely unfortunate in their lack of opportunity to learn?

Only intelligence tests can answer these questions and grade the raw material with which education works. Without them we can never distinguish the results of our educational efforts with a given child from the influence of the child's original endowment. Such tests would have told us, for example, whether the much-discussed "wonder children," such as the Sidis and Wiener boys and the Stoner girl, owe their precocious intellectual prowess to superior training (as their parents believe) or to superior native ability. The supposed effects upon mental development of new methods of mind training, which are exploited so confidently from time to time (e.g., the Montessori method and the various systems of sensory and motor training for the feeble-minded), will have to be checked up by the same kind of scientific measurement.

In all these fields intelligence tests are certain to play an ever-increasing role. With the exception of moral character, there is nothing as significant for a child's future as his grade of intelligence. Even health itself is likely to have less influence in determining success in life. Although strength and swiftness have always had great survival value among the lower animals, these characteristics have long since lost their supremacy in man's

---

*From Lewis M. Terman. *The Measurement of Intelligence.* (Boston 1916) pp. 19–21, 36–40, 65–68, 72–73, 114–116, 140–141.

struggle for existence. For us the rule of brawn has been broken, and intelligence has become the decisive factor in success. Schools, railroads, factories, and the largest commercial concerns may be successfully managed by persons who are physically weak or even sickly. One who has intelligence constantly measures opportunities against his own strength or weakness and adjusts himself to conditions by following those leads which promise most toward the realization of his individual possibilities.

All classes of intellects, the weakest as well as the strongest, will profit by the application of their talents to tasks which are consonant with their ability. When we have learned the lessons which intelligence tests have to teach, we shall no longer blame mentally defective workmen for their industrial inefficiency, punish weak-minded children because of their inability to learn, or imprison and hang mentally defective criminals because they lacked the intelligence to appreciate the ordinary codes of social conduct.

\* \* \*

The Binet scale is made up of an extended series of tests in the nature of "stunts," or problems, success in which demands the exercise of intelligence. As left by Binet, the scale consists of 54 tests, so graded in difficulty that the easiest lie well within the range of normal 3-year-old children, while the hardest tax the intelligence of the average adult. The problems are designed primarily to test native intelligence, not school knowledge or home training. They try to answer the question, "How intelligent is this child?" How much the child has learned is of significance only in so far as it throws light on his ability to learn more.

Binet fully appreciated the fact that intelligence is not homogeneous, that it has many aspects, and that no one kind of test will display it adequately. He therefore assembled for his intelligence scale tests of many different types, some of them designed to display differences of memory, others differences in power to reason, ability to compare, power of comprehension, time orientation, facility in the use of number concepts, power to combine ideas into a meaningful whole, the maturity of apperception, wealth of ideas, knowledge of common objects, etc.

The tests were arranged in order of difficulty, as found by trying them upon some 200 normal children of different ages from 3 to 15 years. It was found, for illustration, that a certain test was passed by only a very small proportion of the younger children, say the 5-year-olds, and that the number passing this test increased rapidly in the succeeding years until by the age of 7 or 8 years, let us say, practically all the children were successful. If, in our supposed case, the test was passed by about two thirds to three fourths of the normal children aged 7 years, it was considered by Binet a test of 7-year intelligence. In like manner, a test passed by 65 to 75 per cent of the normal 9-year-olds was considered a test of 9-year intelligence, and so on. By trying out many different tests in this way it was possible to secure five tests to represent each age from 3 to 10 years (excepting age 4, which has only four tests), five for age 12, five for 15, and five for adults, making 54 tests in all. The following is the list of tests as arranged by Binet in 1911, shortly before his untimely death:—

*Age 3:*
1. Points to nose, eyes, and mouth.
2. Repeats two digits.
3. Enumerates objects in a picture.

**4.** Gives family name.

**5.** Repeats a sentence of six syllables.

*Age 4:*

**1.** Gives his sex.

**2.** Names key, knife, and penny.

**3.** Repeats three digits.

**4.** Compares two lines.

*Age 5:*

**1.** Compares two weights.

**2.** Copies a square.

**3.** Repeats a sentence of ten syllables.

**4.** Counts four pennies.

**5.** Unites the halves of a divided rectangle.

*Age 6:*

**1.** Distinguishes between morning and afternoon.

**2.** Defines familiar words in terms of use.

**3.** Copies a diamond.

**4.** Counts thirteen pennies.

**5.** Distinguishes pictures of ugly and pretty faces.

*Age 7:*

**1.** Shows right hand and left ear.

**2.** Describes a picture.

**3.** Executes three commissions, given simultaneously.

**4.** Counts the value of six sous, three of which are double.

**5.** Names four cardinal colors.

*Age 8:*

**1.** Compares two objects from memory.

**2.** Counts from 20 to 0.

**3.** Notes omissions from pictures.

**4.** Gives day and date.

**5.** Repeats five digits.

*Age 9:*

**1.** Gives change from twenty sous.

**2.** Defines familiar words in terms superior to use.

**3.** Recognizes all the pieces of money.

**4.** Names the months of the year, in order.

**5.** Answers easy "comprehension questions."

*Age 10:*

**1.** Arranges five blocks in order of weight.

2. Copies drawings from memory.
3. Criticizes absurd statements.
4. Answers difficult "comprehension questions."
5. Uses three given words in not more than two sentences.

### Age 12:

1. Resists suggestion.
2. Composes one sentence containing three given words.
3. Names sixty words in three minutes.
4. Defines certain abstract words.
5. Discovers the sense of a disarranged sentence.

### Age 15:

1. Repeats seven digits.
2. Finds three rhymes for a given word.
3. Repeats a sentence of twenty-six syllables.
4. Interprets pictures.
5. Interprets given facts.

### Adult:

1. Solves the paper-cutting test.
2. Rearranges a triangle in imagination.
3. Gives differences between pairs of abstract terms.
4. Gives three differences between a president and a king.
5. Gives the main thought of a selection which he has heard read.

It should be emphasized that merely to name the tests in this way gives little idea of their nature and meaning, and tells nothing about Binet's method of conducting the 54 experiments. In order to use the tests intelligently it is necessary to acquaint one's self thoroughly with the purpose of each test, its correct procedure, and the psychological interpretation of different types of response.

In fairness to Binet, it should also be borne in mind that the scale of tests was only a rough approximation to the ideal which the author had set himself to realize. Had his life been spared a few years longer, he would doubtless have carried the method much nearer perfection.

By means of the Binet tests we can judge the intelligence of a given individual by comparison with standards of intellectual performance for normal children of different ages. In order to make the comparison it is only necessary to begin the examination of the subject at a point in the scale where all the tests are passed successfully, and to continue up the scale until no more successes are possible. Then we compare our subject's performances with the standard for normal children of the same age, and note the amount of acceleration or retardation.

Let us suppose the subject being tested is 9 years of age. If he goes as far in the tests as normal 9-year-old children ordinarily go, we can say that the child has a "mental age" of 9 years, which in this case is normal (our child being 9 years of age). If he goes only as far as normal 8-year-old children ordinarily go, we say that his "mental age" is 8 years. In like manner, a mentally defective child of 9 years may have a "mental age" of only 4 years, or a young genius of 9 years may have a mental age of 12 or 13 years.

An extended account of the 1000 tests on which the Stanford revision is chiefly based has been presented in a separate monograph. This chapter will include only the briefest summary of some of those results of the investigation which contribute to the intelligent use of the revision.

The question as to the manner in which intelligence is distributed is one of great practical as well as theoretical importance. One of the most vital questions which can be asked by any nation of any age is the following: "How high is the average level of intelligence among our people, and how frequent are the various grades of ability above and below the average?" With the development of standardized tests we are approaching, for the first time in history, a possible answer to this question.

Most of the earlier Binet studies, however, have thrown little light on the distribution of intelligence because of their failure to avoid the influence of accidental selection in choosing subjects for testing. The method of securing subjects for the Stanford revision makes our results on this point especially interesting. It is believed that the subjects used for this investigation were as nearly representative of average American-born children as it is possible to secure.

The intelligence quotients for these 1000 unselected children were calculated, and their distribution was plotted for the ages separately. The distribution was found fairly symmetrical at each age from 5 to 14. At 15 the range is on either side of 90 as a median, and at 16 on either side of 80 as a median. That the 15- and 16-year-olds test low is due to the fact that these children are left-over retardates and are below average in intelligence.

The IQ's were then grouped in ranges of ten. In the middle group were thrown those from 96 to 105; the ascending groups including in order the IQ's from 106 to 115, 116 to 125, etc.; correspondingly with the descending groups....

The symmetry for the separate ages was hardly less marked, considering that only 80 to 120 children were tested at each age. In fact, the range, including the middle 50 per cent of IQ's, was found practically constant from 5 to 14 years. The tendency is for the middle 50 per cent to fall (approximately) between 93 and 108.

Three important conclusions are justified by the above facts:—

**1.** Since the frequency of the various grades of intelligence decreases *gradually* and at no point abruptly on each side of the median, it is evident that there is no definite dividing line between normality and feeblemindedness, or between normality and genius. Psychologically, the mentally defective child does not belong to a distinct type, nor does the genius. There is no line of demarcation between either of these extremes and the so-called "normal" child. The number of mentally defective individuals in a population will depend upon the standard arbitrarily set up as to what constitutes mental deficiency. Similarly for genius. It is exactly as if we should undertake to classify all people into the three groups: abnormally tall, normally tall, and abnormally short.

**2.** The common opinion that extreme deviations below the median are more frequent than extreme deviations above the median seems to have no foundation in fact. Among unselected school children, at least, for every child of any given degree of deficiency there is another child as far above the average IQ as the former is below. We have shown elsewhere the serious consequences of neglect of this fact.

**3.** The traditional view that variability in mental traits becomes more marked during adolescence is here contradicted, as far as intelligence is concerned, for the distribution of IQs is practically the same at each age from 5 to 14. For example, 6-year-olds differ from one another fully as much as do 14-year-olds.

\* \* \*

The validity of the intelligence quotient. The facts presented above argue strongly for the validity of the IQ as an expression of a child's intelligence status. This follows necessarily from the similar nature of the distributions at the various ages. The inference is that a child's IQ, as measured by this scale, remains relatively constant. Re-tests of the same children at intervals of two to five years support the inference. Children of superior intelligence do not seem to deteriorate as they get older, nor dull children to develop average intelligence. Knowing a child's IQ, we can predict with a fair degree of accuracy the course of his later development.

The mental age of a subject is meaningless if considered apart from chronological age. It is only the ratio of retardation or acceleration to chronological age (that is, the IQ) which has significance.

It follows also that if the IQ is a valid expression of intelligence, as it seems to be, then the Binet-Simon "age-grade method" becomes transformed automatically into a "point-scale method," if one wants to use it that way. As such it is superior to any other point scale that has been proposed, because it includes a larger number of tests and its points have definite meanings.

\* \* \*

Of the 1000 children, 492 were classified by their teachers according to social class into the following five groups: *very inferior, inferior, average, superior,* and *very superior.* A comparative study was then made of the distribution of IQ's for these different groups.

The data may be summarized as follows:—

**1.** The median IQ for children of the superior social class is about 7 points above, and that of the inferior social class about 7 points below, the median IQ of the average social group. This means that by the age of 14 inferior class children are about one year below, and superior class children one year above, the median mental age for all classes taken together.

**2.** That the children of the superior social classes make a better showing in the tests is probably due, for the most part, to a superiority in original endowment. This conclusion is supported by five supplementary lines of evidence: (*a*) the teachers' rankings of the children according to intelligence; (*b*) the age-grade progress of the children; (*c*) the quality of the school work; (*d*) the comparison of older and younger children as regards the influence of social environments; and (*e*) the study of individual cases of bright and dull children in the same family.

**3.** In order to facilitate comparison, it is advisable to express the intelligence of children of all social classes in terms of the same objective scale of intelligence. This scale should be based on the median for all classes taken together.

**4.** As regards their responses to individual tests, our children of a given social class were not distinguishable from children of the same intelligence in any other social class.

The school work of 504 children was graded by the teachers on a scale of five grades: *very inferior, inferior, average, superior,* and *very superior.* When this grouping was compared with that made on the basis of IQ, fairly close agreement was found. However, in about one case out of ten there was rather serious disagreement; a child, for example, would be rated as doing *average* school work when his IQ would place him in the *very inferior* intelligence group.

When the data were searched for explanations of such disagreements it was found that most of them were plainly due to the failure of teachers to take into account the age of the child when grading the quality of his school work. When allowance was made for this tendency there were no disagreements which justified any serious suspicion as to the accuracy of the intelligence scale. Minor disagreements may, of course, be disregarded, since the quality of school work depends in part on other factors than intelligence, such as industry, health, regularity of attendance, quality of instruction, etc.

\* \* \*

Influence of social and educational advantages. The criticism has often been made that the responses to many of the tests are so much subject to the influence of school and home environment as seriously to invalidate the scale as a whole. Some of the tests most often named in this connection are the following: Giving age and sex; naming common objects, colors, and coins; giving the value of stamps; giving date; naming the months of the year and the days of the week; distinguishing forenoon and afternoon; counting; making change; reading for memories; naming sixty words; giving definitions; finding rhymes; and constructing a sentence containing three given words.

It has in fact been found wherever comparisons have been made that children of superior social status yield a higher average mental age than children of the laboring classes. The results of Decroly and Degand and of Meumann, Stern, and Binet himself may be referred to in this connection. In the case of the Stanford investigation, also, it was found that when the unselected school children were grouped in three classes according to social status (superior, average. and inferior), the average IQ for the superior social group was 107, and that of the inferior social group 93. This is equivalent to a difference of one year in mental age with 7-year-olds, and to a difference of two years with 14-year-olds.

However, the common opinion that the child from a cultured home does better in tests solely by reason of his superior home advantages is an entirely gratuitous assumption. Practically all of the investigations which have been made of the influence of nature and nurture on mental performance agree in attributing far more to original endowment than to environment. Common observation would itself suggest that the social class to which the family belongs depends less on chance than on the parents' native qualities of intellect and character.

The results of five separate and distinct lines of inquiry based on the Stanford data agree in supporting the conclusion that the children of successful and cultured parents test higher than children from wretched and ignorant homes for the simple reason that their heredity is better. The results of this investigation are set forth in full elsewhere.[1]

\* \* \*

It would, of course, be going too far to deny all possibility of environmental conditions affecting the result of an intelligence test. Certainly no one would expect that a child reared in a cage and denied all intercourse with other human beings could by any system of mental measurement test up to the level of normal children. There is, however, no reason to believe that *ordinary* differences in social environment apart from heredity, differences such as those obtaining among unselected children attending approximately the same general type of school in a civilized community, affects to any great extent the validity of the scale.

A crucial experiment would be to take a large number of very young children of the lower classes and, after placing them in the most favorable environment obtainable, to compare their later mental development with that of children born into the best homes. No extensive study of this kind has been made, but the writer has tested twenty orphanage children who, for the most part, had come from very inferior homes. They had been in a well-conducted orphanage for from two to several years, and had enjoyed during that time the advantages of an excellent village school. Nevertheless, all but three tested below average, ranging from 75 to 90 IQ.

The impotence of school instruction to neutralize individual differences in native endowment will be evident to any one who follows the school career of backward children. The children who are seriously retarded in school are not normal, and cannot be made normal by any refinement of educational method. As a rule, the longer the inferior child attends school, the more evident his inferiority becomes. It would hardly be reasonable, therefore, to expect that a little incidental instruction in the home would weigh very heavily against these same native differences in endowment.

\* \* \*

As elsewhere explained, the mental age alone does not tell us what we want to know about a child's intelligence status. The significance of a given number of years of retardation or acceleration depends upon the age of the child. A 3-year-old child who is retarded one year is ordinarily feeble-minded; a 10-year-old retarded one year is only a little below normal. The child who at 3 years of age is retarded one year will probably be retarded two years at the age of 6, three years at the age of 9, and four years at the age of 12.

What we want to know, therefore, is the ratio existing between mental age and real age. This is the intelligence quotient, or IQ. To find it we simply divide mental age (expressed in years and months) by real age (also expressed in years and months). The process is easier if we express each age in terms of months alone before dividing. The division can, of course, be performed almost instantaneously and with much less danger of error by the

---

[1]See *The Stanford Revision and Extension of the Binet-Simon Measuring Scale of Intelligence.* (Warwick and York, 1916.)

use of a slide rule or a division table. One who has to calculate many intelligence quotients should by all means use some kind of mechanical help.

Native intelligence, in so far as it can be measured by tests now available, appears to improve but little after the age of 15 or 16 years. It follows that in calculating the IQ of an adult subject, it will be necessary to disregard the years he has lived beyond the point where intelligence attains its final development.

Although the location of this point is not exactly known, it will be sufficiently accurate for our purpose to assume its location at 16 years. Accordingly, any person over 16 years of age, however old, is for purposes of calculating IQ considered to be just 16 years old. If a youth of 18 and a man of 60 years both have a mental age of 12 the IQ in each case is $12 \div 16$, or .75.

The significance of various values of the IQ is set forth elsewhere. Here it need only be repeated that 100 IQ means exactly average intelligence; that nearly all who are below 70 or 75 IQ are feeble-minded; and that the child of 125 IQ is about as much above the average as the high-grade feeble-minded individual is below the average. For ordinary purposes all who fall between 95 and 105 IQ may be considered as average in intelligence.

# The Big Score*

Inside Chicago's top-ranked Whitney Young High School, the posters started appearing last December. LET'S BE #1! GIVE IT 110%! Usually this sort of rah-rah propaganda supports the basketball team, but this campaign by the principal had a different aim: urging kids to score high on the Illinois Goal Assessment Program, a standardized test that students would take in February. Tests are nothing new to the kids at Whitney Young—they already take three other batteries of standardized exams each year. But for a group of high-achieving 11th graders, the pressure was just too much. These kids say real learning is being shoved aside as teachers focus on boosting test scores. Creative writing? Forget it. Instead, they say, teachers emphasize a boilerplate essay format that exam scorers prefer. So on Feb. 2, eight juniors purposely failed the social-studies portion of the test. The next day 10 failed the science test. Then they sent a letter to the principal: "We refuse to feed into this test-taking frenzy."

As rebellions go, it wasn't exactly the Boston Tea Party. But it's a small sign of the growing anxiety among parents, teachers and kids over the proliferation of standardized tests. Fill-in-the-bubble exams have been part of classroom life for decades, but for most of their history they were no big deal. Scores were tucked in students' folders; at most, they were used to segregate kids into higher- and lower-level classes. That's changed dramatically in the last decade as reformers try to improve school quality by holding educators accountable for learning. Every state has a different testing scheme, but many state legislatures are writing new standards for what kids should learn in each grade and mandating tough new "high stakes" tests to gauge progress. Unlike such old-style standardized

*From Daniel McGinn with Steve Rhodes, Donna Foote, and Anne Gesalman, "The Big Score." From *Newsweek,* Sept. 6, 1999, © 1999 Newsweek, Inc. All rights reserved. Reprinted by permission.

tests as the Iowas or Metropolitans, many of the new exams are linked to the curriculum and feature essays and short answers, not just multiple choice. The biggest difference: low scores can bring real pain. Kids can be held back, forced into summer school or, under rules in 26 states, denied a diploma. Educators can lose pay or be fired; schools can face state takeover. In polls, the tests win wide public support, and more states are jumping on the bandwagon.

Yet there is no easy answer to the most basic question: do these tests help kids learn? As the testing movement has grown, opposing experts have churned out a mountain of conflicting research. Fans of the tests say they're as necessary to schooling as a scale is to dieting. Ideally, they're diagnostic tools, letting teachers know Jack doesn't understand two-digit multiplication and Jill needs help with subject-verb agreement. Yes, it's sad that a single exam might keep a child from graduating, but most European countries already use exit exams, and some U.S. students are kept from graduating for lesser offenses, like flunking gym or cutting too many classes. And as schools ask for money to hire teachers and cut class size, taxpayers have every right to expect a measurable payback. Supporters of the new exams point to encouraging results in Texas, one of the first states to implement this type of reform plan.

Despite those arguments, a growing number of critics say this testing inevitably leads to dumbed-down teaching. "Every hour that teachers feel compelled to try to raise test scores is an hour not spent helping kids become critical, creative, curious thinkers," says Alfie Kohn, author of "The Schools Our Children Deserve." It's those skills, after all, that put the United States ahead of world competitors in areas like entrepreneurship. Last fall the National Research Council warned Congress that schools should refrain from basing important decisions like who gets promoted or graduates solely on test scores, and called for more exploration of the unintended consequences of high-stakes exams. Teachers in the inner cities, where many children are being held back for failing the tests, worry that these exams are overwhelming their already overcrowded and understaffed classrooms. Suburban homeowners have more bottom-line concerns; they fear that dismal test scores will lower home values. For now, those worries will persist. Testing opponents have scored small victories in places like Wisconsin, but momentum is on the side of reformers. As kids return to classrooms this fall, the new exams will be part of the curriculum.

At Madison High School in Houston, the tests have already brought an innovation that makes teenagers cringe: Saturday classes. In 1990 Texas replaced its old tests with a tough new one (its acronym: TAAS); students who failed wouldn't graduate. Early results were abysmal. Madison principal Warner Ervin remembers when dozens of seniors failed. Students were crushed, parents were irate, teachers embarrassed. "It was difficult for everyone," Ervin says. So in 1997, Ervin began requiring every failing kid to attend tutoring sessions, some held on Saturday. The year before the tutoring began, 57 seniors failed; last spring the whole class passed. Results are also improving statewide. Last spring 78 percent of Texas students passed the test, up from 53 percent in 1994. Education is certain to be a key issue in the presidential race, so expect Gov. George W. Bush to tout this track record.

Other states can boast of their own success stories. Take 9-year-old Steven Ip of Brooklyn, one of 17,591 third graders who failed the high-stakes test given to New York City kids for the first time last winter. Steven, whose parents emigrated from China, has solid math skills, but because of his limited English ability, he scored in the 11th percentile

## What Parents Can Do to Help Their Kids Pass

Most parents are understandably anxious when they hear that their child has to take a high-stakes test. Here are some things parents can do to keep everyone in the family on course:

1. **A good vocabulary** is essential for passing most standardized tests, so read to your children early and often. When they read on their own, encourage them by creating a quiet reading spot in the house and making regular library trips.
2. **Learn everything you can** about the test your child will be taking. How will the results be used? How much class time will be taken up in test preparation?
3. **The night before the test,** make sure your child gets enough sleep. Stay calm yourself; he's probably anxious and needs reassurance.
4. **If the results concern you,** seek advice from testing experts. Teachers and guidance counselors are obvious resources. Also check out schools of education at local universities.
5. **Remember that even the best test** is just a snapshot of your child at one particular point in time. It's not the whole picture. Success in life is dependent on many qualities that can't be tested, including creativity, determination, ambition, and luck.

---

on the reading test. So like a record 37,000 New York City kids, he faced mandatory summer school; if he failed his retest in August, he'd be forced to repeat third grade. During five sweaty weeks in a classroom at P.S. 241, teacher Maria Teresa Maisano worked with Steven and seven other students. They read books in class and for homework, learning how to ask questions and find key ideas. When test day arrived, Steven felt prepared. Like roughly 60 percent of the summer students, he passed the exam and can start fourth grade. The city's school chancellor, Rudolph Crew, has been blasted for retaining kids and mandating summer school, but he's standing firm. "This is high anxiety—it's not for the meek of heart," he says. "But I think it's the right thing to do."

Other educators aren't so enthusiastic. At Santa Monica Boulevard Elementary in Los Angeles, the lilting sounds of Spanish fill the playground. But in teacher David Levinson's fifth grade, as in all other California schools, classes must be taught in English. For 31 of his 32 students, English is a second language. "The scores for most of these kids are low and it's not too hard to figure out why," says Levinson. "These tests are extremely unfair." But they're the law, and as a consequence they're beginning to drive the curriculum. "We spend a lot more time teaching to the test and a lot less on the kind of hands-on, learn-by-doing teaching we did in the past," says the school's longtime principal, Albert Arnold. "My teachers are very frustrated, and kids pick up on that." They'll be more frustrated next year when, for the first time, student who fail the test are held back.

California's on-again, off-again testing regimen shows just how messy the transition to exam-driven reform can be. Until the late '80s, California's schools were top-notch. Then in the early '90s, a sinking economy, political bickering over education reform and a growing immigrant population set them back. So the state devised a new test, the California Learning Assessment System. But critics attacked essay questions as too subjective to be fairly graded, and reformers who favor a back-to-basics approach lobbied for more focus on the three Rs. By 1994, the CLAS was dead, and students went untested for three years as legislators debated new standards. Most experts urged them to design a customized exam that test exactly the skills the state's kids should be learning, instead of an off-the-shelf national exam. When standards, curriculum, and test are aligned through the made-to-order tests many states are adopting, "teaching to the test" can become a positive technique, experts say. But California's leaders couldn't wait for a custom exam, so they opted to use a generic test in the interim. Experts say that's been a weak link in their reform plan. "The system in California is imperfect," says Stanford professor Kenji Hakuta. "What's needed are tests that more closely line up to instruction." This disparity is a recurring theme: experts favor a gradual, methodical transition, but political realities often force quick, crude steps to try to show improvement before the next election.

As testing spreads, experts aren't the only ones parsing the quality of exams. When Wisconsin Gov. Tommy Thompson proposed a statewide graduation exam in 1997, he had wide public support. Then parents saw sample questions. "It scared the heck out of them," says state Sen. Bob Jauch. "They weren't sure they could pass it themselves." A strange coalition of opponents emerged, consisting of parents concerned that the tests were too tough, educators who resented the state's giving orders to locally run schools and legislators who'd rather spend the $10 million testing budget on a tax cut. By June, Wisconsin's new test was dead.

Tales like that one give hope to the Chicago kids at Whitney Young who bucked the test last winter. Over the summer they rounded up like-minded students from other schools and named themselves the Organized Students of Chicago. They've already passed out leaflets denouncing the city's testmania; now they're planning teach-ins. The focus on the exams "just seems so totally excessive," says Will Tanzman, 17. Eli Presser, an 18-year-old who graduated last spring but is still active in the group, says the rising number of tests makes students feel "like they're under constant jeopardy—like every single test was going to influence their life." Principal Joyce Kenner ordered the students to perform 10 hours of community service for refusing to take last year's exam. So far, they haven't served it, and may rally more students to boycott the exams this winter.

School officials are sympathetic to charges that they're giving too many tests. "Nobody wants to be test crazy…We don't want you to be drones," says Chicago school board president Gery Chico. But like administrators around the country, he says schools need to face the reality that the status quo, in which thousands of kids languished in classes with virtually no instruction, couldn't continue. Parents like Jay Rehak, who's also a Whitney Young teacher, worry their kids are suffering for the sake of the system. When his daughter faced her first high-stakes exam two years ago, "she came home panicked every night," he says. But University of Chicago researcher Melissa Roderick, who's followed 100 students at five schools through Chicago's pass-the-test-or-stay-back program, says the get-tough approach is needed, the same way financiers impose harsh, short-term measures to stabilize troubled economies. "The tests are getting us moving," Roderick says. "Over time we'll look to other things."

Perhaps. Or maybe this new breed of exam will become a defining part of school days well into the new century. Most states are only beginning to get their curriculum in sync with the new tests, so experts say it will be years before we see whether they deliver improvements

## 'Tests Are an Easy Way Out'

**Two Educators Urge Parents to Look beyond Numbers**

Theodore R. Sizer and his wife, Nancy Faust Sizer, have been on the front lines of the school reform battle for decades. He is founder of the Coalition of Essential Schools, a national network of innovative schools, and has been dean of the Harvard Graduate School of Education and a professor at Brown University. Nancy Sizer was a teacher for 25 years. The Sizers recently finished serving as acting co-principals of the Francis W. Parker Charter Essential School in Devens, Mass., and have written a new book, "The Students Are Watching" *(131 pages. Beacon Press. $21).* They discussed the pros and cons of testing with Newsweek Senior Editor Barbara Kantrowitz.

> **NEWSWEEK:** Are test scores a good way for parents to pick a school for their child?
>
> **THEODORE SIZER:** A lot of those scores rest on very sandy soil. It's limited and often very skewed information. We all know that some kids blossom with tests and some kids don't. And we also know that there are very few correlations between sophisticated standardized testing and long-term intellectual performance and character habits.

**What's a Better Way to Judge a School?**

> **NANCY SIZER:** If I were a parent, I would ask to follow a kid through the school for a day. Ask to see the child's work and have him or her explain it to you.
>
> **T.S.:** At the Parker Charter School, we have just gone through a formal state inspection, a highly orchestrated visit arising from a very carefully prepared document set by the state authorities. We were highly accountable. A group of veteran teachers spent three-and-a-half days with us. The inspectors also talked with the parents in a way that went far beyond any test. You can hide in a test. You can't hide in an inspection.

**Still, Most People Use Scores to Judge a School's Effectiveness.**

> **T.S.:** That's because people are lazy. They're not asking questions. Tests are an easy out. They have this façade of toughness and objectivity. Test put no burden on the people who most often demand them—the politicians.

**Do You Think Teachers Should be Tested?**

> **T.S.:** This is another example of harmful laziness. It's easy to give a test but it only tells you something at the extremes. The totally incompetent teacher and the totally incompetent arithmetic student—they'll pop out in a test. In a good school, you wouldn't have to give a test. You'd know who's having a problem. Testing reduces teaching to mechanics, and as a principal, I don't want mechanical teachers.
>
> **N.S.:** But you're asking an awful lot of the human beings inside schools if you don't have tests. You're asking for principals to be willing to sit down with a teacher and talk to him about things that have gotten out of hand. And you have to reduce the teacher's load so that they can get to know their students better and find out what will really make each student sing as a scholar.

dramatic enough to justify the investment. "We're in the middle of the maelstrom—it's very difficult to see which way it's going to go," says Judith Mathers, a policy analyst at the Education Commission of the States. Until then, pencils in hand, we all plunge ahead.

## QUESTIONS

1. Explain the connection between the emergence of "the one best system" of schooling and the rise of the testing movement in the United States.

2. Compare Alfred Binet's beliefs about measuring human intelligence to those of his U.S. followers, H. H. Goddard, Lewis Terman, and R. M. Yerkes.

3. Explain the idea of a heriditarian theory of IQ.

4. Discuss the impact of the development of the Army Alpha and Beta tests and the testing of 1.75 million U.S. army recruits during World War I.

5. What lessons should be learned from the so-called "perversion" (as used by Gould) of Binet's intent in developing an IQ test in the noble, if misguided, attempt to recruit a natural aristocracy using the Scholastic Aptitude Test?

6. Distinguish between the medical, pedagogical, and psychological methods for measuring intelligence.

7. What role, according to Binet, does judgment play in intelligence?

8. Explain Theodore Sizer's suggestion that our infatuation with testing is due to our laziness. Do you agree or disagree with his assessments? Explain your answer.

## SUGGESTIONS FOR FURTHER READING

David C. Berliner and Bruce J. Biddle, *The Manufactured Crisis: Myths, Fraud, and the Attack on America's Public Schools*. (White Plains, NY: Longman Publishers, 1996).

Stephen J. Gould, *The Mismeasure of Man*. (New York: W. W. Norton & Company, 1981).

Gerald Grant and Christine Murphy: *Teaching in America: The Slow Revolution*. (Cambridge, MA: Harvard University Press, 1999).

Nicholas Lemann, *The Big Test: The Secret History of the American Meritocracy*. (New York: Farrar, Straus, and Giroux, 1999).

Diane Ravitch, *Left Back: A Century of Failed School Reform*. (New York: Simon & Schuster, 2000).

# SUBJECT INDEX

# NAME INDEX

Antin, Mary, 152, 154
Armstrong, Samuel Chapman, 126

Bakke, Allan, 191
Barnard, Henry, 84
Beecher, Catherine, 102
Bender, Wilbur, 220
Binet, Alfred, 218, 220, 225, 237
Bonner, John, 111
Brigham, Carl, 220
Bush, George W., 233

Calvin, John, 3
Chauncey, Henry, 220
Cisneros, Henry, 165, 167
Conant, James Bryant, 220
Cotton, John, 5

Du Bois, W. E. B., 126, 127, 136, 139, 141

Elson, Richard, 102

Fallows, James, 157
Frankfurter, J. A., 41
Franklin, Benjamin, 125
Fry, Joshua, 20

Gobitis, Lillian and William, 39, 41, 43
Gochman, Arthur, 202
Goddard, H. H., 218, 237
Goodsell, Willystine, 102
Gould, Stephen Jay, 219
Grant, Gerald, 88

Hopkins, Mark, 140

Jefferson, Thomas, 19, 20, 29, 58, 67, 79, 113, 121
Johnson, Lyndon, 183
Judge Maris, 42
Justice Black, 53, 57

Justice Brennan, 185
Justice Jackson, Robert, 39
Justice Powell, 191
Justice Stewart, 60
Justice Warren, 173, 177

McGuffey, William Holmes, 102, 104, 109
McLaurin, George, 143
Madison, James, 56, 58, 62
Mann, Horace, 20, 56, 79, 80, 81, 87, 88, 113, 121
Marshall, Thurgood, 172, 178
Mill, John Stuart, 113
Murray, Christine E., 88
Murray, Madalyn, 53

Plessy, Homer Adolf, 143, 144

Rodriguez, Demetrio, 202
Rodriguez, Richard, 164
Ruffner, Viola, 125, 128

Sizer, Nancy Faust, 236
Sizer, Theodore R., 236
Small, Dr. William, 21
Smith, Adam, 114
Sweatt, Heman M., 143

Terman, Lewis, 218, 219, 224, 237
Tyack, David, 80, 102

Washington, Booker T., 125, 127, 136, 137, 138, 139, 141, 142, 143, 153
Washington, George, 101
Webster, Daniel, 80
Webster, Noah, 68, 101, 102
Willard, Emma, 102
Wythe, George, 21

Yerkes, R. M., 218, 219, 237